SCIENTIFIC
CHAMPIONS OF SCIENCE

For Key Stage 3 Science

Peter Ellis • Phil Godding • Derek McMonagle
Louise Petheram • Lawrie Ryan
David Sang • Jane Taylor

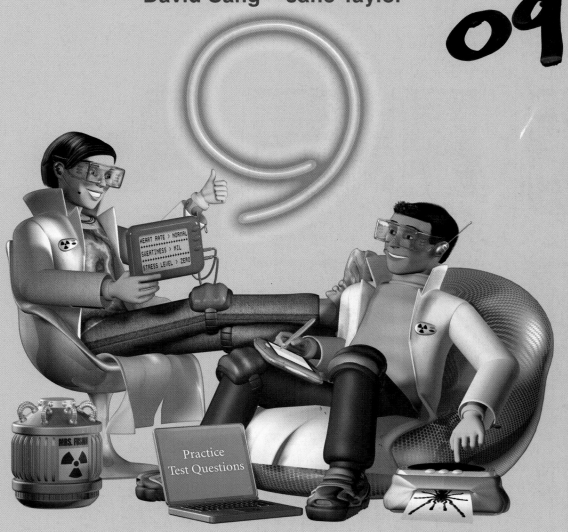

Published in 2005 by:
Nelson Thornes Ltd
Delta Place
27 Bath Road
CHELTENHAM
GL53 7TH
United Kingdom

05 06 07 08 09 / 10 9 8 7 6 5 4 3 2 1

A catalogue record for this book is available from the British Library

ISBN 0 7487 7996 5

Illustrations by Mark Draisey, Bede Illustration
Cover illustration by Andy Parker
Page make-up by Wearset Ltd

Printed in Croatia by Zrinski

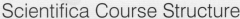

Scientifica Course Structure

0 7487 7996 5
Levels 4–7
Student Book

0 7487 8000 9
Complete teacher
guidance
for Levels 4–7

0 7487 8035 1
Teacher Resource
Pack for total
learning support and
extension

0 7487 8037 8
ICT Power
Pack for
Supercharged
lessons!

0 7487 7997 3
Levels 3–6
Student Book

0 7487 8003 3
Complete teacher
guidance
for Levels 3–6

0 7487 8040 8
Formative and
summative
progression tracking

0 7487 9487 5
CD-ROM
and Online
Test and
Assessment

year
9

0 7487 9205 8
Ultimate SEN
support

0 7487 9015 2
Fantastic science
reading

0 7487 9186 8
Low cost.
take-home
personalise

CONTENTS

Scientifica

LEARN ABOUT
How Scientifica works

See which lesson you are studying

This shows what you should hope to learn in this lesson. If you don't understand these things at the end, read through the pages again, and don't be afraid to ask teacher!

LINK UP TO

You can use the things you learn in Science in other subjects too. These panels will help you watch out for things that will help you in other lessons like Maths, Geography and Citizenship. Sometimes they will contain handy hints about other sections of the book.

ICT CHALLENGE

It's really important to develop good computer skills at school. These ICT Challenges will provide lots of interesting activities that help you practice.

Welcome to Scientifica

Why should Science textbooks be boring? We think Science is amazing, and that's why we've packed this book full of great ideas. You'll find tons of amazing facts, gruesome details, clever activities and funny cartoons. There's lots of brilliant Science too!

Here are some of the main features in Scientifica. There are lots more to discover if you look…

Get stuck in

Whenever you see a blue-coloured panel, it means it's time to start doing some science activities. This blue panel provides a set of simple instructions you can follow. Your teacher may also have a sheet to help you and for you to write on.

Meet the Scientifica crew!

Molly Kewell   Mike Roscope   Pip Ette   Benson Burner   Reese Cycle   Pete Ridish

Throughout the book you may see lots of questions, with four possible answers. Only one is correct. The answers **are in different colours.** If the teacher gives the class coloured cards to vote with, it will be easy to show your vote.

Q1 Did you really understand what you just read?

Q2 Are you sure?

Q3 Won't these questions help you check?

SUMMARY QUESTIONS

At the end of each lesson, there is a set of questions to see if you understood everything.

☆ See those stars at the beginning of each question?

They tell you whether a question is supposed to be Easy (☆), Medium (☆☆) or Hard (☆☆☆).

AMAZING SCIENCE!

Freaky insects, expanding bridges, boiling hot super stars… These are the most fantastic facts you can find!

Find out how scientists worked out what we know so far. Don't worry! There's plenty for the scientists of the future to find out.

IDEAS AND EVIDENCE

Gruesome science

Lethal clouds of poison gas, dead human skin cells, killer electric eels… Sometimes Science can be just plain nasty! Why not learn about that too?

UNIT REVIEW

There are loads of homework questions at the end of each Unit. There are lots of different types too. If you complete all the SAT-style questions, the teacher may be able to tell you what Level you are working at. Do your best to improve as you go along!

DANGER! AVOID THESE COMMON ERRORS

'Er, the Sun goes out like a light-bulb at night, right?' People make mistakes about science all the time. Before you leave the topic, this will help you make sure you're not one of them!

Phenomenal performance

If you do *brilliantly* in the lesson, your *extraordinary* teacher may ask you to turn towards the back of this *fantastic* book. There are lots of *super* activities for you to try in the *Phenomenal Performance* section.

Don't forget!

At the back of the book you will find lots of help for your revision before the Key Stage 3 Tests.

Good luck! – *Lawrie, David and Jane*

Key words

amazing
brilliant
phenomenal

Keywords are a handy way of remembering a topic. Some might be scrambled up though!

9A Inheritance and selection

COMING SOON

9A1 Variation

9A2 Passing on the genes

9A3 Breeding animals

9A4 Breeding plants

9A5 Inherited conditions

Let me see. Eye of bat, tongue of frog, a dollop of DDT... yes! the perfect wasp catcher. I'll sell millions.

What's it all about?

If you inherited the family nose, what are the chances your children will get it too?

In this unit you will learn more about inherited features. You will find out about how we apply genetics – the science of inheritance – to develop new varieties of animals and plants.

We can use this same knowledge to predict whether individuals are likely to suffer from inherited health problems.

 ## What do you remember?

You already know about:
- cell structure.
- human and plant reproduction.
- how individuals vary.

1 Name the parts indicated on this diagram of an animal cell.

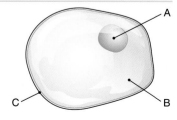

2 Which of these carries inherited information?

gene   alveolus   villus   chloroplast

3 Match the pairs:

fertilisation	pollen grain reaching the female part of a plant
pollination	discharge of the uterus lining every four weeks
ovulation	nucleus of sperm cells and egg cells combine
menstruation	egg cell is released from the ovary

4 Which of these features of a plant is affected by the environment in which it is growing?

size of leaf   colour of flower
shape of leaf   perfume of flower

Ideas about differences

QUESTIONS

The Scientifica crew seem to have forgotten some of what they learned about variation.

a) Cats inherit their coat colour. Patch is black with white patches. Tom is tabby striped. Are they likely to have ginger kittens?

b) What are the little pips on strawberries? Can scientists change the way a plant grows and develops?

c) Pip's bean is bigger than Benson's so she thinks it must be a different sort. Is that true?

d) Suggest some reasons why the beans are different sizes.

LAUNCH

Variation

9A1

LEARN ABOUT

- variations
- presenting data in graphs

Have you ever had your temperature taken? Was it 37°C, as it says in the books? You might be surprised to know that a healthy person may have a body temperature that is slightly different, perhaps 36.8°C. Human body temperature varies slightly from one person to another; 37°C is an average. Body temperature is just one of the many features that varies between people.

Q1 Suggest five ways in which humans vary from each other.

Variation

Your sex is a feature for which there are two possibilities – male or female. There are more possibilities for your blood group. Features that vary in this way show **discontinuous variation**.

Plants have features that vary discontinuously too. Garden peas may make round seeds or wrinkled seeds. Courgettes may make green or yellow fruits.

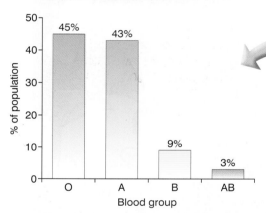

There are four main blood groups in the UK

Your height is not an 'either/or' feature. A pupil in Year 9 can be any height between 150 cm and 180 cm and still be within the normal range of heights for a Year 9 student. This is an example of a feature that shows **continuous variation**. Weight is another feature that varies continuously between individuals.

Q2 Cats can be black, ginger or tabby. Is this an example of continuous or discontinuous variation?

Genes, the environment and you

You have **genes** that control how your hair grows, your blood group and what shape your nose takes. In fact most of our features are controlled by genes. Features such as your blood group are entirely due to the genes you have inherited. Other animals and plants have features that are entirely inherited. For example, the colour of a rose depends on its genes, not on the kind of soil or the climate it grows in.

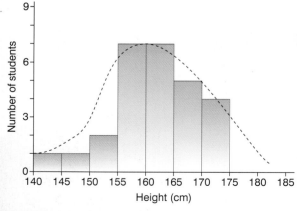

Heights of girls in Year 9

Although the colour of apple blossom growing on an apple tree is due to genes, the size of an apple growing from the tree can be affected by its **environment**. Genes determine whether it produces a large or a small type of fruit. But the amount of sunlight and water, and the temperature in spring, all affect how big the fruit actually grows.

We have features that will be affected by the environment we grow up in. We have all inherited the capacity to use language – but the languages we speak and understand depend on the family environment we grew up in. Your diet will affect how tall you are and visiting an orthodontist may affect how exactly your teeth grow.

Variation

- Measure your body temperature and compare it with others in the class.
  How much variation is there in body temperature? Is the average temperature 37°C?

- Investigate how the hand span of people in your class varies. Stretch your fingers out and measure the distance from the tip of your thumb to the tip of your little finger.

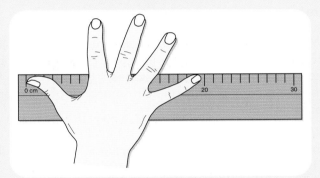

Measuring handspan

Why is it important that everyone holds their fingers out straight? Make a table of your data.
Use your data to plot a graph. What sort of graph should you plot? Explain the pattern that you see.

Q3 Try to think of a feature of humans which is inherited from parents but which is not affected by the environment.

Q4 Think of another human feature which is affected by the environment.

AMAZING SCIENCE!

Scientists still don't know how many genes we have. Estimates range from 30 000 to 60 000.

ICT **CHALLENGE**

Use a spreadsheet to manage your data.

SUMMARY QUESTIONS

1 ☆ What is meant by discontinuous variation?

2 ☆ Which of the four features below could be affected by the environment you live in?

   foot length   **gap between front teeth**   **skin tone**   **eye colour**

3 ☆☆ Sort the following features into those that show continuous variation and those that show discontinuous variation.

   body temperature   **ear lobe shape**   **height**   **eye colour**
   blood group   **your sex**   **flower colour**   **fruit size**
   the languages you speak

Key words
continuous variation
discontinuous variation
environment
gene

Passing on the genes

9A2

Young animals and plants are like their parents because they have inherited features from them. These features vary between individuals. You may have a different blood group from the person next to you as well as a different eye colour.

● Inheriting features

Information for inherited features is carried by **genes** on pairs of **chromosomes** in the nucleus of cells. They are passed on through sperm and eggs. Sperm and eggs are called **gametes**. Pollen and ovules carry genetic information in plants.

Q1 Where are **a)** sperm and **b)** eggs made?

ovaries   uterus   penis   testes

When sperm and eggs are made they receive copies of the chromosomes in the parent's cells. However, they have only half the number of chromosomes. This is because they receive a copy of only one chromosome of each pair in a parental cell.

When a sperm fertilises an egg the chromosomes carried by the egg pair up with the chromosomes carried by the sperm. The fertilised egg now has the same number of chromosomes as the parents' cells, and it has inherited a mixture of its parents' genes.

Q2 A mouse has 40 chromosomes in its body cells. How many chromosomes will there be in an egg cell of a female mouse?

One pair of chromosomes determines which sex you are. Girls carry two X chromosomes. Boys carry an X and a Y chromosome. Women can only pass on a copy of an X chromosome into their eggs. A man can pass on copies of his X chromosome or his Y chromosome to his sperm. Half his sperm will carry his X chromosome, half his Y chromosome. The sex of the child is decided by which sperm fertilises the egg.

● What are the chances?

A baby has two copies of the genes for each inherited feature. It inherits one copy on the chromosome from its father and another copy on the chromosome from its mother.

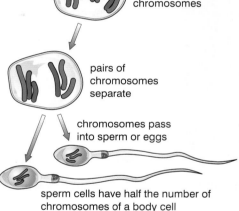

Ahh... you've inherited my eyes

How chromosomes pass into sperms and eggs

parent cell 3 pairs of chromosomes

pairs of chromosomes separate

chromosomes pass into sperm or eggs

sperm cells have half the number of chromosomes of a body cell

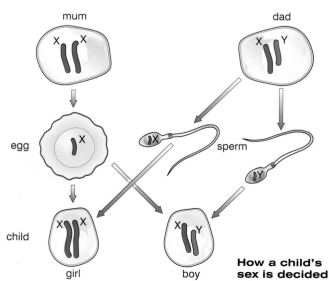

mum

dad

egg

sperm

child

girl   boy

How a child's sex is decided

Sometimes the two genes are the same, for example, both genes are for blue eyes, or for blood group A. Sometimes they are different, say, one brown hair gene and one blonde hair gene. Different forms of genes are called **alleles**.

Some alleles, such as the allele for brown eyes, are **dominant**. If you inherit a copy it will be shown. The other form, in this case blue eyes, is **recessive** and is not shown. You would need to inherit blue eyes from both parents to have blue eyes. In the genetic diagram you can see how this can affect the outward appearance of a person.

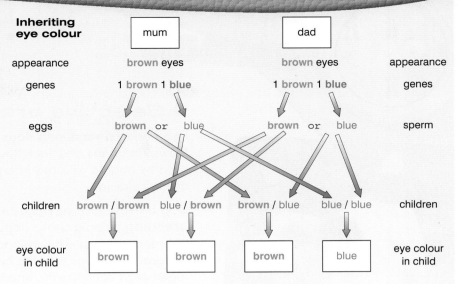

Pass it on

Mr and Mrs Morgan are very proud of their red hair. Their four children all have red hair too. Red hair is a recessive feature to brown hair.

- Look at the family trees in the diagram. Martin is married to Anneka who also has red hair. Mabel married Luke who has brown hair. Try to work out the hair colour of:
  a) Martin's daughter Marie
  b) Mabel's son Michael.

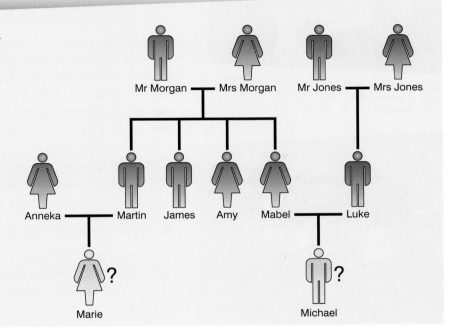

SUMMARY QUESTIONS

1 ☆ Where are chromosomes located?

2 ☆ How do the chromosomes of a sperm cell differ from chromosomes in other cells of the body?

3 ☆ What is an allele?

4 ☆☆☆ Mr and Mrs Bright both have brown eyes. Their brown-eyed son Robin marries Sandra, a blue-eyed girl. The allele for brown eyes is dominant to blue eyes. Are Robin and Sandra's children likely to have brown eyes? Could they have a blue-eyed child?

Key words
allele
chromosome
dominant
gamete
gene
recessive

Breeding animals

● Selective breeding

Five hundred years ago dogs such as Shetland sheepdogs, Newfoundlands and Jack Russell terriers did not exist. They have been bred by people who are interested in producing dogs that are good at a particular job.

Dog breeds, such as Dachshunds, are the result of **selective breeding**. People chose dogs that had particularly desirable features to breed together. They hoped that the pups would inherit these features. The pups with the best combination of features were bred together to continue the improvement.

Jack Russell terriers were bred by Reverend John Russell. He wanted a small sturdy dog with a narrow chest and flexible body for following foxes through narrow tunnels into their dens.

Dachshunds were bred to hunt badgers. They also had to be small, thin and flexible to enter a badger's sett. They were selected to be fearless and persevering, as badgers are extremely fierce animals when threatened. They also needed a deep bark so the hunters above ground could locate them underground. Nowadays they make good pets.

The Jack Russell terrier was bred to have a white coat to stop hunters mistaking it for a fox when hunting

Q1 What are Border Collies used for? What features do they have that make them good at their job?

Sheepdogs use their hunting ability to control sheep

● Increasing productivity

Farm animals have been bred to increase **productivity**. Productivity is the amount of saleable product, for example meat, eggs, milk, wool, that the farmer gets from an animal for the cost of keeping and feeding it.

Selective breeding has increased the productivity of cows. Cows produce more milk per year than they did two hundred years ago. Other important features that breeders consider are the nutrient content of the milk, how easily a cow gives birth to its calves, and whether the shape of the udder is suitable for automated milking machines.

I've bred him to hunt chicken nuggets.

Chicky Bits

Data about a bull's daughters helps farmers choose a bull whose genes will improve their own herd

Farmers who keep a breeding herd do not usually keep a bull. They buy samples of sperm from suitable bulls kept at stud farms. The sperm is used to **artificially inseminate** the cows.

● Breeding for rearing

Many farm animals are reared intensively. Chickens grown for the food market are kept inside in warm sheds. They are bred to have fewer feathers, which allows more energy from their food to go into making their body meat. They are also bred to grow very quickly, so they reach marketable size in a few weeks. Pigs bred for bacon production have longer backs than other pigs. There will be more meat from these pigs for back bacon.

Plenty of rashers on old Spot.

Dogs from the 2.5 kg Chihuahua to the 95 kg St Bernard were all bred from wolves.

The mating game

Farmer Martin and farmer Ruth both want to improve their dairy herds. Martin wants to reduce the amount he pays in vets' fees. Ruth wants to improve the volume of milk her cows produce.

● Look at the stud book entries for three bulls.
  Choose a bull for Martin and one for Ruth to breed with their cows.

	Hereford Bonzer	Hoof Boy	Big Blue
weight at 500 days	610 kg	425 kg	540 kg
number of calves	152	185	146
% difficult calvings	5%	0.0%	1%
daughter's milk production	585 kg	607 kg	682 kg
protein content	20.5 kg	21.1 kg	21.6 kg
milking speed	average	average	very good

Gruesome science

Bull sperm can be frozen for years. A bull can still father calves long after he has become pet food.

SUMMARY QUESTIONS

1 ☆ Why do farmers selectively breed animals?

2 ☆☆ Make a flow chart of the process of selective breeding.

3 ☆☆ What features should a breeder look for in a guide dog for the blind?

4 ☆☆ Try to find out what Newfoundland dogs were bred for.

Key words

artificial insemination
productivity
selective breeding

LEARN ABOUT
■ breeding plants

Plants have features that are controlled by genes. The colour of their flowers, their leaf shape, and how tall the plant can grow are all inherited features. Genes for these features are passed on through pollen and ovules.

● Passing on genes

Pollen and ovules carry chromosomes from the parent plants. When a pollen grain fertilises an ovule, the chromosomes from each parent pair up. The young plant that grows from a seed will have a mixture of features from each parent.

Unlike humans, plants usually produce more than one seed at a time. Each seed inherits its own individual combination of chromosomes, and hence genes, from each parent. We may talk about things being 'as alike as two peas in a pod', but in fact the peas in a pod will grow into plants which are different.

Q1 What is the name of the process that results in a pollen grain reaching the female part of a plant?

dispersal   pollination   ovulation   germination

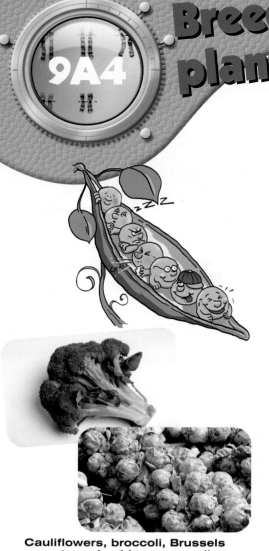

Cauliflowers, broccoli, Brussels sprouts and cabbages are all the result of selective breeding from the same wild ancestors

● Plant breeding

Plant breeders produce new **varieties** of flowers and crops. If you look into a plant catalogue you will find over 20 varieties of lettuce. They have been produced by selective breeding. They are the same species, but they have different leaf colours, shapes and textures. These distinctive features are genetic and are passed on through seeds.

Breeders select plants that have a particularly desirable feature and breed them together. The breeder will place pollen from one of the parent plants onto the stigma of the other parent plant. The seeds it produces are planted and grown on. Any of the young plants showing the desired features are bred together to produce the next generation of seeds. The process may take many generations before strong plants with the desired features are produced.

Plant breeders are usually working towards improving crop productivity. They produce plants that can withstand diseases better, or cope better with adverse weather conditions or give a better crop.

Q2 Bad weather, such as wind and rain, can flatten grain crops, such as wheat, and reduce the yield. What features could a plant breeder develop to help weather resistance?

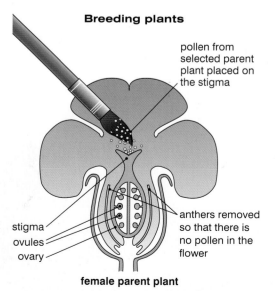

Breeding plants

pollen from selected parent plant placed on the stigma

stigma
ovules
ovary

anthers removed so that there is no pollen in the flower

female parent plant

● Genetic manipulation

It takes many years and thousands of plants to produce a new variety by selective breeding. Some plants, such as cultivated bananas do not reproduce sexually at all so it is almost impossible to selectively breed them. Plant breeders can use scientific knowledge of genetics to solve this problem and speed up the process.

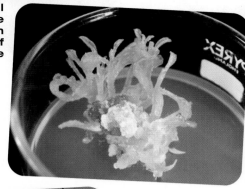

Several identical plantlets are developing from this sample of plant tissue

If we have one plant with the right features we can make thousands more by **cloning** it. Small sections of tissue are grown in a nutrient jelly and sprout into individual plants within weeks. Thousands of new plants can be generated this way from a good parent plant.

Another method uses genetic engineering. A desirable gene is transferred directly into crop plant cells. The plant cells are allowed to develop into new plants carrying the gene. Cotton and maize plants that are poisonous to insects do not need expensive chemicals to reduce insect damage to the crop. These genes can come from other plant species or even other sorts of living things. These plants are **genetically modified**.

These genetically modified cotton plants make a chemical that kills the bollworm, an insect that attacks cotton plants

A bean feast

Haricot, kidney, and runner beans are important food crops. Investigate the variation in three bean varieties.
● What evidence is there that you are looking at three different types of bean?
● Measure the length of a suitable number of beans from each sample and present your data in a table.
● What is the range for each variety?
● It has been said that beans are sorted for size before being packaged for sale. Compare garden-grown and packaged beans. Do your results support this statement?
● What factors could be affecting the size of the beans in your samples?
● If you were keeping beans to sow for next year's crop, which ones would you choose?

SUMMARY QUESTION

1 ✷✷ A plant breeder wants to breed a new variety of potato. He wants it to resist potato blight infections and make good mashed potato. The breeder already has a variety that makes good mashed potato, but it is easily infected with blight. He has another variety that resists blight, but the potatoes stay hard when cooked.
   a) Explain how the breeder could cross the two varieties.
   b) The breeder grew the seeds from the cross and found some grew into plants that resisted blight and made good potatoes. How could the breeder make more of these plants?

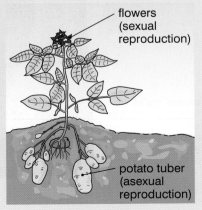

flowers (sexual reproduction)

potato tuber (asexual reproduction)

A potato plant

ICT ⟩ CHALLENGE

Use a spreadsheet to analyse your data.

Key words

clone
genetic modification
pollination
variety

Inherited conditions

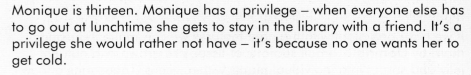

LEARN ABOUT
- how we inherit unfavourable genes

Monique is thirteen. Monique has a privilege – when everyone else has to go out at lunchtime she gets to stay in the library with a friend. It's a privilege she would rather not have – it's because no one wants her to get cold.

Monique has a condition called **sickle-cell anaemia**. Her red blood cells take an unusual sickle shape when they release oxygen in her body tissues. Sometimes they get stuck in the tiniest blood vessels and reduce the flow of blood. Her joints swell up and she suffers a lot of pain in her hands, arms and back. She hates it when she has to miss school because she needs to go to hospital for treatment. The people who care for her are great, but she would rather be with her mates.

Q1 What shape are normal red blood cells?

Monique inherited her condition from her parents. Both of her parents carry a sickle-cell gene. It affects the haemoglobin in her red blood cells. It does not carry oxygen as well as normal haemoglobin does. Both of her parents also have a normal haemoglobin gene so they are hardly affected. Before they had Monique, they did not know that they had the gene. Now all the family members have been tested to find out if they carry the gene too. Monique's cousin Gary has the **sickle-cell trait**. He carries one copy of the sickle-cell gene but has a normal gene as well.

AMAZING SCIENCE!

An octopus has blue blood.

The red blood cells in a person with sickle-cell anaemia become distorted when they lose oxygen. They can easily block capillaries.

Q2 Why does the haemoglobin problem mean that Monique has to stay in to keep warm?

● Unfavourable genes

Some genes have effects we might not be too keen on, for example, having hairy fingers, an extra finger, or webbing between a couple of toes. These effects are not harmful.

There are a few other genes that can have harmful effects if we inherit them. Most of them are **recessive** and people must inherit a copy of the gene from each parent before the condition develops. The genes causing cystic fibrosis and thalassaemia are both recessive. Thalassaemia is a blood disorder and cystic fibrosis affects the lungs and digestive system.

Once someone has been diagnosed as suffering from a genetic disorder, the rest of the family may wonder if they have it too. The family can talk to a **genetic counsellor** who can tell them about tests to see if they have the faulty gene and the probability of the gene being inherited or passed on.

Does my extra finger look big in this?

Counselling Monique's family

Here is Monique's family tree.

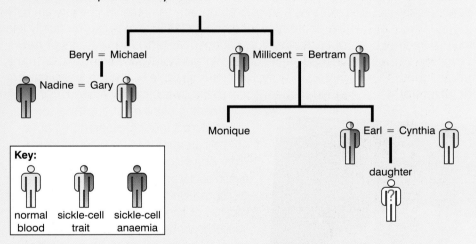

Beryl = Michael

Nadine = Gary

Millicent = Bertram

Monique

Earl = Cynthia

daughter

Key:

normal blood | sickle-cell trait | sickle-cell anaemia

- Could Earl's daughter suffer from sickle-cell anaemia?
- Could Gary's son suffer from sickle-cell anaemia?

Gruesome science

Hundreds of years ago women with an extra finger were thought to be witches.

ICT ⟩ CHALLENGE

Find out about one of these genetic disorders and make a PowerPoint presentation about it to the rest of the class.

SUMMARY QUESTIONS

1 ☆ What haemoglobin genes does someone with sickle-cell trait have?

2 ☆☆ Write sentences that make the meaning of the following terms clear:
dominant   recessive   gene   cystic fibrosis

3 ☆☆ Write out the word equation for oxygen binding with haemoglobin.

Key words

genetic counselling
recessive
sickle-cell anaemia
sickle-cell trait

IDEAS AND EVIDENCE

Breeding endangered animals

Animal and plant breeders use selective breeding to improve certain features and produce populations that all have the same favoured genetic feature. Zoos selectively breed animals with the opposite aim in mind – to produce populations that are as genetically different as possible.

All around the world, animals and plants are threatened by human activity. Zoos hold small groups of **endangered species**. The animals living in zoos form a significant proportion of the total population of that species so zoos can help conserve them.

Zoos cannot keep large groups of any animal. There are usually just three or four adults. Animals bred together within a small zoo population lose some of the variation of the species as a whole. This reduces **genetic diversity**.

Also too much **inbreeding** (mating closely related animals together) can bring genetic problems and recessive genes to prominence. Animals are mated with animals from other zoos. The aim is to produce and keep a healthy, genetically diverse and stable population across many different zoos.

There are species survival plans (SSP) for many endangered species. In the SSP there are 'family trees' and plans for breeding that will result in maximum genetic diversity. A studbook contains the records of every animal in the entire managed population of a species. The family line of each individual is logged. All births and parents of new animals are recorded. So are deaths and transfers. With this information available, it is possible to choose individuals to breed that are not genetically too closely related.

Breeding plans must also take some other factors into consideration. Some animals are physically difficult to move from one place to another. Many mammals live in social and family groups that are disrupted when one member, perhaps the mother of the group, has to leave for a year. The transferred animal is stressed through having to leave a group and establish itself in a new already established group.

The giant tortoises of Galapagos are unique. Tortoises from each island have different shell patterns. Conservation measures reduce competition from introduced species and hunting.

- *Some of the differences between individuals are genetic.*
- *Inherited features are carried by genes and passed on through eggs, sperm, pollen and ovules.*
- *Some features controlled by genes are also affected by the environment.*
- *In selective breeding, individuals with desirable features are chosen to be the parents of the next generation.*
- *Desirable plants may be cloned.*
- *Genes can be transferred between species.*
- *Breeders aim to increase productivity in farm animals and crops.*
- *Some genes can cause problems when they are inherited.*

DANGER! AVOID THESE COMMON ERRORS

Dominant genes are dominant in all individuals possessing them. Genes do not change their dominance or recessiveness.

Selective breeders can only change features that are controlled by genes. If a feature is not genetic then offspring will not inherit it.

Key words

endangered species
genetic diversity
inbreeding

REVIEW QUESTIONS
Understanding and applying concepts

1   What are the two sorts of variation? Give an example of each.

2   a   Give an example of a feature that is controlled entirely by genes.
    b   Give an example of a feature that is affected by environmental factors.

3   Parents pass on inherited features to their offspring.
    a   Name two types of cells that pass on inherited information from parents to offspring.
    b   How are the chromosomes of these cells different from those of normal cells?
    c   Explain why a child has the same number of chromosomes in its cells as its parents.

4   Explain fully how the sex of a child is decided.

Ways with words

5   There are both chromosomes and genes in the nucleus of cells. Write a sentence using both words to show what these terms mean.

Thinking skills

6   Two reasons why scientists selectively breed animals and plants are:
    ● to obtain more milk from a cow at each milking
    ● to develop a sweeter apple.

    Add some more reasons to this list.

Making more of maths

7   Molly counted how many redcurrants there were in the clusters hanging from a branch of her redcurrant bush. She made a bar chart to show her results.

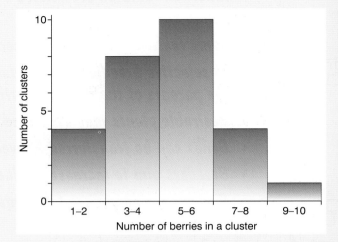

    a   What is the most frequent number of redcurrants in a cluster?
    b   What was the largest number of redcurrants in a cluster?

SAT-STYLE QUESTIONS

1   The diagram shows sperm and egg cells, and what happens just before fertilisation.

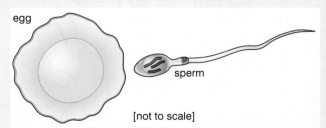

egg

sperm

[not to scale]

    a   Describe one way in which a sperm cell is adapted for its function.   (1)
    b   i)   The chromosomes in the sperm cell are shown in the drawing. Copy the egg cell and add the corresponding chromosomes on it.   (1)
        ii) Draw the fertilised egg and add the chromosomes.   (1)
    c   Explain why identical twins are identical.   (2)
    d   Cigarette smoke affects how the foetus grows in the uterus so that babies born to women who smoke are smaller.
        Name two other factors that could affect how well a foetus or young baby grows. (2)

2 The loganberry is a fruit thought to be the result of breeding together a raspberry and a type of blackberry. It has a larger sweeter berry than either of its parents.

a What word describes the breeding of two different varieties of plant to produce offspring with a particularly desirable feature? (1)

b Suggest one other feature that soft fruit growers might like their loganberries to have. (1)

c Plant breeders are trying to develop currant bushes that carry their fruit at the tips of the branches to make picking easier. Describe the steps they should take in a selective breeding process. (5)

3 Sickle-cell anaemia is an inherited condition in which red blood cells make abnormal haemoglobin (HbS).

A person needs to inherit the HbS gene from both parents to develop sickle-cell anaemia. Someone with sickle-cell trait has one HbS gene and one normal gene, and makes a mixture of normal and abnormal haemoglobin.

Look at the family tree:

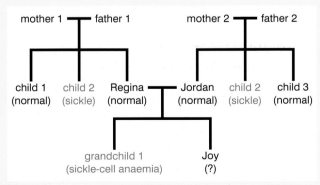

a What haemoglobin genes are carried by
i) Regina? (1)
ii) Jordan? (1)

b What can you deduce about the genes carried by Regina's father and mother? (1)

c Explain how the new baby Joy could have only normal haemoglobin. (1)

d What is the function of haemoglobin in the body? (1)

The HbS gene is common in Western Africa and in people whose families originated there. Malaria is also common in that part of the world and kills many people each year.

When malaria parasites infect, they enter red blood cells and digest haemoglobin. They find it hard to infect cells containing sickle haemoglobin.

e Explain why it may be an advantage to have sickle-cell trait where malaria is common. (2)

4 Mike and Pete were investigating how much variation there is in beans.

They measured the length of 25 beans and recorded their data in a table.

Bean length (mm)	Tally	Number
10–12	I	1
13–15	⑂⑂⑂	
16–18	⑂⑂⑂ I	6
19–21	⑂⑂⑂ III	
22–24	⑂⑂⑂	5

a Copy and complete the table of results. (1)

b What is the most frequent size of bean? (1)

c Use the data to construct a graph. (5)

d Does the data support the idea that beans show continuous variation? (1)

e What factors could have influenced the size of the beans? (2)

Key words

Unscramble these:
severe sic
giner in bed
sorchoomme
raytive

9B

Fit and healthy

Coming soon

9B1 Skeleton
9B2 Muscles
9B3 Eating well
9B4 Unhealthy hearts
9B5 Smoking
9B6 Alcohol and drugs

He's fit!

What's it all about?

'Get fit' we are told – but what is 'fitness' and how can you measure it? Part of being fit is about having a healthy body with all its systems working well.

Fitness is also about being alert and interested in the world around you, and ready to try something new. When you make demands on your body – running for the bus, travelling on a long journey, doing exams – it should be able to cope with all the stresses and strains you put on it.

You already know quite a lot about what your body needs to be healthy. In this unit we look at how your lifestyle can affect your health.

What do you remember?

You already know about:
- nutrients in a balanced diet.
- factors that harm a developing fetus.
- factors that harm your lungs.

1 Which of these is/are nutrients?
carbohydrate   fibre   fat   minerals

2 Which of these should form the largest part of a balanced diet?
carbohydrates   protein
fat   vitamins

3 Which parts of the body are harmed by smoking?

4 How does a developing baby in the uterus get the oxygen and nutrients it needs?

5 Your heart pumps blood. Where does blood go when it is pumped by:
a) the left hand side of the heart?
b) the right hand side of the heart?

Ideas about fitness

LAUNCH

QUESTIONS

The Scientifica crew have learned about how different body systems work. They have the knowledge but they aren't sure how it applies to everyday life.

a) How can owning a dog help you to keep fit?

b) How is the man on the bench harming his health?

c) The girl is not fat but is she healthy?

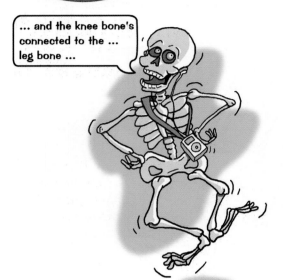

... and the knee bone's connected to the ... leg bone ...

Forensic scientists can learn a lot from buried skeletons. They can discover how long the skeleton has been there – two months or two thousand years. Your skeleton and teeth are the hardest parts of your body. They remain long after the rest of you has decayed. Even the chemicals in your bones tell scientists about where you lived.

Skeleton

Your **skeleton** consists of bones that:

- protect your internal organs, for example, your ribs protect your lungs and heart from damage by crushing,
- are a strong support for the whole body,
- anchor muscles, so that you can move,
- make new red and white blood cells.

Your skull encloses your brain and protects it from damage. Your skull is attached to your backbone, or **spine**. Your spine is made of small bones called vertebrae that fit closely together. They can move against each other slightly, which allows the spine to bend and flex so that you can move about easily. The bones of your arms and legs are attached to your skeleton through bones at the shoulders and hips.

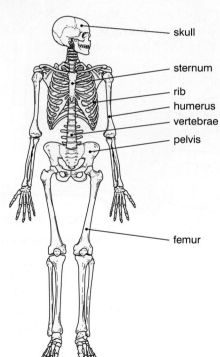

- skull
- sternum
- rib
- humerus
- vertebrae
- pelvis
- femur

The human skeleton

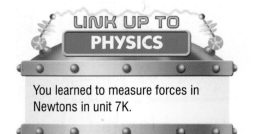

LINK UP TO
PHYSICS

You learned to measure forces in Newtons in unit 7K.

AMAZING SCIENCE!

There are 206 bones in the human body. Sixty of them are in our hands and arms.

Bones

We are making new bone material all the time. If you start to do a new physically strenuous activity, your bones soon strengthen to meet the new demands. If you go off into space however, like an astronaut, your bones will have less work to do because you will weigh less. They will lose mass and become weaker. We need plenty of calcium in our diet for strong bones and vitamin D to help us absorb calcium from our food.

Observing bones and joints

- Look carefully at a model elbow or knee joint.
  Work the joint. Notice how the ends of the bones slide over each other as the joint bends.
  Notice how the ends of the bones are shaped.
  Examine a bone more carefully. Look at the end of the bone. Can you see evidence of cartilage?
  Draw the end of the bone. The centre of the bone is not as solid as the other layers. This reduces the bone mass without losing strength. The centre of the bone holds marrow. Bone marrow makes new blood cells.

- Make a model hinge joint.

We exert so much force on our bones as we move that scientists have had to develop special super-strong metal alloys to repair damaged bones and joints.

Joints

The place where two bones meet together is called a **joint**. Strong ligaments hold the bones together.

Your bones can move and slide over each other smoothly when you bend a joint because the ends are covered in **cartilage**. Cartilage is a slippery, flexible material. The vertebrae in your spine have pads of cartilage in between them. These act as shock absorbers, as well as helping the vertebrae move smoothly.

Q1 In one type of arthritis, cartilage in some joints is damaged and roughened. How can this make the joint stiffer?

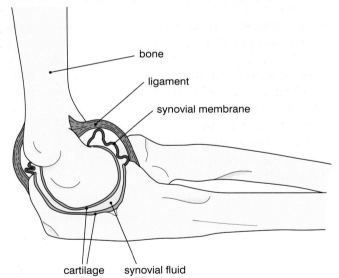

bone
ligament
synovial membrane
cartilage   synovial fluid

A joint

Bend ze knees!

SUMMARY QUESTIONS

1 ⭐ Give two functions of bones.

2 ⭐ What holds bones together at joints?

3 ⭐⭐ What is cartilage? How does it help a joint work smoothly?

4 ⭐⭐ Why is it better to have many small bones in the spine rather than one long bone?

Key words

bone
cartilage
joint
skeleton
spine

Muscles

9B2

LEARN ABOUT
- muscles
- how muscles work

We use **muscles** to move. Muscles force food through the digestive system, force blood through your body and force babies out into the world. Muscles pull your forearm up so that you can eat your pizza.

● How do muscles work?

Muscles are made of special cells that can **contract** (get shorter). When the muscle has finished its job the cells **relax**.

Contracting a muscle uses energy. This energy comes from respiration in muscle cells. Muscles have a good blood supply to bring glucose to them and remove wastes.

● Moving joints

Muscles that move us about are attached to the bones of the skeleton. They are attached by strong **tendons,** which join the end of the muscle to a bone.

Q1 What is the tendon called that joins the calf muscle to the heel bone?

The strongest weightlifters can lift almost 500 kilograms by sheer muscle power.

When a muscle contracts, it pulls on the bone it is attached to. Look at the diagram of the elbow joint. A pair of muscles works to bend and straighten the elbow.

Q2 What happens when the biceps contracts?

Q3 What happens when the triceps contracts?

A pair of muscles, such as the biceps and triceps, that work together to move a joint is called an **antagonistic pair**. One muscle of the pair contracts to **flex**, or bend, the joint. The other muscle contracts to **extend**, or straighten, the joint.

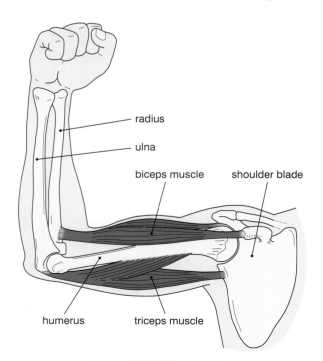

radius
ulna
biceps muscle
shoulder blade
humerus
triceps muscle

AMAZING SCIENCE!

PIZZA

At the upper end of the arm the biceps and triceps are attached to the bones of the shoulder. Muscles in the shoulder stabilise the shoulder joint. The shoulder does not move when we contract the biceps.

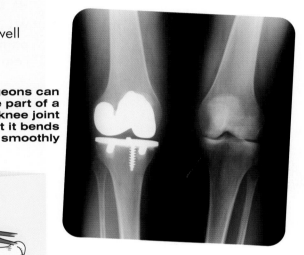

Contracting the biceps muscle pulls the forearm up

● Damaged joints

Saturday afternoon in the casualty department is sport injury time. Even if you warm up and train for your sport, you may expose your muscles, joints and bones to forces they cannot cope with.

Some people tear the ligaments that hold joints together. Others damage the tendons that hold muscles to bones. These injuries will heal in time and physiotherapy helps to restore muscle strength.

Osteoarthritis can develop in joints that are frequently injured, as well as in elderly people. The joint wears out. The bones rub against each other when the cartilage breaks down. Bony lumps and hardened bits of cartilage form and the joint becomes swollen and deformed. People with badly affected knees and hips can become severely disabled.

Surgeons can replace part of a damaged knee joint so that it bends smoothly

Bend the knees

Look at the diagram of a knee joint and the muscles associated with it.

● Explain how the muscles enable us to straighten the knee joint and to bend it.

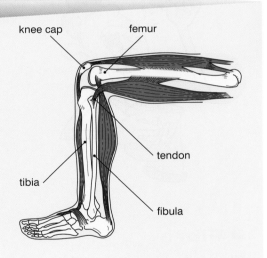

knee cap   femur

tendon

tibia

fibula

LINK UP TO PHYSICS

In unit 9L you will learn about levers. Muscles provide the force to move a lever – a bone.

SUMMARY QUESTIONS

1 ☆ Describe how muscles work.

2 ☆ How do muscles get the energy they need?

3 ☆ What are antagonistic muscles?

4 ☆☆ What is the difference between a ligament and a tendon?

Key words

antagonistic pair
contraction
extend
flex
muscle
relax
tendon

LEARN ABOUT
- balanced diets
- malnutrition
- the effects of an imbalanced diet on health

You know that a diet of cola, chips, crisps and pizza may be tasty, but it is not a **balanced diet**. It does not contain all the nutrients you need and has too high a proportion of fat to be healthy.

Q1 What is missing from this diet?

● Deficiency diseases

We suffer from **deficiency diseases** when we do not eat enough of a particular nutrient. A deficiency disease called **anaemia** is very common. It is the result of not having enough iron in your diet.

Q2 Name another deficiency disease.

The symptoms of anaemia include feeling very tired, lacking energy and looking pale. Iron is needed to make haemoglobin in red blood cells. If you do not have enough iron, you cannot replace worn out red cells efficiently. Your blood will not be able to carry as much oxygen round your body. This affects how much energy can be released in respiration. You look pale because your blood has fewer red cells in it than usual.

● Fibre

Fibre is the tough indigestible material found in plant foods. We cannot digest it but it is vital for a healthy digestive system. Fibre in your food helps to hold water in undigested food passing along your intestines. This keeps faeces soft so they move along the intestine quickly and easily. Scientists have found a link between a lack of fibre in the diet and bowel cancer.

It helps me go more quickly

LINK UP TO FOOD TECHNOLOGY

Find out about healthy products that you can eat as part of a balanced diet.

Are you getting enough?

- Use food labels and nutritional tables to research foods that are rich in iron or in fibre.
- Use what you have found out to plan family menus for
  a) a teenage girl who is anaemic, and
  b) her father, who wants to boost the fibre in his diet.

ICT CHALLENGE

Use a database to research vitamins, fibre and minerals in food.

Food	Fat (g/100 g)	Protein (g/100 g)	Calcium (mg/100 g)
milk	3.8	3.3	120
yoghurt	0.3	1.4	180
cheese	33.5	26.0	800
eggs	10.9	12.3	52
beef	22.0	17.1	8
chicken	17.7	17.6	3
cod	0.2	17.4	16

We need 1.1 g of calcium each day. Explain why children benefit from eating cheese but adults on a diet avoid it. (1 mg = 1/1000 g)

● Malnutrition

Deficiency diseases are the result of **malnutrition**. Some people do not get enough food at all, or not enough energy. Others eat too much food altogether. All of these cause health problems. Underfed children grow more slowly than children who eat a balanced diet. They are more likely to suffer or even die from infectious diseases and parasites such as worms.

Eating too much food and not using up the energy in activity causes **obesity**. Obesity too is linked to health problems. An obese person's extra mass puts more of a strain on the heart and circulatory system, and on joints. It may result in diabetes.

Some young people are also at risk because they are convinced that they must lose weight even though they are not overweight. They will not eat enough food, which restricts the amount of calories they get to a very low level. Sometimes they over-exercise as well. Eventually the damage done causes major health problems. This is an **eating disorder** known as anorexia nervosa.

That stuff will make you fat.

It's not as if I do this every day.

SUMMARY QUESTIONS

1 ☆ Give an example of a deficiency disorder.

2 ☆ Which organ is damaged if you do not eat enough fibre?

3 ☆☆ Explain how a bad diet can cause obesity.

4 ☆☆ People without enough vitamin D in their diet may suffer from a deficiency disease called rickets. Their bones are soft and bend under their mass. Explain how a shortage of this vitamin can lead to soft bones.

Key words
anaemia
balanced diet
deficiency disease
eating disorder
fibre
malnutrition
obesity

Your heart is a busy pump, beating hundreds of times every hour to circulate your blood through your body. Your blood transports materials around your body and remove wastes.

Blood picks up nutrients as it reaches your small intestine and oxygen as it reaches your lungs. It delivers these to cells, where it picks up carbon dioxide and other wastes. If your heart is not up to the job, your body does not get what it needs and accumulates harmful wastes. This will affect your ability to do what you want.

● Unhealthy circulation

There are some problems with the circulatory system that an unhealthy lifestyle makes worse. Some people suffer from **high blood pressure**. Their hearts have to work harder and this worsens other health problems.

Another major problem is atheroma. This is deposits of fatty material inside the arteries. They disrupt the smooth flow of blood. Blood can stick to the artery walls and form clots. Clots will block the flow of blood to the tissues and cause major damage. The artery walls harden at the same time. A **coronary thrombosis** occurs when blood clots block the blood vessels supplying the heart muscle. This disrupts the heart beat and blood supply to the rest of the body.

● Blood clotting

Healthy arteries have very smooth walls but atheroma roughens the surface. Platelets washed against the rough surface break open and start the clotting process. A blood clot protects your body from blood loss and infections. When you receive an injury, tissues are damaged. In the damaged area, platelets in your blood break open and release a substance that solidifies a protein in your blood. Tangled threads form that trap red blood cells and make a plug that stops blood escaping.

● How lifestyle affects the heart

Heart disease is made worse by an unhealthy lifestyle, including the following:

Smoking
Cigarette smoke contains carbon monoxide. Carbon monoxide reduces the amount of oxygen that blood cells can carry. Cigarette smoke also contains nicotine that raises the heart rate and increases blood pressure.

Poor diet
Eating too much, eating too much animal fat and eating too much sugar are all linked to atheroma. If you are very overweight, your heart has to work harder to supply your body.

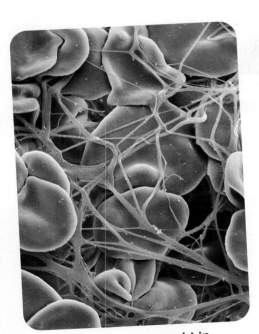

Red blood cells are caught in sticky threads to make a blood clot that seals a wound

Lack of exercise
Exercise protects the heart whether you are overweight or not. If you are not physically active you are likely to put on weight.

Stress
High levels of emotional stress raise your blood pressure and keep high levels of stress hormones in your blood.

How healthy is your heart?

Measuring your heart rate can be used to monitor fitness. Your pulse goes up when you are physically active and rapidly returns to your resting rate if you are fit.

Measuring the time it takes for your pulse to return to normal shows how fit you are.

● Sit on a chair quietly for a few minutes. Take your pulse.
Stand up and then run on the spot for 1 minute. Take your pulse immediately.
Sit down again and take your pulse at intervals until it returns to normal.
How long did it take?
Compare your results with others in your group.

● Look at the graph of Lara's pulse rate. Estimate how long it would take for her pulse to return to normal.

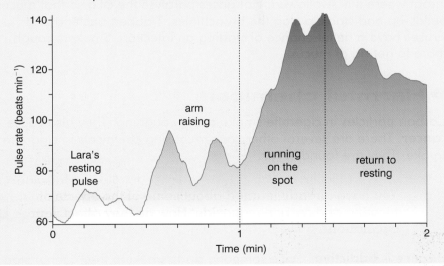

Whether you are resting or active, your brain needs 750 cm³ of blood delivered to it every minute.

 CHALLENGE

Use data logging equipment to record and display your pulse rate during several activities. Print out the graph and label it.

SUMMARY QUESTIONS

1 ☆ Blood is pumped to the lungs and the body organs by the heart. What substances does the blood collect from
 a) the lungs b) the small intestine?

2 ☆ Give one advantage and one disadvantage of blood clotting.

3 ☆☆ Explain how adopting a healthier lifestyle can lead to a healthier heart.

Key words
blood clotting
coronary thrombosis
high blood pressure

LEARN ABOUT
- the effects of cigarette smoke
- how medical ideas advance

Everyone knows that smoking harms the lungs, hinders breathing and will kill you. So, how does it cause these problems?

Smoking and breathing

You have lungs to take in oxygen and remove carbon dioxide from your body. This gas exchange takes place in alveoli, small air sacs in your lungs. We need hundreds of thousands of alveoli to provide us with enough surface area to exchange enough gases for our needs. Cigarette smoke is a very hot gas mixture that contains harmful substances. It damages the lungs and bodies of smokers and of those people around them in several ways.

Hot gases

Hot gases in smoke affect **ciliated cells** lining the airways. Dust and microbes in the air we breathe are trapped by mucus in the airways. In healthy airways, cilia sweep mucus and its trapped debris up to the throat where it is swallowed. Hot gases paralyse the cilia so that mucus builds-up and starts to clog the bronchioles. Trapped bacteria and viruses have a better chance of starting an infection. Smokers cough more to get rid of mucus.

Harmful chemicals

Carbon particles in cigarette smoke cause coughing. They also cause **cancer**. There are several other cancer-causing chemicals in cigarette smoke. They are found in **tar**.

Q1 You have already learned about some of the effects of nicotine and carbon monoxide. How do they affect your circulation?

Nicotine is **addictive**. Once someone starts smoking they cannot stop without experiencing unpleasant effects.

Smoking affects other parts of the body. Pregnant women who smoke are more likely to have a stillborn or premature baby. This is because chemicals in smoke can pass across the placenta and harm the fetus or slow its growth.

Tobacco has been used for hundreds of years and smoking became an accepted activity during the 20th century. Smoking did make people cough more and have worse chest infections, but the most harmful effects were not recognised for many years. Evidence began to accumulate that smoking caused serious harm.

Cilia will see them off.

Now _we_ look sillier!

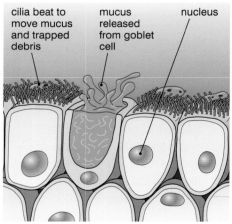

cilia beat to move mucus and trapped debris

mucus released from goblet cell

nucleus

Cells lining the trachea

Gruesome science

There are over forty different cancer-causing chemicals in cigarette smoke.

● Attitudes to smoking, 2002 survey

88%	of people	want restrictions on smoking in restaurants
86%	of people	think there should be restrictions on smoking at work
87%	of people	think there should be restrictions on smoking in other public places, such as banks and post offices
70%	of current smokers	said they would like to give up smoking
68%	of smokers wanting to give up	thought it would be better for their health if they did so
55%	of non-smokers	mind if other people smoke near them

Source: Smoking related behaviour and attitudes, 2002, Her Majesty's Stationery Office

Do your own survey. Ask five adults. Pool your groups' data.

Do your results match the national survey?

How did we find out that smoking was harmful?

Proving just how much harm smoking causes was difficult. Scientists investigating the problem could not do experiments on people to find out the harmful effects, so they did experiments using animals instead.

● Why can't we do experiments on people to find out if smoking is harmful?

● Why is the evidence collected from animal studies not enough on its own?

A committee of experts, led by Sir Richard Doll, was asked to look at research evidence from many sources about smoking and health.

Look at the graphs, which show some of that evidence.

● What does each graph show?

● Evidence like this shows **correlations**. They do not prove a cause. What other factors may be influencing the health of these people?

Gruesome science

In 1995, smoking was involved in 120 000 deaths: one in five of all deaths in the UK.

ICT ▶ CHALLENGE

Research the harmful effects of passive smoking.

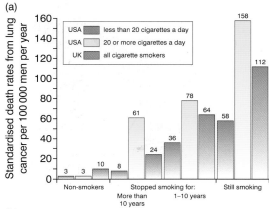

(a)

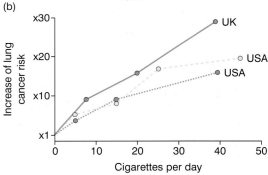

(b)

Source: Smoking and Health, Royal College of Physicians of London (1962), Pitman Publishing Co.

SUMMARY QUESTIONS

1 ☆ Name two harmful substances in cigarette smoke. Explain how each is harmful.

2 ☆ Give the scientific names for the wind pipe, air sacs, voice box.

3 ☆☆ Explain how ciliated cells protect us from infections.

4 ☆☆ Why do people find it hard to give up smoking?

Key words

addiction
cancer
ciliated cells
correlation
tar

LEARN ABOUT
- how alcohol affects behaviour
- how drugs affect your body

Cola seems to be the world's favourite drink. Why is it so popular? One of the ingredients in cola is **caffeine**, which certainly makes you feel refreshed. Caffeine is found in tea and coffee too. Caffeine is a stimulant. It makes you feel a bit more energetic.

● Drugs

Caffeine is a drug. A **drug** is any substance that changes the way the body works, physically or mentally. Your doctor may prescribe you with medications containing drugs when you are ill, or you may get something from the chemist. These drugs are to help your body with a medical problem. The amount you can take is carefully controlled.

Q1 Paracetemol is a drug used as a pain-killer. Can you name another sort of medical drug?

● Recreational drugs

People take recreational drugs because of the effect they have on their body. People smoke because it is calming, they drink coffee or cola because it is stimulating, and they drink alcoholic drinks because it makes them more relaxed. These are accepted recreational drugs, even though they may have adverse effects on your behaviour and reactions.

Q2 There are rules about who is allowed to smoke or to drink alcohol, and when and where smoking and drinking can take place. What are they?

It is illegal to use some recreational drugs. They have too many harmful effects to allow people to use them freely. They include drugs such as amphetamines, heroin, cocaine, cannabis and ecstasy. Drugs such as heroin can kill you. Solvents used to make glue can also be lethal because they chill the blood circulating in the brain.

Drugs such as cocaine, heroin and the nicotine in cigarette smoke are **addictive**. The body develops a physical need for them and suffers ill effects without them. They cause cravings. People need to take more and more of the drug to meet this craving.

LINK UP TO CITIZENSHIP

In Citizenship you learn about the social harm caused by drugs.

● Alcohol

Alcohol affects the nervous system. It slows down your reaction time, even though you may feel more confident. If you are driving or doing a complicated job, you are more likely to have an accident.

Alcohol is absorbed from the stomach into the blood stream. Its effects are felt very quickly. People drinking beer, wine and other alcoholic drinks start by feeling cheerful, but alcohol is actually a depressant. As they continue to drink they lose their inhibitions and may become more aggressive and violent if they drink too much.

Excessive drinking leads to health problems, sometimes leading to alcoholism. The liver hardens and cannot function effectively. Excessive drinking also causes permanent memory damage. A pregnant woman is advised not to drink because alcohol harms her developing fetus.

A useful measure of the amount of alcohol in a drink is a 'unit'. This is equivalent to the alcohol in a small glass of wine or half a pint of beer. It takes about one hour for your liver to get rid of one unit of alcohol. Doctors advise that men should drink not more than 21 units per week and women not more than 14 units.

Caffeine and reaction time

Investigate the effect on reaction time of drinking a cola drink containing caffeine.

You will need to think about the following:

- How will you measure reaction time?
- What would make a suitable control experiment?
- How much data do you need to collect?
- What volume of cola drink should be consumed?
- How long should you wait for it to take effect?
- People may expect their performance to improve if they think they have had a drink containing caffeine. This may change the way they perform.
- People get better at physical tasks with practice.
- Some people are sensitive to caffeine.

Q3 What is meant by a car driver being 'over the limit'?

Q4 How long after drinking would this person be fit to drive a car?

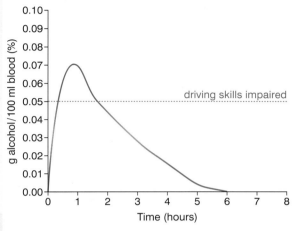

Blood alcohol levels after taking alcohol

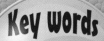 **CHALLENGE**

Measure reaction time using data logging equipment. Then analyse your data using a spreadsheet program.

SUMMARY QUESTIONS

1 ☆ What is meant by 'addictive drugs'? Give an example of an addictive drug.

2 ☆ How does alcohol affect car drivers?

3 ☆ How does drinking excessive amounts of alcohol for a long time harm the body?

Key words

addiction
alcohol
caffeine
drug

Read all about it!

IDEAS AND EVIDENCE

Drugs and athletics

Long ago, people living in the Andes Mountains discovered that they could do more work in the thin air if they chewed coca leaves. The leaves contain the stimulant cocaine, which enabled them to push their tired bodies further.

There is a powerful incentive for people who use their body to make a living to improve their performance by using drugs. Sportsmen, body-builders and models have all abused drugs in the effort to outperform their rivals.

Anabolic steroids are usually used to treat people who have underdeveloped testes. They are synthetic substances related to male sex hormones. They are misused in sport to increase the size of an athlete's muscles as well as muscle strength. They increase the amount of protein that is made. With training and a particular diet, they increase an athlete's lean muscle. They also shorten the time it takes an athlete to recover from hard work, and increase aggressiveness. Abusers may take doses up to 100 times more than a standard medical dose. Other hormones, such as human growth hormone, are also abused in the effort to go faster, be bigger, jump higher.

There is a health price to pay for this abuse. Anabolic steroids interfere with normal hormone production in men and women. This can cause tumour growth and psychiatric problems. Men suffer acne, kidney and liver problems, shrinking testes and enlarged prostate gland, grow breasts and lose their hair.

In women these drugs can cause masculinisation, abnormal menstrual cycles, excessive hair growth, deepening of the voice, and kidney and liver problems. Teenagers taking these drugs, in a bid to improve their appearance or performance, may suffer stunted growth. The hormones stop their long bones, such as leg bones, from growing.

Increasing muscle size makes weightlifters stronger so they can do more work

Sportsmen and women also use stimulants to keep them going when they are exhausted. Drugs which improve performance are called **performance enhancers**. Sports authorities have known about this sort of drug abuse for a long time, but it was difficult to detect when an athlete was cheating. It took the deaths of two cycle racers in the 1960s from amphetamine abuse to spur the development of effective anti-doping measures. There are techniques such as **gas chromatography** that detect traces of drugs in blood and urine. There are now sensitive tests for many banned performance enhancers.

Testing positive for a banned drug will cost an athlete a medal

- Bones support the body, anchor muscles and protect organs from damage.
- Muscles work in antagonistic pairs to flex and extend a joint.
- Deficiency diseases and malnutrition are the result of an inadequate diet.
- Anorexia can cause girls to stop having periods and they can even end up in hospital.
- A poor diet and lack of exercise can damage the heart and blood vessels.
- Drugs adversely affect the way the body works.
- Some drugs are addictive and cause cravings.

DANGER! AVOID THESE COMMON ERRORS

Some people think that you need protein for energy. In fact we use carbohydrate or fat for energy – we only use protein when we are starving.

Muscles contract and relax: they cannot expand. When we lift something up or climb the stairs, we use our joints to bend our arms and legs. Our bones do not bend.

Key words

anabolic steroid
gas chromatography
performance
enhancers

REVIEW QUESTIONS
Understanding and applying concepts

1   Look at the diagram of the knee joint.

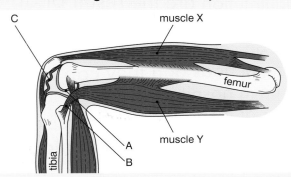

a   Which muscle straightens the leg when it contracts?
b   Which muscle bends the knee when it contracts?
c   What are the parts labelled A, B and C?

2   Cigarette smoke contains many harmful substances. Match the cigarette smoke component to the harm it does.

nicotine   carried instead of oxygen in red blood cells

heat   causes lung cancer

tar   causes addiction to smoking

carbon monoxide   paralyses ciliated cells

3   Which deficiency diseases are caused by a shortage of
a   vitamin C   b   iron?

4   Explain how a poor diet and lack of exercise can cause heart problems.

5   a   What is the role of alveoli?
b   How does cigarette smoke damage the lungs?

6   a   How does alcohol affect the body?
b   Which organs are damaged by excessive alcohol consumption?

Ways with words

7   Write a short article for a Sunday magazine that would persuade middle-aged men to adopt a healthier lifestyle.

8   Make a leaflet for pre-teens about having healthy eating while still having fun.

Making more of maths

9   Researchers gave a volunteer a large alcoholic drink. They took a blood sample from him every 30 minutes for several hours.
    The table shows the volunteer's blood alcohol level in the samples they took.

Time after drinking (hours)	Start	$\frac{1}{2}$	1	$1\frac{1}{2}$	2	$2\frac{1}{2}$	3	$3\frac{1}{2}$	4
Alcohol in blood (mg)	0	0.8	1.5	1.8	1.2	0.7	0.5	–	–

a   Plot a graph of the change in blood alcohol over time.
b   The volunteer felt ill after 3 hours and went home. Extend the graph to predict how the blood alcohol level would have changed for the next two readings.
c   The researchers discovered that the first signs of alcohol intoxication were detectable when the blood alcohol reached 0.4 mg.
    At what time would the first signs of intoxication in the volunteer be seen?

Thinking skills

10   Make a concept map of damaging your lungs. Make sure you include the following terms on your map:

heat   nicotine   blood pressure   tar
alveoli   emphysema   red blood cells
mucus

SAT-STYLE QUESTIONS

1 The diagram shows the lungs.

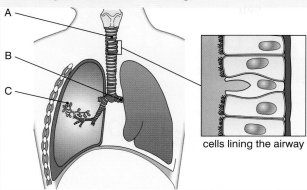

cells lining the airway

a Identify the parts labelled A, B and C. (3)
b Cells like the ones shown in the diagram are found lining the airways. What is the function of these cells? (1)
c Describe three ways in which smoking harms people. (3)
d An unborn baby cannot breathe air. How does it obtain the oxygen it needs? (2)
e How can harmful substances, such as nicotine in cigarette smoke, pass from a mother's lungs to her unborn baby? (2)

2 Annie has a packed lunch. She wanted to find out which carton drink would be the best to go with her sandwiches.

She used a petri dish containing agar jelly mixed with a blue dye. Vitamin C makes the blue dye change to colourless. Annie cut six small holes in the jelly then put in samples from five different small cartons of drink. She also used a sample of orange juice from a carton that had been open for a few days.

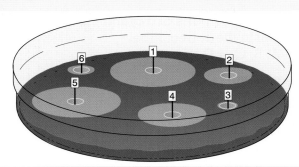

She left the petri dish for one hour, so that the vitamin C in the drinks had time to react with the dye. After one hour, Annie measured each clear area and recorded her results in a table.

Hole	Type of juice	Diameter of clear area (mm)
1	orange juice	25
2	old opened orange juice	14
3	pineapple juice	6
4	tropical fruit juice	20
5	cranberry juice	26
6	blackcurrant and apple juice drink	8

a Name the process by which vitamin C spreads through the jelly. (1)
b Describe one thing Annie should have done in her experiment to ensure her test was fair. (1)
c **i)** Which juice drink contained the most vitamin C? (1)
   ii) Which juice drink contained the least amount of vitamin C? (1)
   iii) Annie knew that blackcurrants are a good source of vitamin C, so she was surprised by the results for the blackcurrant and apple drink. Give one reason why the drink could have a low vitamin C content. (1)
d The opened carton of orange juice contained less vitamin C than the new carton. Pick the correct reason.
   A Vitamin C evaporates.
   B Air slowly breaks down vitamin C.
   C Vitamin C crystallises on the bottom of the carton. (1)
e What problem do people suffer if they do not have enough vitamin C in their diet? (1)
f Name one other item Annie could include in her lunch box to make it a healthy lunch. Explain why this makes her lunch healthy. (1)

Key words

Unscramble these:
klestnoe
graticela
I got a scannit
coin tine
face fine

Plants and photosynthesis

What's it all about?

Plants make a green background to our lives. We sit, walk the dog and play football on grass, make daisy chains, and smell the flowers.

But plants are more than just something nice to look at. Our lives depend on them. Plants take energy from the Sun and transform it into food that we can eat. They make the oxygen that we breathe. Life would be very different without plants.

In this unit you will learn more about plants, photosynthesis, and how they make foods.

What do you remember?

You already know about:
- plant structure.
- the conditions that plants need to grow well.
- respiration.
- cell structure.

1 Which part of a plant absorbs light for photosynthesis?

root   stem   leaf   flowers

2 Rearrange these words into the word equation for respiration.

oxygen   carbon dioxide
water   glucose

3 Match the parts of a plant cell to the correct label A, B, C or D.

cell wall
chloroplast
vacuole
nucleus

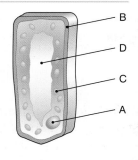

4 Pick out the best conditions for plant growth.

moist   dry   warm   cool
shady   sunny

Ideas about plants

The Scientifica crew are visiting the botanical gardens to find out about plants. Most of them haven't seen plants like these before. They have learned about plants but seem to have forgotten some of what they knew.

a) Do plants get food from the soil?

b) Are plants alive? What are the life processes?

c) Do plants breathe?

d) Why does a fish need plants in its pond?

The Amazon water lily grows the largest leaves. They can reach 120 centimetres across.

Some people have a Swiss cheese plant, or *Monstera*, at home. It is a vine that clambers a few metres up trees in moist tropical forests. Trees in these forests grow 30 metres tall. There are hundreds of different species thickly covering every bit of ground. You can see a leaf of *Monstera* in the photograph.

A Swiss cheese plant or *Monstera*

Q1 Why do you think the leaf of a Swiss cheese plant is so large and such a dark green?

● Leaves

Leaves make food for a plant. The process is called photosynthesis because plants use light energy from the Sun to make food. A plant needs enough light for photosynthesis if it is to grow well.

As well as light, plants also need supplies of the raw materials they use to make food. They need carbon dioxide and water. These come from the environment round a plant. Carbon dioxide comes from the air. Water comes from the soil.

Oxygen is a waste material that is made in photosynthesis. It is released into the atmosphere.

● Leaf structure

A plant's structure allows it to carry out photosynthesis efficiently. Its leaves are large and flat and at right angles to the direction of sunlight. This is a perfect position for catching as much light as possible. Also its leaves are arranged so that they do not overlap and shade each other. In shady places, plants grow larger leaves to capture the same amount of light. Leaves are also very thin, so that gases can pass in quickly from the air to the cells.

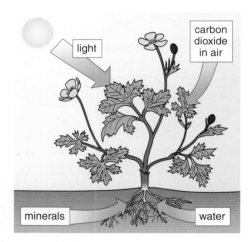

light

carbon dioxide in air

minerals

water

A leaf is an organ made of several different kinds of cells. Inside the leaf is a factory for making food. The top layer of cells, the **epidermis**, is transparent. It has a waxy waterproof layer over it that stops the leaf from drying out. Light passes through the epidermis to the next layer of cells, the **palisade layer**. Inside the leaf, most cells are green. They contain green chloroplasts where food is made.

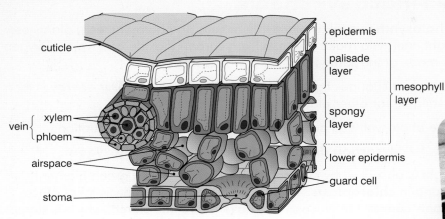

Palisade cells are specialised for photosynthesis. They are provided with water by the **veins** in a leaf. Below the palisade layer is a layer of cells called the spongy mesophyll. In this layer the air spaces act as reservoirs for the gases that palisade cells need.

There is another layer of epidermis on the lower surface of the leaf. This is waterproof too. Gases such as carbon dioxide enter and leave a leaf through tiny pores called **stomata**. **Guard cells** by each stoma shut the stomata at night.

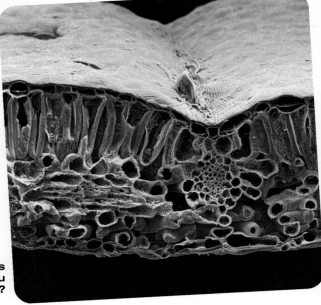

A section across a leaf – can you identify the layers?

Looking at leaves

- Test a leaf for the presence of starch.
- Use a microscope to examine a leaf section. Identify the palisade layer, the epidermis and stomata.
- Draw and label the tissues in a leaf, on an outline of leaf section.

ICT CHALLENGE

Use the Internet to find pictures of leaf sections and leaf surfaces.

SUMMARY QUESTIONS

1 ☆ Where do plants get the carbon dioxide and water they need for photosynthesis?

2 ☆ What do plants add to the air as a result of photosynthesis?

3 ☆☆ How does a plant's structure make it efficient at photosynthesising?

Key words

palisade layer
epidermis
guard cells
stomata
vein

Photosynthesis

Photosynthesis

Photosynthesis takes place in leaf cells. In photosynthesis, plants use light energy to make **glucose** from carbon dioxide and water. Oxygen is made at the same time. It is a waste product.

The plant changes light energy to chemical energy. This energy is then available for other plant activities.

The photosynthesis process can be written as a word equation:

carbon dioxide + water → glucose + oxygen

Light is absorbed by **chlorophyll**. Chlorophyll is a green pigment found in **chloroplasts.** These are where photosynthesis takes place. Plants convert the glucose they have made into starch, which is stored until it is needed.

Palisade cells

The palisade layer is made up of **palisade cells**. These are cells that are specialised for photosynthesis. Each palisade cell is packed with chloroplasts and has a long, thin shape. This shape ensures that most of the light is captured as it passes through the leaf.

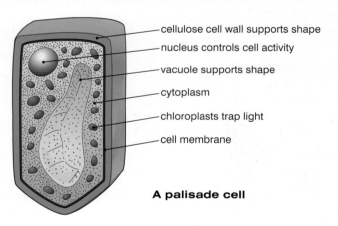

cellulose cell wall supports shape
nucleus controls cell activity
vacuole supports shape
cytoplasm
chloroplasts trap light
cell membrane

A palisade cell

Each palisade cell is close to an air space in the leaf. Carbon dioxide from the air can pass into the air spaces through stomata. Oxygen from photosynthesis passes into the air spaces too. Plants, like every living thing, respire. A small amount of the oxygen they have made in photosynthesis is used for respiration. The rest diffuses out of the leaf through stomata into the atmosphere.

Plants absorb red and blue light to make glucose. Green and yellow light are reflected – that's why plants look green.

bubbles of oxygen

pond weed

You can sometimes see bubbles of oxygen released by waterweed

Q1 How would you test the gas in the test tube to see if it is oxygen?

Monitoring photosynthesis

We can monitor photosynthesis by looking for oxygen production or starch production.

- *Elodea* is a pondweed. In bright light it photosynthesises and releases oxygen. The oxygen forms bubbles that rise to the surface. You can use the rate at which bubbles are produced from *Elodea* to monitor photosynthesis.
  Investigate the rate at which *Elodea* produces bubbles when it is under bright light.
  Then slip black paper round the container and look at the difference in bubble rate. Why has this happened?

- Look for starch in variegated leaves. Variegated leaves are green with white areas. The white parts of the leaf do not have chloroplasts in their cells. Can these white parts make starch?

- In the dark, plants use their stores of starch for energy. If a plant is kept in the dark for several days it will use up all its stores. Cut two pieces of black paper about 8 cm by 8 cm. Cut a simple shape in the centre of one to make a template. Use paper clips to fasten your

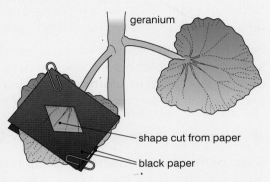

geranium

shape cut from paper

black paper

pieces of paper over a leaf of a plant that has been kept in the dark. Stand the plant in a light place to photosynthesise for a day. Detach the leaf and look for starch.

Let me out! I've run out of starch

What can you say about light and starch production?

CHALLENGE

Use a data logger and oxygen probe to monitor oxygen production.

SUMMARY QUESTIONS

1 ☆ Write out the word equation for photosynthesis.
2 ☆ Name two substances made in photosynthesis.
3 ☆ What is the role of chlorophyll?
4 ☆ How do plants store sugar?

Key words

chlorophyll
chloroplast
glucose
palisade cell
photosynthesis

Biomass

● Biomass

As you grew older, you got taller and heavier. Plants also get taller and heavier as they grow. They use glucose from photosynthesis to make the materials they need to grow.

The increase in mass of a plant comes from:

● new materials it has made,
● water it has taken in.

The water content of a plant varies enormously. A cabbage put in a bucket of water will absorb water and put on a few hundred grams after a couple of hours – but it hasn't grown.

Because the water content varies, scientists prefer to dry plant material to remove the water before they measure its mass. The total dry mass of a plant is called its **biomass**. Growing plants increase in biomass because of the new materials they have made.

● New materials made by plants

Some of the glucose made by a plant is used in **respiration**. The rest is used to make new materials or is stored in the plant. Plants make **protein** from glucose and from the minerals they absorb. They also make **cellulose** for their cell walls, **oil**, and **starch**. Plants make cells in roots, shoots and flowers using these new materials.

Starch is stored in roots and seeds. Peas and some other seeds are stores of protein, while peanuts are stores of oil. Fruits are often full of sugar or oil to attract animals that disperse the seeds inside.

Gruesome science

Castor oil beans contain a protein, ricin. It is so poisonous that 1 mg, the amount in a couple of beans, will kill an adult.

How sugar is used in a plant

LINK UP TO BIOLOGY

In unit 8B, you saw that glucose is used in respiration by all cells.

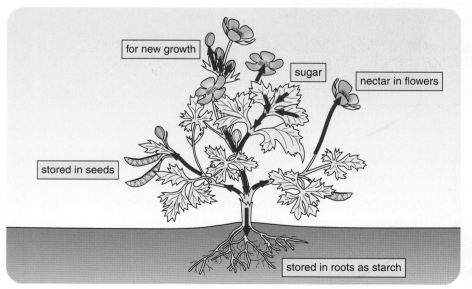

for new growth

sugar

nectar in flowers

stored in seeds

stored in roots as starch

Q1 **a)** Which of these seeds and fruits do you think might have oil stores?

sunflowers   rice grains   olives   plums

b) What do you think the others store?

Peanuts are a source of cooking oil as well as peanut butter and other foods

Ideas about growth

Hundreds of years ago scientists were measuring plants and investigating what they needed to grow. Some people thought that plants got their food from the soil. A scientist, Jean-Baptiste van Helmont, carried out one of the first studies. It was reported in 1648. He tried to find out what plants used to grow.

What van Helmont did
He weighed a plant pot and filled it with a weighed amount of dried soil. He weighed a young willow sapling and then planted it in the pot. He covered the surface of the soil to stop dust settling in the pot and adding to the mass.

The plant was watered by the rain. He used distilled water in dry spells. The plant grew. Five years later he weighed it again. It had gained almost 75 kg in mass, yet the soil had only lost 50 g.

Conclusions
Van Helmont realised that the plant had not taken all the materials it needed to grow from the soil. He concluded that the plant gained mass because the plant transformed water into new materials.

● Why did he come to this conclusion?
● Why didn't he think of photosynthesis as the source of new mass?

Van Helmont used the evidence he had collected and explained it using the science of the time. He didn't think about photosynthesis, because it hadn't been discovered. Carbon dioxide was not identified until 1750. Oxygen had not been discovered. If he knew as much as you do, he would have come to a different conclusion!

Scientists have to rethink their ideas and explanations as they discover more about the world and the way it works.

Which plants are good sources of protein?

● Use the food tests you have learned to look for protein in plant material.

SUMMARY QUESTIONS

1   ☆ Explain how glucose is used in respiration.
2   ☆ Write out the word equations for photosynthesis and for respiration.
3   ☆☆ How can photosynthesis lead to an increase in biomass?

Key words

biomass
cellulose
oil
protein
respiration
starch

Roots

LEARN ABOUT
- how plants take in water
- why plants need minerals

Roots

If you could see into the ground you would see that a tree's roots spread out almost as much as the branches do. It's like an iceberg – you can only see a part of the structure.

Plants are fixed in the ground by their roots. Roots keep plants stable even in gale force winds or when a goat is tugging at their leaves.

Some plants have long **tap roots** that draw water from deep underground. Others have spreading **fibrous roots** that can absorb rain water falling on soil around them. Roots branch into many smaller roots. This gives them a large surface area in contact with the soil.

Roots cannot photosynthesise. Their cells respire using glucose from the leaves and oxygen from minute air spaces in the soil around them.

Plants and minerals

The most important function of a root is to take up water and **minerals** from the soil. Minerals are used to make new materials from glucose, such as protein. Plants grow poorly in soil with few minerals.

Minerals are dissolved in moisture in the soil. Minerals and water pass into the roots through **root hairs**. Specialised root hair cells close to the tip of a root are adapted to absorb water and minerals.

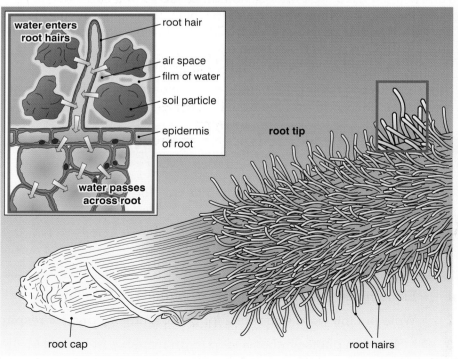

A root hair cell

Gruesome science

The Venus fly trap gets some of its minerals by digesting flies. Its leaves snap shut over flies in less than a second.

Plants and water

Water passes through plants in a one-way flow, carrying dissolved minerals with it. It is absorbed by the roots. It passes up the stem and out into leaves through specialised cells called **xylem**. Water evaporates into the air from the leaves. The air spaces inside a leaf are saturated with water vapour, which passes out into the air through stomata.

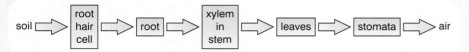

soil ⟹ root hair cell ⟹ root ⟹ xylem in stem ⟹ leaves ⟹ stomata ⟹ air

How water passes through a plant

A plant uses some water during photosynthesis to make glucose. Water also swells the cytoplasm in plant cells so they push against each other. This makes plant tissues firm. If a plant is short of water, its cells become floppy and the leaves droop.

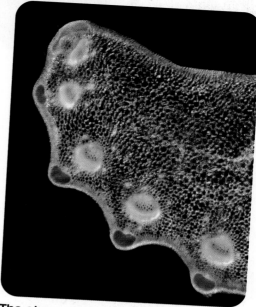

The strong walls of xylem, seen round the edge of the celery stalk, help to hold it upright

Moving water

- Use plant stems, such as celery, that have been standing in a beaker of water containing a blue dye. The stain dyes the cells it passes through as it is pulled up the stem.
  Carefully cut thin slices of the stem and examine them with a hand lens, binocular microscope or ordinary microscope. Look for patches of cells that have been dyed.
  Draw a diagram of your stem section showing where the xylem is.

- Carefully paint a thin layer of pale nail varnish on the lower surface of a leaf.
  After it has dried, peel off a small strip of varnish. Place it on a microscope slide so that the surface that was next to the leaf surface is uppermost.
  Finish making the slide by adding a drop of water and a cover slip. Using a microscope, look for stomata.
  Draw two or three sets of guard cells and the stomata between them.

AMAZING SCIENCE!

Evaporation from the leaves helps redwood trees pull water from the roots up to almost 100 metres above the ground.

SUMMARY QUESTIONS

1 ✹ What sort of plant cells absorb water and minerals from the soil?

2 ✹ Why do plants need minerals?

3 ✩ How are roots adapted to do their job?

4 ✩✩ Water-logged soil and flooded soil has little air in it. Why does this kill the roots of many plants?

Key words

fibrous root
minerals
root hairs
tap root
xylem

Why are plants important?

LINK UP TO BIOLOGY

In unit 8B, you found out that respiration is the release of energy from glucose.

● Ecosystems

You can keep a colony of tiny crustacea called brine shrimps in a mini-aquarium. They feed on minute algae that live in the water. As long as the algae have plenty of light and receive some minerals occasionally, the colony will live and breed for years without any outside help. It is a self-contained **ecosystem**.

Brine shrimps feed on algae in warm salty ponds

How does this ecosystem work? It works in the same way as any natural ecosystem. The animals and plants supply each other's needs.

The algae photosynthesise using light energy. They grow and reproduce using the materials they have made. They release oxygen into the water.

Brine shrimps eat the algae. They digest starch and other nutrients they have taken in. Brine shrimps use oxygen from the water for respiration. The oxygen is supplied by photosynthesising algae.

Q1 What substance is produced when an animal digests starch?

Carbon dioxide is a waste product of respiration. Brine shrimps release carbon dioxide into the water as they respire. The algae use this carbon dioxide in photosynthesis. And so the cycle goes on.

Plants are the basis of food chains. They provide the carbohydrates that other species need in the form of glucose, other sugars, starch and cellulose. Without plants there could be no animals, and animal respiration provides the carbon dioxide that plants need.

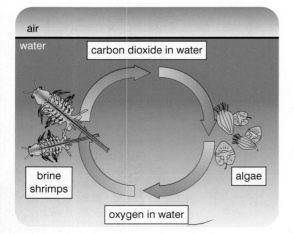

air
water
carbon dioxide in water
brine shrimps
algae
oxygen in water

● Equations

You can see that the process of **photosynthesis** is the reverse of aerobic **respiration** by comparing their equations.

Photosynthesis

carbon dioxide + water ⟶ glucose + oxygen

light **energy**

Aerobic respiration

glucose + oxygen ⟶ carbon dioxide + water

energy released

Plants and animals in balance

Joseph Priestley showed that plants make something that animals need.

Q2 What would happen if the plant in (b) were kept in the dark?

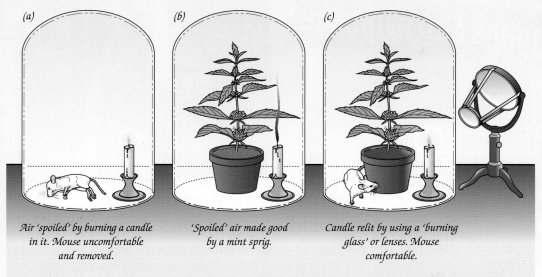

(a) Air 'spoiled' by burning a candle in it. Mouse uncomfortable and removed.

(b) 'Spoiled' air made good by a mint sprig.

(c) Candle relit by using a 'burning glass' or lenses. Mouse comfortable.

Conclusion: The injury which is done to the atmosphere by the respiration of such a large number of animals... is, in part at least, repaired by vegetable creation.

Joseph Priestley's work

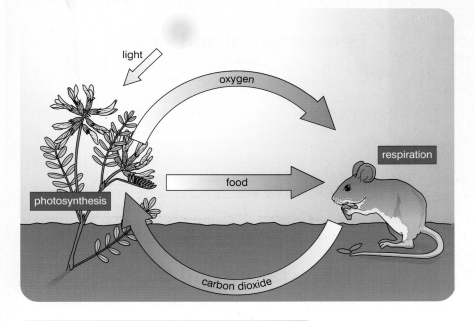

light

oxygen

respiration

food

photosynthesis

carbon dioxide

Sweet harmony

- Make a poster showing how the plants and animals in a pond are in balance.

SUMMARY QUESTIONS

1 ☆ Give two ways in which water plants help the fish in a pond to stay alive.

2 ☆☆ What would happen in the brine shrimp aquarium if it were kept in the dark?

Key words

ecosystem
energy
photosynthesis
respiration

Deforestation

The clearing of forests is called **deforestation**. Forests are cut down for:

- agriculture, to feed more people. Poor farmers clear small areas of forest. Several square miles are cleared for cattle ranching or cash crops to be sold on the world market.
- commercial **logging** for valuable woods such as ebony, for timber and for wood pulp.
- firewood, building, and animal fodder.

All species are affected when their habitats disappear during logging

What happens after a forest is cleared?

Most of the **minerals** in a tropical forest are in the plants, not in the ground. Farmers burn the trees they have cut down to release minerals and make the soil fertile. Minerals are quickly washed away by rain. Within a few years, the ground is unsuitable for crops. The farmers move on. The forest grows back very slowly because there are so few nutrients in the soil. It takes decades for a forest to re-grow.

Worse damage is caused by clear-cut logging. There are almost no nutrients in the bare ground because the trees are removed. We do not know how long it takes for the forest to re-grow.

Deforestation and carbon dioxide

Forests take **carbon dioxide** from the atmosphere and use it to produce biomass. Carbon dioxide is released back into the atmosphere when a forest is cut and burned. About one-third of all carbon dioxide released from human activity is from deforestation. It increases the carbon dioxide concentration in the air and contributes to global warming.

Deforestation and water

In a forest, the treetops touch to form a solid canopy. The air beneath is cool and moist. Water drawn up from the soil evaporates from leaves into the air below the canopy and has a cooling effect. Moisture condenses to form clouds and rain that returns to the ground. About half of the rain in a tropical rain forest is recycled within the forest.

Once the forest is cleared, water does not return to the ground as rain. The ground is drier. More of the Sun's energy warms the ground instead of evaporating water. The air above it gets hotter. Without a protective layer of vegetation more soil is eroded by wind and rain. Eroded soil enters waterways and silts up rivers, lakes and dams.

Deforestation and biodiversity

Tropical rain forests contain over half of the Earth's species. Many rain forest plants and animals live in small areas of specialised habitat. They are very vulnerable to extinction through deforestation. Few of these species have been studied in depth, which means we don't know the value of what we are losing. They are certainly part of food webs and so other organisms that depend on them also face extinction.

Find out what these terms mean:
- cash crops,
- clear-cut logging,
- global warming.

- Leaves photosynthesise. Their shape makes them very efficient.
- Palisade cells are adapted for photosynthesis.
- Light energy is trapped by chlorophyll.
- The word equation for photosynthesis can be written as

$$\text{carbon dioxide} + \text{water} \rightarrow \text{glucose} + \text{oxygen}$$

- Glucose is made into fats, starch and proteins.
- Plants absorb water and minerals through their root hairs.
- Plants respire.

Plants make glucose. They turn it into food using minerals from soil.

Plants are alive. They grow, they respire, they are sensitive to the conditions around them...

Yes, they reproduce, excrete wastes, make foods to nourish themselves...

And, they move their petals to open and close their flowers.

Plants don't breathe but they exchange gases through stomata.

I need the oxygen that water plants make, and I eat the plants.

DANGER! AVOID THESE COMMON ERRORS

Plants make their own food materials. The minerals they take from the soil are not foods. They are used to make substances such as protein.

Plants respire slowly all the time. They use oxygen and produce carbon dioxide. It is easier to show that plants are respiring in the dark, because photosynthesis stops and carbon dioxide is released instead of being used in photosynthesis.

Key words

biodiversity
carbon dioxide
deforestation
logging
minerals

REVIEW QUESTIONS
Understanding and applying concepts

1 Copy the following sentences and fill in the missing words.

A leaf's function is to ... Its shape makes it very efficient. ... cells are adapted for photosynthesis. They have large numbers of ... and a long, thin shape. Light energy is trapped by ... The word equation for photosynthesis is written as

... ... + water → ... + oxygen

Fats, starch and proteins are made from ..., which is made during photosynthesis. New materials contribute to the increase of ... in a growing plant. Plants absorb ... and ... through their root ... Plants respire all the time using ... and ... made in photosynthesis. They release ... ... During the daytime this waste is used in photosynthesis.

2 What is the name of the process in which plants make glucose?

3 Why do living things need carbohydrates such as glucose?

4 Give two parts that are found in plant cells but not in animal cells.

5 List two substances that plants make from glucose.

6 What happens to stored starch in a plant if the plant is kept in the dark for three days?

7 What is the function of root hairs?

8 Name two substances that plants need to take in from the soil.

9 The diagram shows duckweed plants floating in a pond.
   Describe one way in which duckweed is adapted for photosynthesis.

Ways with numbers

10 The graph shows the carbon dioxide concentration in the air among the plants in a greenhouse during one day in the summer.

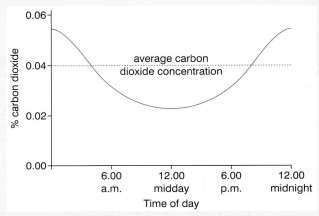

a Describe how the carbon dioxide concentration changes between 4 am and 11 pm.
b Explain why the concentration changes.

Thinking skills

11 Make a concept map of photosynthesis.

SAT-STYLE QUESTIONS

1 Grant keeps brine shrimps in a large bottle on his windowsill. Brine shrimps are small crustaceans that feed on tiny algae in salty ponds.

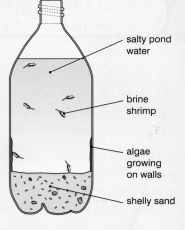

salty pond water

brine shrimp

algae growing on walls

shelly sand

a Which organism is the producer? (1)

b Brine shrimps and algae both produce carbon dioxide. Which process in the brine shrimps and algae produces carbon dioxide? (1)

c Sometimes on very hot days Grant sees very small bubbles of gas form near where the algae grow on the walls of the bottle. What is the name of this gas? (1)

d Grant adds a few drops of a 'plant food' fertiliser to the bottle once every two months. Why does he do this? (1)

e Explain why the amounts of oxygen and carbon dioxide in the bottle stay the same over the course of a month. (2)

2 The diagram shows cells found in a plant.

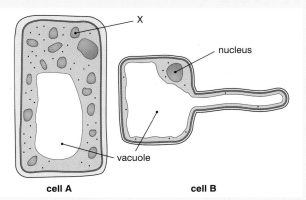

cell A   cell B

a i) What is the function of cell A? (1)
 ii) Give two ways cell A is adapted for its function. (2)
 iii) What is the green substance in the part labelled X? (1)

b In which part of the plant would you find:
 i) cell A (1)
 ii) cell B? (1)

c i) What is the function of cell B? (1)
 ii) How can you tell that cell B cannot make sugars? (1)

3 Rosie and Eleanor used an oxygen sensor to monitor the oxygen produced by some waterweed in a beaker.

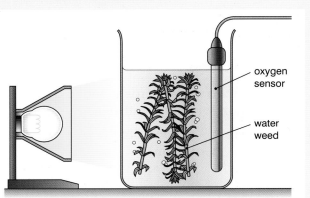

a What is the process that produces oxygen? (1)

They shone a bright light on the beaker for a time, and then placed a cylinder of black paper over the beaker. After 6 minutes, they removed the cylinder of paper, so that the bright light could shine on the beaker again.

The print-out of the data from the probe is shown below:

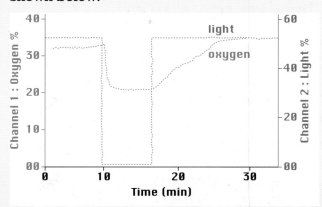

b i) What was the measurable outcome (the dependent variable)? (1)
 ii) Which factor was changed (the independent variable)? (1)

c Between which times was the black paper over the beaker? Explain your decision. (2)

d What would happen if Rosie switched the lamp off at 20 minutes? (1)

Key words

Unscramble these:
tomatas
she posh so nitty
shari toro
scrath
please call di

9D

Plants for food

What's it all about?

How many plants have you used today? The ones you have eaten, of course, like wheat in your bread, potatoes for your chips, and so on. But you have used lots of others too. The wood holding up parts of your house and forming your furniture came from plants. There is probably cotton in your clothes. Did you drink tea or fruit juice this morning, or wash with soap that smelled nice? Maybe you had a medicine made from plants.

The world's population is booming. Farmers growing crops such as corn, rice and cotton need to produce more and more. There is a simple pattern – the more of us there are, the more plants we need to grow.

In this unit you will learn more about the factors which plants need in order to grow, and the steps that farmers can take to increase crop production.

 ## What do you remember?

You already know about:
- photosynthesis.
- food chains.
- why plants need minerals.

1 Which part of a plant takes in minerals?

root   stem   leaf   flower

2 Which term describes an apple tree?

consumer   producer
herbivore   prey

3 What are the raw materials for photosynthesis? Where does a plant obtain each of these?

4 Rearrange these words to make a word equation for photosynthesis.

glucose   carbon dioxide
water   oxygen

Ideas about growing crops

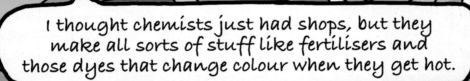

The speech bubbles in the comic read:

"I'm going to agricultural college. I need to know how to grow crops better when I get a farm."

"I went to Holland last summer. There are greenhouses instead of fields over there."

"I'm going to be a protester. Farmers make a right mess with all the poisons they spray on the fields."

"I thought chemists just had shops, but they make all sorts of stuff like fertilisers and those dyes that change colour when they get hot."

QUESTIONS

The Scientifica crew need to make their option choices for GCSE, so they are researching careers they are interested in.

a) What will Molly's crops need in order to grow well, when she becomes a farmer?

b) Benson was talking about pesticides that farmers spray on their crops. What are pesticides for?

c) Why might someone grow crops in a greenhouse instead of fields?

d) What other things do chemists make that are useful to farmers?

9D1 Plants and food

Bananas are a good mid-morning snack to keep your energy levels up. They are a starchy food. A few other foods rich in **starch** are potatoes, rice, and sweet corn. What do they have in common? They all come from plants.

Q1 List some other foods rich in starch. How many are made from plants?

(a) Pine resin protects the tree against pest attacks

Plants make starch from glucose. Glucose is made in photosynthesis. It is converted to other materials that plants use in their growth. Plants make:

- cellulose for cell walls,
- fat and oil for waterproofing layers and energy stores,
- protein for new cells,
- vitamins for cell processes,
- coloured substances for their flowers and leaves,
- perfumes to attract pollinating insects,
- protective chemicals, such as resins, to guard against attacks by pests and diseases.

(c) Mint oil is used to flavour everything from toothpaste to tea

(d) The thick waxy layer helps to keep water inside the leaf, even in drying winter winds

(b) Indigo blue fabric was coloured with a dye extracted from plants

● Profit from plants

People have discovered how to use many of the materials that plants make. We collect some plant products from the wild, such as brazil nuts and forest trees. But most plants are grown as **crops**. Plants that are widely used for commercial purposes are described as **economically important** plants.

Here are just a few of the uses we have found for them:

- *Fibres:* Plants are a good source of tough fibres. Fibres from cotton, coconut, jute and flax are woven into fabrics. Other fibres go into ropes, carpets or are made into paper.

- *Timber:* Trees are tall and heavy. Their trunks need to be strong but flexible enough to bend with the wind. The **timber** from the wood in trees is used in buildings, boats, furniture and tools.
- *Flavours:* We make plant extracts to drink, like tea, coffee, cola, chocolate, and fruit squashes. We also use them for flavourings and smells, such as vanilla, strawberry, rose, mint, and pine.

Q2 Think about how we use plants. List 20 ways in which we use plants.

Timber...
paper...
chairs...
floors...
perfume...
shelves...

Selective crop breeding

Farmers are often interested in increasing the yield of just one part of the plant. This is usually the part that is harvested. However, plants use the materials they make to grow other parts as well, and to make seeds. Plant breeders try to breed plants that use more of their energy to make more of the product that we want and less of the other parts. For example, pea plants are bred to have fewer tendrils, and cereals like wheat to have shorter stems.

What do plants make?

- Investigate whether foods from plants contain starch using the starch test you have learned.
  Did they all contain starch?
  List your foods in two groups – those with starch and those without starch.
  Find out what is stored in the plant materials that did not contain starch. How could you test for these?
- Test for cellulose some of the materials made from plants, such as paper and cotton.
- Find out about one economically important plant: how it is grown, and the use we make of it. Make a presentation about your plant. Some ideas are cotton, potatoes, lavender, pine, tea, coffee, cocoa, bananas, sugar, quinine, vanilla.

AMAZING SCIENCE!

Attar of roses is the most expensive perfume ingredient. Fifteen thousand roses are used to make $10\,\text{cm}^3$, which costs about £500.

ICT **CHALLENGE**

Use the Internet to research a plant. Use a suitable program to make a presentation about the plant.

SUMMARY QUESTIONS

1 ☆ What substance does a potato store?

2 ☆ Give three uses of plants.

3 ☆ List four substances plants can make from glucose.

4 ☆ As a plant gets older, it increases in biomass. Where has this increase in biomass come from?

Key words

crop
economically important
plant breeding
starch
timber

Fertilisers

LEARN ABOUT
■ minerals
■ fertilisers

At some times during the year the countryside gets very 'whiffy'. This is because farmers spray their fields with well-rotted manure. Farmers who don't have cows to provide manure buy **fertilisers** to do the same job. They are adding something to the soil, so that grass or crops will grow better next season.

Why do plants need fertiliser?

Plants need minerals from the soil to make proteins, cellulose and all the other substances required to make new cells. The most important minerals that plants use are **nitrates** for making protein, **potassium** and **phosphates**. If there isn't enough of one of these important minerals, plants will not grow well. Manure and artificial fertilisers contain minerals. They release nutrients into the soil and plants take them up through their root hairs.

The plant on the right does not have enough nitrogen compounds, so it has not grown as well as the plant on the left

What makes a good fertiliser?

A fertiliser should contain compounds of nitrogen, phosphorus and potassium to supply a crop's mineral needs. Animal dung and compost made from decayed plant material are good fertilisers. Microbes in the soil break them down and release the minerals slowly over time. Dung and compost also absorb water and stop the soil from drying out too quickly.

Commercial fertilisers are mixtures of soluble chemicals designed to provide plants with the minerals they need in the correct proportions. These are simple to spray over the ground, but need to be applied every year.

Farmers can also grow crops, such as clover and alfalfa, which can be ploughed into the ground to enrich the soil. These are described as 'green manure'.

LINK UP TO CHEMISTRY

You can read more about the effects of fertilisers on wildlife in 9G3.

● Fertilisers and the environment

Commercial fertilisers are soluble compounds that are sprayed onto fields. If it rains heavily afterwards they are washed away by the rain and drain through the soil into rivers.

This can boost the growth of plants and algae in the water for a while. When these plants die they rot. The rotting process uses up oxygen in the water and can affect animals living in the water.

Clover plants have bacteria in their roots that can make nitrogen compounds for them

Algae have grown and bloomed in water containing fertiliser. Later they will die and rot.

How does fertiliser affect growth?

- Look at samples of commercial fertiliser. Each carries a list of its chemical ingredients.
  Which substance will supply plants with nitrogen?
  Which substance contains phosphorus?

- Plan and carry out an investigation to find out how fertiliser affects the growth of cress seedlings or duckweed.
  How will you change the amount of fertiliser the seedlings receive?
  How will you measure growth?
  How many plants should you use?

Gruesome science

Many seeds, for example tomato seeds, are not digested when animals eat them. They pass through the digestive system and are planted with a dollop of fertiliser when they emerge from the other end.

 CHALLENGE

Find out why plants need magnesium for healthy growth.

SUMMARY QUESTIONS

1 ☆ List three types of fertiliser.

2 ☆ Why do farmers put fertiliser on their crops?

3 ☆ Name two minerals found in fertiliser.

4 ☆ How can fertiliser draining into ponds harm pond life?

5 ☆☆ Why do farmers have to keep on adding fertiliser to their crops?

Key words

fertiliser
nitrate
phosphate
potassium

Growing more crops

You'll groan when you're grown

Gardeners take care of their fruit and vegetables. The better the plants grow, the more food they produce. A well-grown apple tree will produce more apples, a looked-after lettuce grows more leaves, and healthy rhubarb produces more stems.

Plants grow using the energy and materials produced from photosynthesis. The more they photosynthesise, the more they can grow. The more crop plants grow, the more product a farmer can harvest. The mass a farmer harvests from an area is described as its **yield**.

Q1 Carol had a large tree growing in her garden near her vegetable patch. One windy day it started to topple so she cut it down. She noticed that she grew much better vegetables the next year. Why did her vegetables grow better after the tree was removed?

● Weeds

Weeds are plants, usually wild plants, growing somewhere that we don't want them. Weeds **compete** with crop plants. Weeds take minerals and water from the soil. They often grow taller or grow more quickly than crop plants. They shade the slower-growing crop plants. The crop plants cannot photosynthesise as much. They are smaller because they have less energy for growth, so they store less starch in roots and seeds. The farmer's yield is reduced.

Farmers can hoe weeds or pull them out. Large areas are usually sprayed with **weed killers**, called **herbicides**. Many crops, such as wheat and barley, are grassy plants. Farmers can use herbicides that only kill plants with broad-leaves such as dandelions and poppies.

AMAZING SCIENCE!

There are mammoth vegetables, such as onions at 2.7 kg and pumpkins weighing 200 kg.

ICT **CHALLENGE**

Use the Internet to find out about the effect of weed killers on the natural environment.

Before they plant their own seeds, farmers let weed seeds sprout so that they can be killed with herbicides

Environmental effects

Weed plants are part of natural food webs. Animals such as butterflies lay their eggs on them and take their nectar. Other animals eat the leaves and seeds.

When weeds are killed, there is less food available for herbivores. These herbivores must compete for other sources of food, including the crop plants. As a result the numbers of herbivores will decrease as there isn't enough food to sustain them. Consequently the numbers of animals that prey on them will decline too.

Measuring the effects of competition

- Plan an investigation into the effects of competition.
  Mustard and cress grow at different rates. Find out what happens to the yield of cress seedlings when they grow by themselves and when they grow with mustard 'weeds'.
  Remember to use dry mass when measuring yield.

- Carry out a weed survey in an area of the school grounds.
  Consider the various ways of controlling weeds.
  a) Which would be the best way for your school grounds?
  b) What safety precautions should be taken in the school grounds to minimise harm to:
  i) people
  ii) food webs?

Poppies are a common weed in crops. They provide nectar for insects and their seeds are food for birds.

Strict safety rules help to protect people working with weed killers

Gruesome science

Even if you pulled out 99% of the weeds that germinated each year, it would still take over thirty years to rid one acre of ground of its weeds.

SUMMARY QUESTIONS

1 ✷ Why are crop plants grown in weedy patches usually smaller than plants grown in well-weeded patches?

2 ✷ Give two environmental factors that can slow down a plant's growth.

3 ✷✷✷ Some gardeners grow African marigolds between their vegetables to deter greenfly. Why do you think the African marigolds do not compete with the vegetables?

Key words

compete
herbicide
weed
weed killer
yield

Pests

9D4

Animals that eat wild plants are often very partial to the domesticated version too and become pests. Our food plants become a part of natural food chains.

Many common crop pests are insects. They include aphids, caterpillars of moths and butterflies, locusts, weevils and seed beetles. Their mealtime habits can ruin a crop or stored plant foods, which reduces the yield. In this way crop pests are competing with humans for food. Insects can also spread viruses and other diseases from one plant to another.

If the weather is favourable and there are plenty of healthy plants, caterpillars grow quickly and devastate plants. Insects such as aphids reproduce very rapidly and their **population booms**.

Even a small amount of damage by insects is enough to stop people wanting to buy fruit

LINK UP TO
BIOLOGY

In unit 8D you looked at predator–prey relationships.

Q1 Can you think why farmers spraying large fields should contact local bee-keepers before they spray?

● Controlling pests

Insect pests are controlled by using an insecticide. It is sprayed over crops or over stored grain. Most insect pests die in a short time when this is done.

Another method of control is by encouraging natural **predators** such as ladybirds, lacewings and small birds. These feed on insect prey. Using a natural predator to keep insect pests down is an example of **biological control**. It takes longer to control the pests because it takes time for the predator population to build up.

● Environmental issues

The insects that feed on crops are part of the local food web. When they are killed, other members of the web are affected. The predators that normally eat them are forced to compete for other prey.

Insecticides may kill beneficial insects at the same time as the pests. This can lead to an odd situation – the number of pests sometimes increases when they are sprayed. Some pests survive the spraying and reproduce rapidly. There are fewer natural predators around to eat them. So there can be a pest population boom before the predator population recovers.

● Bioaccumulation

Pesticides, such as insecticides and herbicides, are **toxic** chemicals. If they are sprayed on crops, they can enter food chains when the plants take them in or if traces remain on the vegetation.

Animals feeding on these plants take in the toxic pesticides. Generally the amount they take in is not enough to kill them, but it can stay in their body because it isn't broken down. Predators further up the food chain eat these animals. The predators take in the stored pesticide. Because they eat many prey animals, they accumulate a lot of toxic material in their bodies.

Top carnivores, such as birds of prey and seals, can take in so much of these substances that it affects their health and their ability to survive or reproduce successfully. This is called **bioaccumulation**.

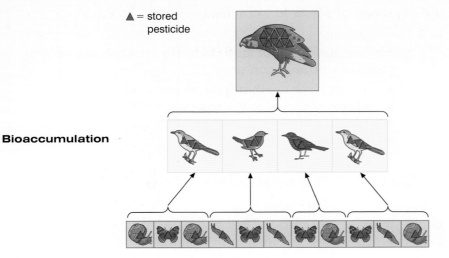

▲ = stored pesticide

Bioaccumulation

Gruesome science

A locust can eat its own mass of vegetation in a day – about 5 grams. But they hang out in swarms of about 30 million – no wonder they can strip a field overnight!

ICT ▸ *CHALLENGE*

In Africa, elephants are a serious pest. Find out how farmers try to stop elephants eating their crops.

Peregrine falcons almost died out in Britain because of pesticides

The case of the disappearing falcon

● Use the Internet and other resources to find out about the effect DDT had on the peregrine falcon population.
Use your research to write an article for the *Handsbridge Chronicle* about the first sighting of peregrine falcons again for 20 years. Include the reasons why DDT was, and still is, used in many places around the world.

SUMMARY QUESTIONS

1 ☆ Give one way in which insects can damage crops.

2 ☆ Describe two ways of controlling insect pests.

3 ☆ Give one reason for not using insecticides.

4 ☆☆ In what way are insect pests in competition with humans?

Key words

bioaccumulation
biological control
pesticide
population boom
predators
toxic

Intensive care for plants

9D5

LEARN ABOUT
- growing plants in glasshouses
- changing the rate of photosynthesis

How can gardeners help plants along so that they grow better? They can do this by making sure that their plants have plenty of the things they need for photosynthesis. You already know that plants use light, carbon dioxide and water for **photosynthesis**. They also need to be at a suitable temperature.

In the early spring, gardeners warm the soil by using **cloches**. Cloches are like mini-greenhouses, trapping warmth. The extra warmth allows seeds to germinate more quickly, and plants begin to grow. Farmers use big sheets of plastic to warm fields.

Q1 Explain how each of these helps to increase the yield of crops a gardener can grow:
- cutting back overhanging shrubs and trees
- adding compost to the soil
- catching rain water in a water butt
- weeding.

Greenhouses and glasshouses

In the winter it is cold. There is less light, so plants cannot photosynthesise very quickly. They stop growing, and they may even drop their leaves and become dormant if they use more glucose in respiration than they make in photosynthesis. We want food supplies all the year round, so some farmers grow crops in large greenhouses called **glasshouses**. Tomatoes, celery, cucumber and flowers are grown in glasshouses.

In the glasshouse, artificial lighting supplements natural daylight. Soil warming cables or heaters raise the soil temperature and watering is done automatically. This enables plants to be grown all year round in near perfect conditions.

Glasshouses are useful for growing flowers like chrysanthemums. As these normally flower in the autumn, the lighting is arranged to mimic autumn nights to bring them into flower all year round. Also it is easier to control insect pests and diseases in the enclosed glasshouse than it would be in a field.

Q2 Can you think of any ways to increase the carbon dioxide concentration inside a glasshouse?

Crops can be grown under ideal conditions all year round in a glasshouse

How much photosynthesis?

CHALLENGE

Find out about growing crops in glasshouses.

● Waterweed, *Elodea*, releases bubbles of oxygen as it photosynthesises. The plant in the experiment had plenty of everything it needed for photosynthesis except light. The graph shows what happened when the waterweed was given more light.

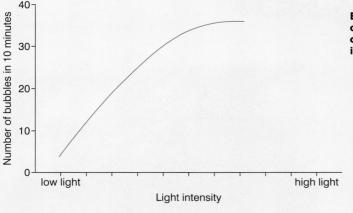

Bubble rate of *Elodea* with different light intensities

AMAZING SCIENCE!

Farmers in volcanic Iceland are using geothermal heat and CO_2 from a natural bore hole for their glasshouses.

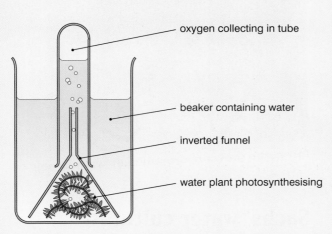

oxygen collecting in tube

beaker containing water

inverted funnel

water plant photosynthesising

a) Describe the pattern shown in the graph.

b) Chemical reactions happen more slowly when the conditions are colder. What would have happened to the number of bubbles produced if the water in the beaker was colder?

c) If the water in the experiment was warmed up by another 10°C, what do you think would happen to the number of oxygen bubbles produced in 10 minutes?

SUMMARY QUESTIONS

1 ☆ What are the best conditions for photosynthesis?

2 ☆ Give two environmental factors that can affect the rate of photosynthesis.

3 ☆☆ Why do plants make less starch in winter than in summer?

Key words

cloche
glasshouse
photosynthesis

IDEAS AND EVIDENCE

Growing without soil

Sometimes growing plants in fields is not very easy. An alternative is to grow plants without soil in a system called **hydroponics**.

When you grow cress seeds on cotton wool in an eggshell, or a hyacinth bulb over a bowl of water, you are using a hydroponic system. There are enough minerals in tap water to keep your plants alive for a few weeks.

In a hydroponic system, plants are kept in a warm, bright greenhouse. They grow in a large tank. The tank may contain a solution or be packed with granules of a chemically inactive substance. The plants are watered with a solution that contains all the **minerals** they need in the correct proportions. Air is pumped through the tank to ensure that the roots get enough **oxygen**.

Scientists use hydroponic systems to research how plants grow, but they can also be used in agriculture. They are useful in deserts where it is too hot and dry outside or in very northerly places where it is too cold and dry.

Tomatoes grown hydroponically without soil

Q1 People have suggested that growing plants hydroponically would be useful on a space station to supply fresh salads. What other advantages would such a system have?

Sachs' water cultures

Once scientists realised that plants needed more than just water to grow, they investigated further. They needed sensitive chemical techniques to analyse plant tissue to find out what was in it. These were developed during the 19th century.

Scientists dried plant material and analysed it to find out which elements were present. They discovered that plants contained minerals.

Julius von Sachs and Wilhelm Knop separately investigated the effects of minerals on plant growth. They each grew plants in water containing known amounts of particular minerals and noted how various combinations of minerals affected growth. They showed that plants needed minerals such as nitrogen, calcium and magnesium ions. Both scientists developed specialised solutions, called **water culture solutions,** for growing plants in.

- We use plants to make products as well as eating them.
- Fertilisers, either natural or artificial, supply plants with nitrates and other minerals.
- Weeds compete with crop plants for light, water and minerals.
- Increasing the amounts of raw materials can increase the rate of photosynthesis.
- Herbicides and pesticides reduce crop losses.
- Toxic materials can accumulate in food chains and harm wildlife.

DANGER! AVOID THESE COMMON ERRORS

Plants need nitrogen and carbon combined in compounds such as potassium nitrate or carbon dioxide. They cannot use nitrogen or carbon as the elements.

Key words

hydroponics
minerals
oxygen
water culture solution

REVIEW QUESTIONS
Understanding and applying concepts

1 Copy and complete the following sentences:

Plants are used for . . . , . . . and . . . (Give three suitable uses.)

Manure is a natural . . . that supplies . . . to the soil. It releases . . . , which are important for making protein.

Weeds compete with crop plants for . . . , water and . . .

When light intensity is increased, the rate of photosynthesis . . .

Herbicides are used to kill . . .

. . . reduce the damage done to crops by caterpillars and other insect pests.

Toxic substances, such as pesticides, can . . . in food chains and harm the . . . at the end of the food chain.

2 Which sort of cell is adapted for taking in water and nitrogen compounds from the soil? Give one feature that adapts it for this job.

3 Write out the word equation for photosynthesis.

4 List the environmental factors that affect photosynthesis.

5 How can insecticide end up in a predatory bird such as the peregrine falcon?

Ways with words

6 Write three sentences that use the words:

herbicide   insecticide   pesticide

SAT-STYLE QUESTIONS

1 a Draw a pyramid of numbers for the following food chain:

plankton → sand eels → cod → seals   (4)

b Seals are warm-blooded and feed their young on milk. To which group do seals belong?

**fish   amphibians   reptiles
     mammals**   (1)

Seals use their stored body fat to supply their energy needs when nursing young pups. Scientists have discovered that their milk contains high levels of pesticides. These come from pesticides sprayed on crops to kill insect pests.

c Explain how pesticide sprayed on crops can end up in seals.   (4)

2 In European agriculture, farmers usually remove weeds from fields in which they are growing crops.

a Why do European farmers remove weeds from their fields?   (1)

Farmers in some hot African countries do not weed carefully between crops, and often plant several different types of crops jumbled together in a field. Agricultural experts from Europe working in Africa encouraged the African farmers to pull up the weeds and to plant just one type of crop in a field. But they were surprised to discover that in hot places fields with jumbled plants were more productive than weeded fields.

b What does 'productive' mean?   (1)

c Give one reason why the weeds may not have affected the growth of the crops.   (1)

d Suggest one reason why the jumbled crops grew better.   (1)

3 Duckweed is a very small plant that grows on the surface of ponds. It grows new leaves from the centre, and clumps split to become two plants. Duckweed absorbs minerals from the water through its roots.

Duckweed

Class 9T grew duckweed in two aquaria. One was filled with a water culture solution containing minerals. The other was filled with distilled water. They counted the number of leaves regularly. You can see their results in the graph.

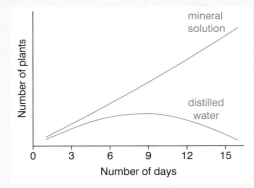

a The class predicted that duckweed would not grow very well in distilled water. Why do you think they made that prediction? (2)

b Explain why the duckweed in distilled water grew for a short time then died. (1)

A few of the children brought bottles of mineral water to school. They compared the mineral composition of their water with the water culture solution.

Mineral composition of various solutions

Mineral salt	Grams in 1000 cm³ solution			
	Distilled water	Sachs' water culture solution	Mineral water Still	Sparkling
potassium nitrate	0	1.0	0.06	0.06
calcium phosphate	0	0.5	0	0
magnesium sulphate	0	0.5	0.07	0.08
calcium sulphate	0	0.5	0.14	0.04
sodium chloride	0	0.25	0.13	0.17
iron sulphate	0	0.001	0	0
hydrogen carbonate	0	0	0.26	0.30

c Use the information in the table to predict how duckweed would grow in still mineral water. Explain your prediction. (2)

d Which are the three most important elements for plants that are provided by the solutions? (3)

4 Match each leaf structure with its function:

palisade layer — carries water
stomata — main site of photosynthesis
xylem — gases can diffuse to and from each cell

air space — allow water and gases in or out of a leaf (4)

Key words

Unscramble these:
relist fire
chiberide
eattrin
nearlism
cotix

Reactions of metals and their compounds

My favourite metal is gold.

Mine too.

What's it all about?

We all use metals every day of our lives. Just think of a normal day, getting up and going to school. How many times do you use things made of metals?

In this unit you will look in more detail at metals and their compounds – especially how they react with acids. You'll find that it's not just metals themselves that are useful. The compounds of metals are used in lots of different ways too.

What do you remember?

You already know about:

- the names and properties of some metals that are elements.
- how atoms join (bond) together in different ways when chemical reactions take place.
- the chemical symbols for some elements and the formulae of some compounds.
- the way we can represent chemical reactions by word equations, symbol equations and particle diagrams.
- how to test for hydrogen and carbon dioxide.

1 Which of these elements is a metal?

chlorine   carbon   helium   sodium

2 What is the chemical symbol for iron?

I   Ir   F   Fe

3 Which of the following represents a compound?

Co O_2 CO_2 C

4 How would you test for carbon dioxide gas?

A lighted splint pops.
Lime water turns milky.
A lighted splint is extinguished.
A glowing splint re-lights.

Ideas about metals and their compounds

Look at the cartoon above and discuss these questions with your partner.

a) Do you think that **all** metals conduct electricity? Are there any exceptions? Will any elements that are non-metals conduct electricity?

b) What is the chemical name of the salt Pete is about to eat? Do you know its chemical formula? Is he right in thinking that there is only one compound called a salt?

c) How would you answer Mike's question? Think about elements and the compounds they make.

d) Do **all** metals have high melting points? Can you think of any metals that don't?

Why are metals useful?

LEARN ABOUT

- the properties of metals and non-metals
- the range, source and uses of metals
- presenting results of research

This wooden barbecue just isn't as good as a metal one!

Metals

Life without metals would be difficult to imagine. We find their properties ideal for a wide variety of uses. Look at the general properties of metals below:

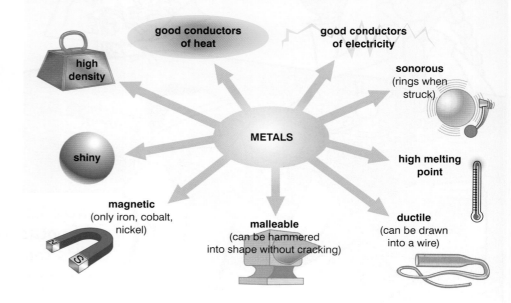

good conductors of heat

good conductors of electricity

sonorous (rings when struck)

high density

METALS

shiny

high melting point

magnetic (only iron, cobalt, nickel)

malleable (can be hammered into shape without cracking)

ductile (can be drawn into a wire)

ICT CHALLENGE

Useful metals
a) Take each property of the metals and link it to a use of metals that relies on that particular property.
b) Find out about one of the metals in the Periodic Table. Write a technical information card, like the one for gold opposite. You can use books, posters, videos, ROMs and the Internet to gather your data. Present your information to best effect, using ICT if possible.

Here is an information card about a metallic element you know well: gold.

Name: gold
Symbol: Au
Metal/non-metal/metalloid: metal
Appearance: shiny, yellowish metal
Melting point: 1064°C
Boiling point: 2850°C
Density: 19.28 g/cm³
Chemical reactivity: low
Sources: Veins of gold running through rock (sometimes deposited as grains on riverbeds). Mainly mined in South Africa and USA.
Uses:
- Jewellery and ornaments.
- Gold coated electrical connections in the computer, telecommunication and home appliance industries.
- Gold plated shields and reflectors to protect equipment on satellites.
- Reflectors to concentrate light energy in lasers used for eye operations and to kill cancerous cells.
- Gold coated contacts in the sensors that activate air bags in cars.

Q1 Which properties of gold make it useful in computers?

Non-metals

Less than a quarter of the elements are non-metals. Some are solids, others are gases and one, bromine, is a liquid at 20 °C.

Look at the general properties of non-metals below:

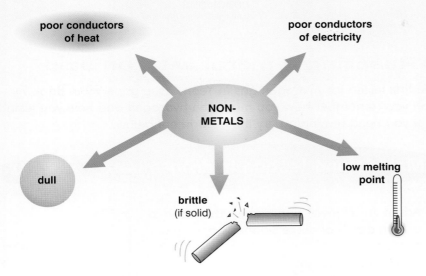

poor conductors of heat

poor conductors of electricity

NON-METALS

dull

brittle (if solid)

low melting point

Q2 Name a yellow non-metallic element that is brittle.

We should really say that '**Most** non-metals are poor conductors of heat and electricity.' The exception to the rule is one form of the element carbon, called **graphite**.

You will use graphite at school on most days – it is mixed with clay in your pencil 'lead'. There are free electrons within graphite. These can drift through the graphite as it conducts electricity.

Graphite is a form of carbon

SUMMARY QUESTIONS

1 ☆ Draw a table to compare the properties of elements that are metals with those that are non-metals.

2 ☆☆ Find out more about the non-metallic element, carbon.
Write a paragraph on each form of carbon you discover.

Key words

ductile
graphite
malleable
sonorous

Metals plus acids

LEARN ABOUT

- metals reacting with dilute acids
- word equations and balanced symbol equations
- identifying patterns in reactions
- making predictions about other reactions

Reacting a metal with an acid

You first tested for hydrogen gas in Year 7 (see page 99 in Book 7). Can you remember how you made the hydrogen and how you tested it? If you need reminding, try the experiment below.

Making and testing hydrogen gas

- Add a small piece of magnesium ribbon to a 2 cm depth of dilute sulphuric acid in a test tube.
  a) What do you see?

- Hold a boiling tube upside down above the mouth of the test tube.
  Hydrogen gas is less dense than air so it will displace air from the boiling tube.

- Test the gas collected in the boiling tube with a lighted splint.
  b) What happens?

- Now repeat the experiment above but use dilute hydrochloric acid instead of sulphuric acid.
  c) Do you get the same result?

hold boiling tube to collect hydrogen

dilute sulphuric acid

magnesium ribbon

Salts

The reaction between a metal and any dilute acid produces hydrogen gas.

Look at the formulae of the three acids we commonly use in school.

Can you see the element that each acid contains? In fact, all acids contain **hydrogen**. It is released as a gas (H_2) if a metal reacts with the acid.

But what happens to the rest of the atoms in the reactants? We have the metal, of course, and the remaining atoms from the acid. These usually form a solution of **a salt**.

In general we can say:

acid + a metal → a salt + hydrogen

A salt *is a compound formed when the hydrogen in an acid is replaced (wholly or partially) by a metal.*

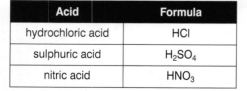

Acid	Formula
hydrochloric acid	HCl
sulphuric acid	H_2SO_4
nitric acid	HNO_3

We can show the reaction between magnesium and sulphuric acid like this:

Word equation:

magnesium + sulphuric acid → magnesium sulphate + hydrogen

Balanced symbol equation:

$$Mg + H_2SO_4 \rightarrow MgSO_4 + H_2$$

The salt formed is called magnesium sulphate. Its formula is $MgSO_4$.

So sulphuric acid makes salts called **sulphates**.
Hydrochloric acid makes salts called **chlorides**.
The salts we make from nitric acid are called **nitrates**.

This is summarised in the table below:

Acid	Salts made	Formula ends in . . .	Example
hydrochloric acid	chlorides	. . . Cl	zinc chloride, $ZnCl_2$
sulphuric acid	sulphates	. . . SO_4	copper sulphate, $CuSO_4$
nitric acid	nitrates	. . . NO_3	sodium nitrate, $NaNO_3$

Why can't I be the metal in the salt for a change?

Q1 Look at the examples of salts in the table. Try to make up a rule about naming salts.

Predicting reactions

- Your teacher will add a small piece of calcium metal to dilute hydrochloric acid. Before that, **predict**:
  a) what you think will happen in the tube
  b) the products that will be formed.

- Your teacher will repeat the experiment, but with dilute sulphuric acid this time.
  c) Make your predictions again.
  d) Explain your observations after you have seen what happens.

Preparing a sample of magnesium chloride

You can prepare a sample of the salt by reacting a metal with an acid. Your teacher will give you a sheet to help. But first, try to plan the experiment yourself.

SUMMARY QUESTIONS

1 ☆ Copy these sentences. Complete them by filling in the gaps.
   If a metal reacts with dilute . . . we get a . . . formed plus . . . gas.

   We can test for the gas with a . . . splint. The gas burns with a squeaky . . .

2 ☆ Write down the general equation for the reaction between a metal and an acid.

3 ☆☆ **a)** Name the salt that forms when:
   i) zinc reacts with dilute sulphuric acid
   ii) iron reacts with dilute hydrochloric acid.
   b) In Year 7, you tested a common metal that did not react with dilute acid. Name the metal.

Key words

chloride
hydrogen
nitrate
prediction
a salt
sulphate

Fizzing carbonates

LEARN ABOUT

- balancing chemical equations
- acids reacting with metal carbonates
- evidence of chemical reactions

Balancing equations

In 9E2 you looked at this reaction:

magnesium + hydrochloric acid → magnesium chloride + hydrogen
$$Mg + 2HCl \rightarrow MgCl_2 + H_2$$

Notice the number 2 in front of the HCl in the symbol equation. It means we have 2 molecules of HCl in the equation. This is called a **balanced equation**.

We need to balance chemical equations to make sure that we have the same number of atoms before and after a reaction. (Remember: no new atoms can be created or destroyed in a reaction – they just 'swap partners'!) We balance an equation by putting numbers in front of formulae, if necessary.

Q1 Why is it necessary to balance the equation for the reaction between Mg and HCl?

We can show the particles of reactants and products using a model that represents atoms as circles. This helps us to count the atoms on each side of the equation. Look at the **particle diagram** below:

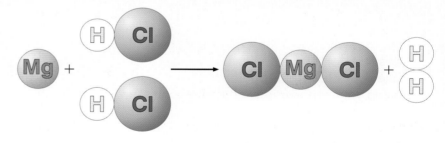

$$Mg + 2HCl \longrightarrow MgCl_2 + H_2$$

So we have:

reactants (left-hand side) → products (right-hand side)
1Mg, 2H's, 2Cl's   1Mg, 2H's, 2Cl's

You can **never change the formula** of a substance just to make an equation balance.

Remember from Year 8 that each atom has a 'combining power'. The number of bonds an atom can form determines the formula of its compounds. So you can't change magnesium chloride from $MgCl_2$ to $MgCl$, or change hydrogen gas from H_2 to H, just to help you balance an equation!

Warning: Magnesium chloride isn't really a molecule made of 3 atoms (see page 76). However, this model helps us to see how to balance equations.

The speech bubble reads: It's very important to balance your atoms on either side, you know.

● Acids plus carbonates

In Year 8 you came across a metal **carbonate**. It was in limestone, which contains calcium carbonate, $CaCO_3$.

Investigating metal carbonates and acids

● You are given the following apparatus and solutions:

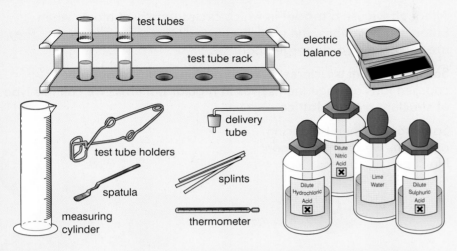

test tubes

test tube rack

electric balance

delivery tube

test tube holders

splints

spatula

measuring cylinder

thermometer

Dilute Nitric Acid

Lime Water

Dilute Hydrochloric Acid

Dilute Sulphuric Acid

You also have a range of different metal carbonates. These include copper carbonate, sodium carbonate, potassium carbonate and magnesium carbonate.

Your task is to explore what happens in reactions between the carbonates and the acids.

You should record similarities and differences systematically.

Make sure you measure any temperature changes that take place.

Let your teacher check your plans before you try them out.

The chemical formula of copper carbonate is $CuCO_3$. When it reacts with sulphuric acid (H_2SO_4) we get:

$$\text{copper carbonate} + \text{sulphuric acid} \rightarrow \text{copper sulphate} + \text{water} + \text{carbon dioxide}$$

$$CuCO_3 + H_2SO_4 \rightarrow CuSO_4 + H_2O + CO_2$$

Q2 How is limestone weathered by rain water?

LINK UP TO GEOGRAPHY

You can learn more about limestone landscapes in Geography.

Q3 Count up the atoms on each side of the equation. Explain why this equation is balanced.

Q4 Write down the general equation for the reaction between a carbonate and an acid.

SUMMARY QUESTIONS

1 ☆ Copy these sentences. Complete them by filling in the gaps:

When a metal carbonate . . . with an acid we get a . . ., water and . . . . . . formed. We can test the gas given off with . . ., which will turn . . .

2 ☆☆☆ Write the word equation and balanced symbol equation for the reaction between hydrochloric acid and
   a) sodium carbonate, Na_2CO_3
   b) zinc carbonate, $ZnCO_3$ (Hint: $ZnCl_2$ is one of the products).

Key words

balanced equation
carbonate
particle diagram

LEARN ABOUT
- acids reacting with metal oxides
- salt formation as evidence of a chemical reaction
- word and symbol equations

The particles in salts

Although we use a **model** in which circles represent atoms when balancing equations, the particles in a salt are not really atoms. They are **ions**, which are charged particles.

Salts have giant structures in which millions of these oppositely charged ions arrange themselves in regular patterns. We call this type of structure a **giant lattice**.

So although when balancing equations we might represent NaCl as:

It is more realistically shown by part of its giant lattice. This will contain an equal number of Na^+ and Cl^- ions:

Q1 Why do scientists use models?

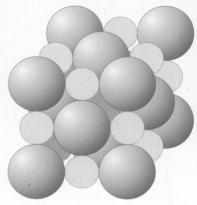

Part of sodium chloride's giant lattice

In just 6 grams of sodium chloride there are over 60 000 000 000 000 000 000 000 Na^+ and Cl^- ions.

Metal oxides plus acids

Metal oxides are another important group of metal compounds.

Metal oxides tend to be basic (the opposite of acidic). So they react with acids in **neutralisation** reactions. You will probably remember this from Unit 7E.

Many metal oxides do not dissolve in water. But they will dissolve in dilute acid during a neutralisation reaction. These metal oxides are called **bases**. (Soluble metal oxides are bases that we call alkalis.)

The general equation is:

acid + metal oxide (base) → a salt + water

For example:

hydrochloric acid + zinc oxide → zinc chloride + water
$$2\,HCl + ZnO \rightarrow ZnCl_2 + H_2O$$

Come on, let's go and react with an acid.

That's so basic!

Preparing copper sulphate crystals

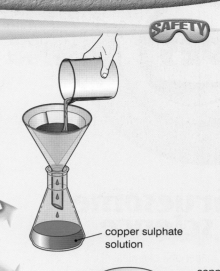

Now you can try out the reaction between copper oxide and dilute sulphuric acid. You can then prepare a sample of the salt formed in the reaction.

- Pour 20 cm^3 of dilute sulphuric acid into a small beaker. Then add a spatula of black copper oxide.
- Stir with a glass rod. Add more copper oxide, one spatula at a time until no more will dissolve.
- Warm the beaker gently on a tripod and gauze.
  !DO NOT boil the mixture! Allow to cool.
- Filter off the excess copper oxide from the solution.

copper sulphate solution

- Pour the solution into an evaporating dish. Heat it on a water bath as shown.
  Stop heating when you see a few small crystals appear around the edge of the solution.

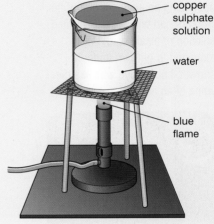

copper sulphate solution

water

- Leave the solution at room temperature for a few days. As the water evaporates off, the copper sulphate will **crystallise** out of the solution.
- Draw a diagram to show the shape of your copper sulphate crystals.

blue flame

  a) How can you tell that a reaction took place? What do we call this type of reaction?
  b) How can you tell when excess copper oxide has been added?
  c) How did you remove the excess copper oxide?
  d) Write a word equation and a balanced symbol equation for the reaction.
  e) Why is the solution left for several days at the end of the experiment?

 CHALLENGE

Monitoring pH changes
a) What do you predict will happen to the pH of an acid when a metal oxide is added?
b) Repeat the first step in the experiment to make copper sulphate crystals. But this time use a pH sensor to measure the initial pH of the sulphuric acid. Then monitor any changes in pH as you add small amounts of copper oxide until it is in excess.
c) Check your data against your prediction. Evaluate your prediction.

SUMMARY QUESTIONS

1 ☆ Copy these sentences. Complete them by filling in the gaps.

When we react a base, such as a metal ..., with an acid we get a ... and ... formed.

We can grow ... from the solution left by allowing the ... to ... slowly.

2 ☆☆☆ Write the word equation and balanced symbol equation for the reaction between zinc oxide and sulphuric acid.

Key words

base
crystallise
giant lattice
ion
model
neutralisation

LEARN ABOUT
- obtaining a neutral solution
- the uses of a range of salts
- using preliminary work to try out a plan
- evaluating the methods used

Gruesome science

A manager of a chemical plant, describing an accident one of the workers had with a concentrated solution of alkali, said 'We managed to get him under a shower, but his eye was like the white of an egg.'

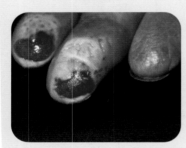

The results of an accident with a concentrated solution of sodium hydroxide

◉ Acids plus alkalis

In 9E4 you saw how copper oxide (a base) neutralises an acid. You didn't need the pH sensor to tell you when the reaction was complete. You could see because the insoluble copper oxide no longer dissolved once all the acid had been neutralised.

However, some metal oxides are soluble in water. An example is sodium oxide. So we can't tell when the sodium oxide is in excess just by looking at the reaction mixture.

Q1 What would be formed if sodium oxide was added to hydrochloric acid?

In Book 7 you might have seen a **burette** used in a neutralisation reaction between an acid and an alkali. An alkaline solution is formed if we add a soluble metal oxide to water:

$$\text{sodium oxide} + \text{water} \rightarrow \text{sodium hydroxide}$$
$$Na_2O + H_2O \rightarrow 2 NaOH$$
$$\text{an alkaline solution}$$

Remember that: **acid + alkali → a salt + water**

For example:

$$HCl + NaOH \rightarrow NaCl + H_2O$$

In the following experiment you can carry out a **neutralisation** reaction with the help of a burette. The burette enables you to make very small additions of one solution to another. An indicator is usually used to tell us when the reaction is just complete.

This technique is called **titration**.

Titrating acid and alkali

SAFETY

- Collect $20 \, cm^3$ of potassium hydroxide solution in a conical flask.
- Add a few drops of phenolphthalein solution.
- Fill a burette with dilute hydrochloric acid using a funnel.
- Add the acid to the potassium hydroxide solution, swirling the flask as you proceed. (Your teacher will show you this technique.)
- When the indicator shows signs of changing colour, add the acid from the burette a drop at a time. Stop when the solution turns colourless. (This is difficult to do, so you will probably have to repeat the titration a few times.)
- Record how much acid is needed to neutralise the alkali.

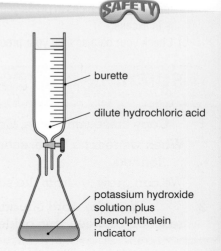

burette

dilute hydrochloric acid

potassium hydroxide solution plus phenolphthalein indicator

The largest natural crystals on Earth have been discovered in Chihuahua, Mexico. The crystals of selenite, a form of calcium sulphate, are over 6 metres long. They were found in a cavern, down a silver and zinc mine. One mineral hunter was crushed to death by one of the huge crystals as he tried to hack it from the roof of the cave. There are now plans to leave the crystals in the cave and allow tourists to see them in their natural glory.

Making your own salt crystals

- Choose an example of a salt to prepare from the list below:
  – magnesium sulphate
  – copper chloride
  – zinc nitrate
  – copper nitrate
  – potassium sulphate
  – sodium nitrate.

- You can use any of the apparatus commonly found in the laboratory. You must check the safety information on any reactants you plan to use and on any products made.

- Think about:
  – How will you know when all the acid has reacted?
  – How will you separate any unreacted solids if necessary?
  – What will you do to make large crystals of your salt?
  a) Write down your plan in note form, including safety precautions.

- Before starting any practical work, **you must check your plans with your teacher**.
  b) Having made your salt, write down an account of your experiment. Include any changes to your original plan. Write down why you had to make them. Say whether they were effective in producing a good sample of your chosen salt.

ICT ✦ CHALLENGE

Uses of salts
There is a wide variety of the compounds we call salts. Some of these salts have uses in industry or in our everyday lives.
Use the Internet to find out the uses of *two* of the following salts:
aluminium sulphate
magnesium sulphate
sodium stearate   silver bromide
calcium phosphate
iron sulphate   potassium nitrate

Well I think that experiment was quite a success!

SUMMARY QUESTIONS

1 ☆ Copy the sentences. Complete them by filling in the blanks.
An acid plus an . . . gives a . . . plus water. This is called a . . . reaction.

2 ☆☆ Name the products when magnesium hydroxide reacts with nitric acid.

3 ☆☆☆ Write the word equation and balanced symbol equation for the reaction between lithium hydroxide (LiOH) and dilute hydrochloric acid.

Key words
burette
neutralisation
titration

Alloys

An alloy is a mixture of metals. Alloys are chosen by materials scientists to have the best properties for a particular job. To make the alloy, you melt the metals and mix them together. The metals do not react together. That's why we can describe the alloy as a mixture (and not a compound).You can read about some examples below.

Common alloys

Name of alloy	Metals the alloy contains	Example of use
brass	copper and zinc	door handles
duralumin	aluminium, copper and magnesium	aeroplanes
solder	lead and tin	making electrical circuits

Some other alloys you use every day are the alloys in coins. These alloys must be very hard-wearing. They also have to be **malleable** enough to be stamped with complex patterns:

Coin	Metals the alloy contains
5p, 10p, 50p	copper (75%), nickel (25%)
20p	copper (84%), nickel (16%)
£1	copper (70%), zinc (24.5%), nickel (5.5%)

Memory metals

Some of the latest 'smart materials' to be developed are called memory metals. These special alloys of nickel and titanium seem to 'remember' their original shape. They can switch back to this shape at a certain temperature. You might have seen adverts for unbreakable sunglasses. Their frames are made from memory metals.

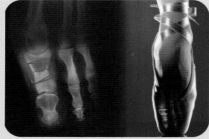

A memory metal is used to hold together a ballet dancer's fractured big toe. The staple (in blue) is trying to return to its original shape (in red).

Here are some uses of memory metals:

- Braces for teeth.
- Fire sprinklers.
- Underwires for bras.
- Thermostats on coffee pots.
- Holding ligaments to bones.
- Joining hydraulic lines in fighter planes.
- Supporting and keeping blood vessels open.

SCIENTIFIC PEOPLE

Gemma designs the spokes on mountain bikes as part of her job as a materials scientist. Here are some of the things she must find out before deciding on the ideal alloy for the job:

- What are the steps in manufacturing a unique blade-shape?
- At what times and temperatures should the alloy be heat-treated to toughen it?
- What are the best surface-finishes?
- How long will the spoke last?
- Do mechanical tests confirm strength and durability requirements?

Steels

Steels are alloys of iron – the most common metal used in construction. Normal steels have small amounts of carbon mixed with the iron. However, you can also get special alloy steels, such as stainless steel which contains chromium and nickel mixed with the iron. A very hard steel is made by alloying iron with tungsten metal.

How does alloying make a metal stronger?

We can use the particle model to explain how mixing metals in alloys makes them stronger. Look at the diagram:

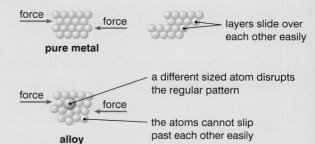

force → ← force
pure metal
layers slide over each other easily

force → ← force
alloy
a different sized atom disrupts the regular pattern
the atoms cannot slip past each other easily

With different sized atoms mixed in, the layers can't slip past each other so smoothly. It's a bit like little stones catching under a door when you try to open it!

- A salt is a crystalline compound. In most salts a metal takes the place of all or some of the hydrogen in an acid.
  The common acids form these salts:

Acid	Salts made
hydrochloric acid	chlorides
sulphuric acid	sulphates
nitric acid	nitrates

- Here are the general equations you should know:

$$metal + acid \rightarrow a\ salt + hydrogen$$
$$metal\ carbonate + acid \rightarrow a\ salt + water + carbon\ dioxide$$
$$metal\ oxide + acid \rightarrow a\ salt + water$$
$$metal\ hydroxide + acid \rightarrow a\ salt + water$$

> Now I know that carbon, a non-metallic element, in the form of graphite, is a good conductor of electricity.

> Common salt... sodium chloride...is only one of thousands of metal compounds called salts.

> Remember that elements are totally different to the compounds they make!

> I see there are lots of metals that have strange properties... but they ALL conduct electricity.

DANGER! AVOID THESE COMMON ERRORS

Although we can generalise about the properties of metals and non-metals, there are lots of exceptions. A good example is graphite. It is a form of the non-metallic element carbon, but it is a good electrical conductor.

Unlike most metals, lithium, sodium and potassium have low densities and low melting points. Then there is mercury, it is a metal that is a liquid at 20 °C.

Remember that when you get crystals from a salt solution, you evaporate the water from the solution. Don't say that you 'evaporate the solution'!

Key words

balanced equation
crystal
crystallise
ductile
general equation
malleable
neutralisation

REVIEW QUESTIONS
Understanding and applying concepts

1 **a** You have a conical flask containing dilute acid on top of an electric balance. You add a piece of magnesium ribbon. What do you think will happen to the mass from the start of the reaction to its completion? Explain why.

b You repeat the experiment in part **a**. This time the reaction takes place in a sealed vessel. What difference would you expect in the mass before and after the reaction? Explain why.

2 Write the word equation and balanced symbol equation for each of the following reactions. (Refer to the combining powers table in question 6 to work out formulae of the salts formed. The combining power of chlorine is 1.)

a calcium + hydrochloric acid
b zinc + sulphuric acid
c magnesium carbonate + hydrochloric acid
d sodium carbonate + hydrochloric acid
e calcium oxide + sulphuric acid
f magnesium oxide + hydrochloric acid
g sodium hydroxide + hydrochloric acid
h potassium hydroxide + nitric acid

3 Zinc oxide is a white powder that is insoluble in water. It reacts with dilute sulphuric acid.

a How can you observe when the reaction has finished?
b What type of substance do we call zinc oxide?
c Write the word equation for the reaction.
d Write the balanced symbol equation for the reaction.
e How would you prepare crystals of the salt formed in the reaction?

Ways with words

4 Zinc reacts with dilute hydrochloric acid. Write a sequence of instructions to explain how to balance the equation for this reaction.

Making more of maths

5 **a** Do some research to find the numbers of non-metals that are solid, liquid or gas at 20 °C.
b Display your data as a pie chart.

6 In this unit you have probably noticed groupings of atoms, such as the SO_4 sulphate grouping, in the formulae of some salts. We can think of these groupings as having a combining power just like atoms. The table below shows the common groupings:

Grouping	Formula	Combining power
sulphate	SO_4	2
carbonate	CO_3	2
nitrate	NO_3	1
hydroxide	OH	1

Here are the combining powers of some metals:

Metal	Symbol	Combining power
sodium	Na	1
potassium	K	1
calcium	Ca	2
copper(II)	Cu	2
magnesium	Mg	2
zinc	Zn	2
aluminium	Al	3

Some examples of salts are sodium sulphate, Na_2SO_4, and magnesium nitrate, $Mg(NO_3)_2$. Notice the brackets that are put around groupings of atoms if there is more than one in a formula.

sodium sulphate – Na_2SO_4

a Draw a table with the metals listed down the side, and with sulphate, nitrate and chloride (combining power = 1) across the top. Then fill in the formulae of the salts for all the possible combinations.

b Look back to the carbonates listed in the experiment on page 75. Write a word equation and a balanced symbol equation for each of their reactions with sulphuric acid.

Thinking skills

7 In a titration, Jason found that $15\,cm^3$ of sodium hydroxide solution was neutralised by $25\,cm^3$ of dilute nitric acid.

Using the same solutions, he repeated the titration, starting with $18\,cm^3$ of sodium hydroxide solution. What volume of dilute nitric acid was needed this time to neutralise the alkali?

Extension questions

8 Write a technical information card about one example of an alloy. You can use books, posters, videos, ROMs and the Internet to gather your data. Present your information clearly.

9 **a** Explain why the method in question 3 would not work if you reacted sodium oxide with sulphuric acid.

b How would you change the method to prepare a sample of sodium sulphate crystals from sodium oxide?

SAT-STYLE QUESTIONS

1 Sam and Becky were preparing a sample of copper sulphate crystals. They started by reacting copper oxide with dilute sulphuric acid.

a What do we call the reaction between an acid and a base? (1)

b Put these steps into the correct order.

A Pour $20\,cm^3$ of sulphuric acid into a small beaker.

B Pour the solution into an evaporating dish. Heat it on a water bath.

C Warm the beaker gently on a tripod and gauze.

D Add more copper oxide, one spatula at a time, until no more will dissolve.

E Leave the solution at room temperature for a few days.

F Add a spatula of black copper oxide. Stir with a glass rod.

G Stop heating when you see a few small crystals appear around the edge of the solution.

H Filter off the excess copper oxide from the solution. (3)

c Write a word equation for the reaction between copper oxide and sulphuric acid. (1)

2 Calcium forms an oxide whose formula is CaO. Calcium oxide reacts with water to form $Ca(OH)_2$.

a i) What is the name of $Ca(OH)_2$? (1)

ii) Would you expect a solution of $Ca(OH)_2$ to be acidic, neutral or alkaline? (1)

b i) What is the name of the salt formed when $Ca(OH)_2$ reacts with dilute nitric acid? (1)

ii) Write a word equation for the reaction in **b** part i). (1)

iii) $Ca(OH)_2$ also reacts with dilute hydrochloric acid. Write a balanced symbol equation for this reaction. (2)

3 A compound whose old name is 'potash' (K_2CO_3) is reacted with nitric acid (HNO_3) to make potassium nitrate (KNO_3).

a What is the chemical name for K_2CO_3? (1)

b Write a balanced equation for the reaction between potash and nitric acid. (2)

Key words

Unscramble these:
slartyc
cutelid
saintlionratue
ballameel

9F

Patterns of reactivity

You told me these were pure gold... so how come they've gone dull?

What's it all about?

In this unit you will look more closely at the differences between metals when they react with oxygen, water and acids. You can use these differences to make an order of reactivity.

Then you will link the uses and extraction of metals to their position in this order of reactivity.

What do you remember?

You already know about:

- the differences between elements and compounds.
- how we represent elements by symbols, and compounds by formulae.
- how we represent chemical reactions by word equations and balanced symbol equations.
- the tests for hydrogen, carbon dioxide and oxygen.
- many metals reacting with oxygen to form oxides.
- the general equation for the reaction if a metal reacts with dilute acid.

1 Which of these is a compound?

chlorine   nitrogen   water   aluminium

2 Complete this word equation.

$$zinc + oxygen \rightarrow ?$$

zinc hydroxide   zinc oxide
zinc carbonate   zinc nitrate

3 Which gas is given off when magnesium reacts with dilute sulphuric acid?

hydrogen   sulphur dioxide
oxygen   carbon dioxide

4 What is the test for oxygen gas?

A lighted splint pops.
Lime water turns milky.
A lighted splint is extinguished.
A glowing splint re-lights.

Ideas about reactivity

QUESTIONS

Look at the cartoon above and discuss these questions with your partner.

a) What other things might affect the cost of sodium metal?

b) Do you think there is a mistake in Molly's book? Explain your answer.

c) The armour is from the Middle Ages and is hundreds of years old. Is it likely to be made from aluminium?

d) Is Reese right about the reaction of metals with water? Do you know any metals that do react well with water?

Why do metals tarnish?

LEARN ABOUT

- how air and water affect many metals
- how metals are affected in different ways
- some metals that are soft and can be cut

AMAZING SCIENCE!

The metal zirconium is used in chemical factories. It is resistant to corrosive attack from most acids, salt solutions, strong alkalis, and even some molten salts.

Strange metals

We usually think of metals as hard, tough materials. However, some are soft and can be cut with an ordinary kitchen knife.

Look at the photos below showing some freshly cut lithium and potassium. Compare them with pieces of metal exposed to the air for a few minutes.

Freshly cut lithium

The same piece of lithium a few minutes later

Q1 What happens to the freshly cut surface of the metals in the photos when they are exposed to the air?

Q2 Give one property of lithium and potassium that suggests they are metals, and one property that is unusual for a metal.

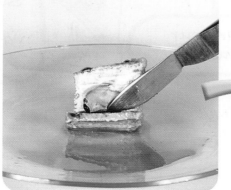

Freshly cut potassium

A piece of potassium exposed to air for a few minutes

When the atoms at the surface of a metal react with substances in the air, the metal loses its shiny appearance. We say that the metal becomes **tarnished**.

Often the metal will form a dull coating of the metal oxide on its surface as it reacts with oxygen in the air. However, water vapour, carbon dioxide, pollutant gases such as sulphur dioxide, and even nitrogen can get involved in tarnishing some metals.

Looking at some common metals

Here are some examples of other metals that tarnish in air:

This roof contains copper. The green colour comes from copper compounds, which are formed as the copper tarnishes.

A rusty bicycle chain. The red/brown rust is a compound of iron.

On the other hand, the metal gold does not tarnish in air. Gold coins found in shipwrecks, hundreds of years old, can still be in mint condition.

Q3 Which of the metals mentioned above tarnish and which don't?

Q4 Why do you think there is a difference between the three metals?

Ah, har, mi hearties. We've found the long-lost gold.

Rusting

The rusting of iron and steel (which contains mainly iron) costs millions of pounds each year. *Iron needs both air (oxygen) and water in order to rust.* **Rust** is a form of iron(III) oxide.

Metals react with oxygen and other substances in the air at different rates. Sometimes they don't react at all. Some, such as lithium and potassium, react quickly. Others react slowly, like copper. Gold is so **unreactive** that it doesn't tarnish in air.

SUMMARY QUESTIONS

1 ☆ Copy these sentences. Complete them by filling in the gaps.
   When metals react with gases in the . . . their surface loses its . . . appearance. We say that the metal's surface is . . .
   Many metals react . . . in the air to form oxides.

2 ☆☆ a) How do we protect iron from rusting? Think of at least three methods that we can use.
   b) How does each method of protection work?

Key words
rust
tarnish
unreactive

Comparing reactivity

9F2

LEARN ABOUT
- how some metals react with cold water
- differences in reactivity between metals
- hazards associated with some metals

Now that's what I call a reaction!

● Metals plus water

Most metals don't react **vigorously** with water. Just think of your saucepans at home! However, there are differences in the reactivity of metals.

Magnesium and copper in cold water

- Clean the surface of a strip of magnesium ribbon with emery paper.

- Wind the ribbon into a coil and place it in the apparatus shown below.

- Repeat this with a piece of copper foil.

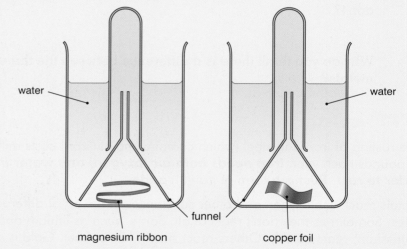

water   water

funnel

magnesium ribbon   copper foil

- Leave the apparatus for a week.
  a) What do you observe after a week? Which metal shows no sign of a reaction?

- Test any gas collected with a lighted splint.
  b) Which gas is produced?
  c) Where did this gas come from?
  d) Which of the two metals is more reactive with water?

Q1 What do you think will happen if lithium, sodium or potassium is added to cold water? These are the metals from 9F1 that tarnished readily. They are found in Group 1 of the Periodic Table.

Q2 Predict what might be formed in any reaction that takes place between these metals and cold water.

Some metals react very slowly with cold water but **react more readily with steam**. Examples are magnesium, iron and zinc.

$$zinc + steam \rightarrow zinc\ oxide + hydrogen$$
$$Zn + H_2O \rightarrow ZnO + H_2$$

Reactive metals

● Watch your teacher demonstrate the reactions of lithium, sodium and potassium with water.
   a) Record your observations of each reaction. Include the name of the gas given off and the solutions formed.
   b) How are the reactions similar?
   c) How do the reactions differ?
   d) What safety precautions did your teacher take when using these metals?
   e) What is the hazard warning sign on each jar of the metals? Why is it there?
   f) Why are the lithium, sodium and potassium stored under oil in their jars?
   g) Put the metals in an order of reactivity with water, listing the most reactive one first.

The alkaline solutions formed as the Group 1 metals react with water are called **hydroxides**. An example is lithium hydroxide, LiOH.

$$\text{lithium} + \text{water} \rightarrow \text{lithium hydroxide} + \text{hydrogen}$$
$$2\,Li + 2\,H_2O \rightarrow 2\,LiOH + H_2$$

Q3 Write the word equations and balanced symbol equations for the reactions of sodium and potassium with water.

Caesium (Cs) reacts violently with water, smashing the glass trough

SUMMARY QUESTIONS

1 ☆ Copy these sentences. Complete them by filling in the gaps.
   The metals in Group . . . of the . . . Table react . . . with cold water.
   They give off . . . gas and form . . . solutions of the metal . . .
   . . . was the most reactive metal we tested with water, followed by . . . and then . . .

2 ☆☆☆ **a)** Find out the name of another metal in Group 1 of the Periodic Table.
   b) Predict how it would react with cold water. Give a word equation and a balanced symbol equation for this reaction.

Key words

hydroxide
vigorously

Sorry, sir but he's been waiting a very long time for this copper to react with dilute acid!

AMAZING SCIENCE!

Less than 200 tonnes of aluminium were produced in 1885. A hundred years later, world production had climbed to almost 22 million tonnes.

Aluminium resists corrosion

What's the order?

You have seen how a range of metals react (or don't react) with water. You used your observations of these reactions to place some metals into an order of reactivity. But with some metals the reactions are very slow. This makes it difficult to put them in order of reactivity. Instead, we can look at their reactions with dilute acid to judge their positions in an order.

Q1 What is usually formed when a metal does react with dilute acid?

Q2 How can we use the reaction between metals and acids to put metals into an order of reactivity?

Q3 Which metals would you not try adding to acid? Why not?

The weird case of aluminium

Aluminium fits into the order of reactivity between magnesium and zinc. So why do we use aluminium to make cans for acidic fizzy drinks?

Reactions of aluminium

a) Predict the reactions you would expect between:
   i) aluminium and water, and
   ii) aluminium and dilute acid.

● Try adding some aluminium to water first of all, then to dilute acid.
   b) What do you observe?
   c) How were your observations surprising?

Aluminium is protected on its surface by a **tough layer of aluminium oxide**.

Once the outer oxide layer has covered the metal, the aluminium atoms beneath are protected from water, dilute acids and oxygen. So aluminium appears to be an unreactive metal. That's why this fairly reactive metal can be used outside, for example in patio doors. It does not corrode badly like unprotected iron.

Gathering quantitative data

In this investigation you should plan to collect more data to test out your order of reactivity. This time, measurements will play a big part in the results you record. This is called **quantitative** data (involving numbers) as opposed to the **qualitative** data that are based on observations.

You will be looking in more detail at the metals zinc, magnesium and aluminium and their reactions with dilute acid. So 'type of metal' is your **independent variable.**

● Think about these questions to help your planning:
  – What could you measure as each reaction proceeds? This will be your **dependent variable**.
  – Which variables will you keep the same (**control variables**) to make your tests as fair as possible?
  – How will you make your investigation safe?

● Let your teacher check your plan before you start your practical work.

A list of elements in order of reactivity is called the **Reactivity Series**.

Constructing and using the Reactivity Series

● Look back through this unit and make a list of metals in order of reactivity. Start with potassium at the top. This is your Reactivity Series.

  a) Using your previous knowledge and your Reactivity Series, predict the answer to this question:

  What you would expect to see if you heated the following metals, then plunged them into a gas jar of pure oxygen gas:

  i) magnesium   **iv)** zinc
  ii) copper   **v)** sodium
  iii) calcium   **vi)** iron?

● Your teacher will show you some of these reactions.

Gruesome science

Aluminium alloys are light and strong and are used to make the latest battleships. However, if hit by a missile, the aluminium hull can actually burst into flames, which results in many casualties with serious burns.

Potassium reacts vigorously in oxygen. The white smoke contains fine particles of potassium oxide.

SUMMARY QUESTIONS

1 ☆ Copy these sentences. Complete them by filling in the gaps.
   Metals can be listed in . . . of reactivity using their reactions with . . ., dilute acid and . . . This is called the . . . Series.

2 ☆☆ Explain why aluminium appears to be in a false position in the Reactivity Series.

Key words

aluminium oxide
control variables
dependent variable
independent variable
qualitative
quantitative
Reactivity Series

Metals in competition

LEARN ABOUT
- displacement reactions
- making and testing predictions using the Reactivity Series
- recording and identifying patterns in observations
- using a model to explain results

⬤ Displacement from solution

So far you have put the metals in order of reactivity on the basis of their reactions with water, dilute acids and oxygen. Now you can use the resulting Reactivity Series to predict what happens when we put the metals 'into competition' with each other.

Metals fight it out!

- Set up the boiling tubes shown in the diagram.
- Leave the metals and solutions to react for about 15 minutes.
  a) Record your observations.
  b) Think about the reactants in each tube and what they could form. (Remember that chemical reactions involve a rearrangement of the particles in the reactants to form the products.) Try to explain in your own words what might be happening in each reaction.

! Wash your hands after using lead nitrate !

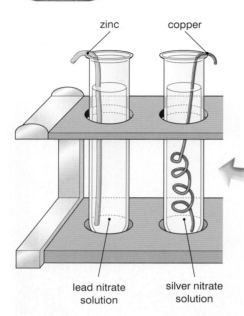

zinc   copper

lead nitrate   silver nitrate
solution   solution

Next you can look at an example using a 'model' to help explain competition between metals.

If we have silver nitrate solution and copper, we set up a competition between silver and copper. Both copper and silver want to form a compound, but it is silver that starts off with the nitrate as a compound in solution.

However, copper is more reactive than silver. It appears above it in the Reactivity Series. We can think of it as 'stronger' than silver. Therefore it 'takes the nitrate' for itself, going into solution to join it. The silver is 'kicked out' of solution and is left as the element alone.

Remember that this is just a model to help us visualise what is happening. The cartoon below might also help.

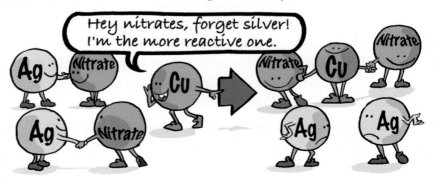

Hey nitrates, forget silver! I'm the more reactive one.

The word equation is:

copper + silver nitrate → copper nitrate + silver

We call this a **displacement** reaction.

> **Exam tip:** If you are asked to explain this reaction, an ideal answer would be:
>
> 'Copper is **more reactive** than silver, therefore it **displaces** the silver from silver nitrate solution. We get silver metal and a solution of copper nitrate formed.'

If we had added silver to copper nitrate, there would have been no reaction.

Silver is not reactive enough to displace copper from its solution.

silver + copper nitrate ↛ no reaction

Q1 Write the word equation for zinc reacting with lead nitrate.

● Displacing metals from their oxides

We can also carry out displacement reactions between metals and metal oxide powders. As both reactants are in the solid state, they need mixing thoroughly so that reacting particles can get next to each other. We also need to heat the mixture to start off the reaction.

Thermit reaction

a) Predict the word equation for the reaction between aluminium and iron(III) oxide.

● Watch your teacher demonstrate the spectacular reaction between aluminium powder and iron(III) oxide.
b) How is the reaction started off?
c) What is formed in the reaction?
d) Why does the iron melt in the reaction?

Predicting displacement from solution

You have powders of the metals magnesium, copper, iron and zinc. You also have access to solutions of magnesium sulphate, copper sulphate, iron(II) sulphate and zinc sulphate.

● Predict which metals will react with which solutions. Your teacher will give you a sheet to help.

The thermit reaction is used by railway workers to weld tracks together. The molten iron drips down into the gap and solidifies when it cools down. The iron can then be filed down to make a smooth joint.

SUMMARY QUESTIONS

1 ☆ Copy these sentences. Complete them by filling in the gaps.
    A . . . reactive metal will . . . a . . . reactive metal from its compounds.
    We call this a . . . reaction.

2 ☆☆☆ Write a word equation and balanced symbol equation for the reaction between aluminium and iron(III) oxide (Fe_2O_3).

Key words

displacement
thermit reaction

Uses and sources of metals

LEARN ABOUT
- linking the source, extraction and use of metals to their position in the Reactivity Series
- carrying out research and presenting its results

Summary of reactions of metals

The table summarises the reactions of some important metals we have met so far:

Order of reactivity	Reaction when heated in air	Reaction with water	Reaction with dilute acid
potassium	burns brightly, forming metal oxide	fizzes in cold water, giving off hydrogen, leaving an alkaline solution of metal hydroxide	explodes
sodium			
lithium			
calcium			fizzes, giving off hydrogen and forming a salt
magnesium		reacts with steam, giving off hydrogen and forming the metal oxide (but no immediate reaction with cold water)	
aluminium			
zinc			
iron			
tin	oxide layer forms without burning	slight reaction with steam	reacts slowly with warm acid
lead			
copper		no reaction, even with steam	no reaction
silver	no reaction		
gold			

Q1 Which metal does not burn when heated in air but does get covered by an oxide layer? This metal does not react with steam or dilute acid.

Q2 Which metal reacts readily with cold water and is safe to add to dilute acid?

Platinum is the most expensive metal in the world. It is more than twice the cost of gold (which is only third on the price list!). A metal called rhodium is second.

Look up the names of any metal you don't know in this Reactivity Series

Uses and sources of metals

In 9E1 on page 70 we looked at some properties of metals and linked these to their uses. These are called the **physical properties** of metals. Examples include a metal's good electrical conductivity or high melting point.

In this unit we have looked at the **chemical properties** of metals in more detail. In the next activity, you can link some uses, sources and methods of extraction of metals to their chemical properties.

An example is the **occurrence** of gold in nature as the metal itself. Only a metal very low down in the Reactivity Series could exist in nature as the element itself. Most metals we use occur as compounds found in ores. An **ore** is rock from which we can extract a metal economically.

Gold can be found as the element itself because of its low reactivity. This nugget has a mass of over half a kilogram.

Gold was discovered and used by ancient civilisations

Discovery of the Group 1 metals
Lithium – 1817
Sodium – 1807
Potassium – 1807
Rubidium – 1861
Caesium – 1860
Francium – 1939

ICT   CHALLENGE

Finding links with the Reactivity Series
Working as a group, collect together some examples of:
– uses of metals
– the occurrence of metals in nature
– the way we extract metals from their ore
– the date of their discovery

that depend on their position in the Reactivity Series. You can use a range of source materials, e.g. books, videos, ROMs, posters, leaflets, the Internet.

Write an account to summarise your findings in each area. Make sure you structure your work logically and use paragraphs to develop each idea.

Q3 Comment on the data in the box on the left.

SUMMARY QUESTIONS

1 ☆ Copy these sentences. Complete them by filling in the gaps.
  Only metals of . . . reactivity can be found in nature as the . . . itself.

  Other metals have to be . . . from their . . . by chemical reactions, including electrolysis.

2 ☆☆ a) Gold has been used for thousands of years. Why?
  b) Find out how gold is mined.

Key words
chemical property
occurrence
ore
physical property

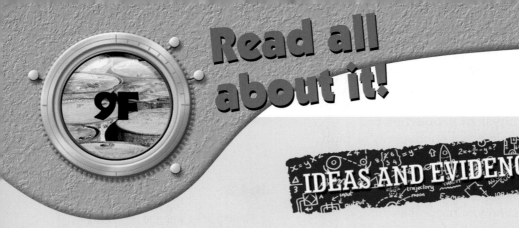
IDEAS AND EVIDENCE

Humphry Davy – element hunter!

Humphry Davy was a brilliant experimental chemist. He loved his chemistry but his long hours in the laboratory and exposure to gases eventually killed him.

Humphry was born on 17th December 1778 in Penzance, Cornwall. Unfortunately his father died when he was sixteen and he felt he had to get a job to help support his family. He became an appentice to a surgeon-apothecary (a kind of cross between a doctor and a pharmacist).

Having completed his apprenticeship, he moved to the Medical Pneumatic Institution of Bristol. Here he studied the effects of gases on the body. His main research was on an oxide of nitrogen, now known as 'laughing gas'. In one experiment he 'breathed in 16 quarts of the gas in seven minutes'. That's over 18 litres, and Humphry 'became completely intoxicated'! You might have come across this gas as an anaesthetic used by dentists.

Humphry's reputation was growing, and in 1801, the Royal Institution in London invited him to be one of their public lecturers. He was a real showman and his lectures became very popular with upper-class audiences in the capital. Many women attended and Humphry was a great favourite. At this time, science was seen as a 'male-only' subject, so his lectures were frowned upon by some.

A cartoonist of the day makes fun of a lecture by Humphry Davy and colleagues demonstrating the effects of laughing gas

It was the invention of the first battery that helped Humphry make his name. He could generate his own electricity using the first primitive cells. He made huge batteries and could really impress his audiences with sparks, bangs and flashes. More importantly, he started experimenting by passing electricity through solutions. He knew that the French scientist Antoine Lavoisier thought some alkaline solids contained unknown metals. But when he passed electricity through solutions of these solids, he found hydrogen gas but no metals. His success came when he tried the experiments with molten compounds, not solutions.

In 1807, he discovered potassium by passing electricity through molten potash (potassium carbonate). The silvery blobs of metal were amazing. When Humphry dropped a piece in water it 'skimmed about excitedly with a hissing sound, and soon burned with a lovely lavender light'. Humphry was obviously pleased with his discovery of the new metal. His brother said he 'danced about and was delirious with joy'. He also discovered sodium in the same year by passing elecricity through molten sodium chloride.

I'm glad I didn't discover caesium!

He went on to use his batteries the following year to isolate magnesium, calcium, strontium and barium. He also discovered boron using potassium to displace it from one of its compounds. Humphry wasn't the first to discover chlorine (that was done by Carl Wilhelm Scheele in 1774) but he did prove it was an element. He named it chlorine after the Greek 'chloros' meaning yellow-green. No wonder Humphry was knighted in 1812. In the same year he married a rich widow.

However, he died in 1829 after years of ill health caused by inhaling many gases in the cause of his scientific research.

We get sodium from molten sodium chloride, not salt solution. So the energy needed to melt sodium chloride and then pass electricity through it makes sodium expensive.

Of course, some of the metals near the bottom of the Reactivity Series don't react with dilute acid.

I doubt it. No reactive metals had been discovered in those days, Mike.

Remember the metals at the top of the Reactivity Series... they react very well with water!

- The list of metals in order of reactivity is known as the **Reactivity Series** (sometimes called the Activity Series) (see page 94).
- A metal higher up the Reactivity Series can displace a less reactive metal from its compounds. For example, in solution:

    zinc + copper sulphate → zinc sulphate + copper
    Zn + $CuSO_4$ → $ZnSO_4$ + Cu

    This is called a **displacement reaction**.
- Another example is the **thermit reaction** (used by rail workers to weld track together):

    aluminium + iron(III) oxide → aluminium oxide + iron
    $2\,Al$ + Fe_2O_3 → Al_2O_3 + $2\,Fe$

DANGER! AVOID THESE COMMON ERRORS

Aluminium is classed as a reactive metal despite its apparent lack of reactivity. That's because the metal is covered in a tough layer of aluminium oxide that protects it from chemical attack. When the oxide layer is removed, aluminium does react as you would expect from its position in the Reactivity Series.

Remember to explain displacement reactions by referring to the metals involved as 'more reactive' or 'less reactive' – not 'stronger' or 'weaker'. The idea of metals having 'a tug-of-war' is only a model we use to help us understand displacement reactions.

Key words

dependent variable
displacement
independent variable
qualitative
quantitative
Reactivity Series
tarnish

UNIT REVIEW

9F

REVIEW QUESTIONS
Understanding and applying concepts

1 Calcium is a metal that is more reactive than magnesium, but less reactive than lithium.
   a Predict
      i) what you will see when a piece of calcium is added to half a beaker of water
      ii) the names of any products that are formed.
   b Write a word equation for the reaction between calcium and water.
   c Put the metals lithium, sodium, potassium and calcium into their order of reactivity with water.
   d i) Give two similarities between the reactions of sodium and potassium with water.
      ii) Give two differences between the reactions of sodium and potassium with water.

2 Imagine that a new metal, given the symbol X, has been discovered. It lies between calcium and magnesium in the Reactivity Series.
   a Describe its reaction when heated in air and give a word equation and symbol equation. (The combining power of X is 2.)
   b Describe the reaction of X with dilute sulphuric acid and give a word equation and symbol equation.
   c Why can't you be sure how X will react with water?
   d X is added to copper sulphate solution. Explain what you would expect to happen.

Another new metal, Y, does not burn in air but does form a layer of oxide on its surface. It doesn't react with water or steam, but there is a slight reaction with warm dilute acid.

   e Where would you place metal Y in the Reactivity Series?
   f Explain what you would expect to happen if metal Y was added to magnesium sulphate solution.

3 This is a picture of the statue of Eros at Piccadilly Circus in London:

The statue is made of aluminium. Aluminium was a very expensive metal in 1893 when the statue was erected.
   a The fine features on the statue have suffered little damage in over a century of exposure in central London. Explain this.
   b Why was aluminium such an expensive metal at the end of the 1800s?

4 a Which of these will react together?
      i) copper oxide + zinc
      ii) magnesium oxide + lead
      iii) lead oxide + copper
      iv) silver nitrate solution + copper
      v) zinc + lead nitrate solution
   b Write a word equation for any reactions you expect to take place in part a.
   c Write a balanced symbol equation for the reactions in part b.
   d What do we call this type of reaction?

5 Draw a concept map linking these terms together. Remember to label the links to explain your thinking.

   hydrogen   metal   Reactivity Series
   potassium   water   dilute acid
   copper

Extension question

6 Use reference sources to find out and explain the role of:
   a sodium in the extraction of titanium metal
   b hydrogen in the extraction of tungsten metal.

Include word equations and symbol equations in your answers.

SAT-STYLE QUESTIONS

1 Here are some reactions of four metals:

Metal	With cold water	With dilute sulphuric acid
iron	no immediate reaction	starts fizzing, giving off a gas
silver	no reaction	no reaction
sodium	floats, then melts as it skims across the surface of the water, giving off a gas	too dangerous to attempt
nickel	no reaction	a few bubbles of gas are given off if the acid is warmed

a List the four metals in their order of reactivity (most reactive first). (1)

b i) Name another metal that reacts in a similar way to sodium with water. (1)

ii) Which gas is given off in this reaction? (1)

iii) What will be the pH of the solution that remains after the reaction?

   1   3   7   14 (1)

iv) Why should the reaction between sodium and dilute sulphuric acid not be tried in a school laboratory? (1)

c i) Name the gas given off when iron reacts with dilute sulphuric acid. (1)

ii) What is the other product formed in this reaction? (1)

d Look at the test tubes below:

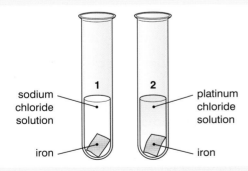

In test tube 2 the iron was slowly covered in a light grey deposit.

i) Name the light grey deposit. (1)

ii) Explain why the light grey deposit formed. (1)

iii) What do we call the type of reaction observed in test tube 2? (1)

iv) Write a word equation for the reaction in test tube 2. (1)

v) Why did no reaction take place in test tube 1? (1)

2 This question is about four metals – labelled A, B, C and D (these are not their chemical symbols). The metals and solutions of their sulphates were mixed on a spotting tile:

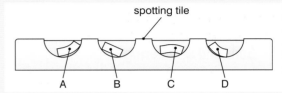

The table shows the results:
✓ shows that a reaction took place
✗ shows that no reaction took place.

	A	B	C	D
A sulphate	✗	✓	✓	i)
B sulphate	✗	✗	✓	✓
C sulphate	✗	ii)	✗	iii)
D sulphate	✗	✗	✓	✗

a Use the table to list the metals A, B, C and D in order of reactivity (most reactive first). (1)

b Use your answer to **a** to decide whether a tick (✓) or a cross (✗) goes in the boxes i), ii) and iii) in the table. (2)

c i) Copper metal reacts with silver nitrate solution. Write the word equation for this reaction. (1)

ii) Platinum does not react when placed in a solution of silver nitrate. List the three metals – platinum, copper and silver – in order of reactivity. Start with the most reactive. (1)

d Copper is used to make household water pipes and iron is used to make boilers. Explain which of these two metals will corrode first. (1)

Key words

Unscramble these:
starhin
clapmeetdins
vitantatique

9G

Environmental chemistry

COMING SOON

9G1 Soils and weathering
9G2 Acid rain
9G3 Monitoring pollution
9G4 Global warming

Don't blame me... It's global warming!

What's it all about?

In this unit you will find out about different types of pollution – how they are caused, their effects and how we can reduce the problems they bring.

You will also learn about:
- rocks, soils and building materials
- chemical weathering that alters rocks and building materials over time
- how the activity of humans and natural processes affect our atmosphere and water resources
- acid rain and global warming
- how we monitor and control environmental conditions.

 # What do you remember?

You already know about:
- the differences between soils which depend on the rocks that formed them.
- how to find the pH of a solution, and how we use the pH scale.

1 Which indicator do we use to find the pH of a solution?

litmus   methyl orange
methyl red   universal indicator

2 What colour will this indicator be in a solution with a pH value of 7?

red   blue   green   purple

3 How do we describe a solution whose pH value is 6?

weakly acidic   weakly alkaline
strongly acidic   strongly alkaline

4 Soil that lies on a bed of chalk is likely to contain a lot of . . .

sodium chloride   potassium nitrate
calcium carbonate   lithium sulphate

Ideas about pollution

Look at the cartoon above and discuss these questions with your partner.

a) Is unpolluted rain water neutral? Explain your answer.

b) Is air pollution just a modern-day problem? When do you think humans started causing major pollution problems?

c) Do you think that the hole in the ozone layer causes global warming? What do you know already about these problems?

9G1 Soils and weathering

LEARN ABOUT

- different soils and the plants that grow in them
- reducing the acidity of soils
- rocks and building materials changing over time
- factors that affect the changes in materials

There are different soil types and these are suited to different plants

Different soils

In Book 8 you saw how rocks can be:

- weathered (broken down),
- transported (moved from the place they were weathered),
- eroded (worn down), and then
- deposited as sediments.

These sediments form the basis of soil.

Q1 What will affect the different types of soil we find in different places?

Q2 As well as deposited rock fragments, what else do we find in soils?

The characteristics of each type of soil are determined by:

- the size of the rock **fragments** it contains,
- the chemical composition of the rock fragments,
- the amount of other organic materials mixed in it. This organic material is called **humus** and comes from living things.

For example, a clay soil contains very tiny grains of weathered rock. This means that there are few gaps between the grains for water to drain through and the soil gets waterlogged.

Compare this with a sandy soil, which feels gritty to the touch. Water drains through it quickly because of its larger fragments of rock. The sandy soil does have a disadvantage – heavy rain can wash away the soluble nutrients. We say that they are **leached** from the soil.

Which type of soil?

- Your teacher will give you a sheet. Do all the tests on the sheet to identify the soil type.

You only find blue hydrangeas growing naturally in acidic soil

Acidic soil

The pH of different soils can also vary. Acidic soil contains lots of organic material because it doesn't rot down in the acidic conditions. The bacteria that aid decomposition cannot thrive in the acidic soil.

You might expect a peaty soil to be rich in nutrients, as animals and plants return their nutrients to the soil. However, the nutrients tend to be 'locked up' in the organic matter as it doesn't decompose easily. So we need to add fertilisers. This gives us an excellent soil for growing plants, as peaty soil holds moisture well.

Neutralising acidic soil

SAFETY

- Your teacher will give you a sheet to test the pH of soils. Then you can neutralise an acidic soil using a base, such as slaked lime (calcium hydroxide).

You don't think this soil is too acidic, do you?

Weathering

Weathering is the breakdown of rock by physical or chemical means. In Book 8 you found out about the physical effects of changes in temperature and 'freeze–thaw'. You also looked at chemical weathering by the reaction of rocks with acidic rain water. The process of weathering also affects building materials.

This obelisk has stood in Egypt for about 3500 years

Cleopatra's Needle was built at the same time but was transported to London in 1878

Bricks and mortar damaged by weathering

Gruesome science

In 1983, two workers digging peat from a bog came across what looked like an old leather football. In fact it was the preserved head of a woman who had died 1750 years earlier. There were still bits of hair and scalp left, as well as some brain and an eyeball.

ICT ⟩⟩ CHALLENGE

Soil information sheet
Use secondary sources and the information in this unit to produce a fact sheet for a garden centre about growing plants in different types of soil.

Q3 Comment on the weathering in the photos above.

Chemical weathering takes place more quickly if you have more concentrated acid. This happens in places affected by acid rain or in the ground beneath vegetation. High rainfall and high temperatures also speed up the breakdown of rocks by chemical weathering.

SUMMARY QUESTIONS

1 ☆ Copy these sentences. Complete them by filling in the gaps.
   The . . . of different rocks produces different types of . . .
   We can . . . acidic soil with a basic substance such as slaked . . .

2 ☆☆ Conduct a survey of weathering around your school or at home. Include the corrosion of metals and the decomposition of wooden structures.

Key words

fragments
humus
leach
weathering

Acid rain

9G2

LEARN ABOUT
- the causes of acid rain
- the effects of acid rain
- reducing the effects of acid rain

Causes of acid rain

There is a small proportion of carbon dioxide in the air (just less than 0.04%). Much of this comes from *natural processes*, such as:

- volcanic activity,
- respiration in living organisms,
- the death and decomposition of living things.

This is enough to make rain water naturally acidic, as we saw in 9G1. Its pH value is about 5.6.

However, pollution has made rain in many places *more acidic*. Burning **fossil fuels** adds more carbon dioxide to the air. There are also impurities of sulphur present in fossil fuels. When we burn them, e.g. coal in power stations, the sulphur reacts with oxygen. It forms **sulphur dioxide** gas:

$$\text{sulphur} + \text{oxygen} \rightarrow \text{sulphur dioxide}$$
$$S + O_2 \rightarrow SO_2$$

Sulphur dioxide is the main cause of **acid rain**. The sulphur dioxide reacts with water and oxygen in the atmosphere to make **sulphuric acid**. The acidic solution falls back to ground in rain, snow and fog.

More industrial processes release sulphur dioxide, and cars also contribute to the problem of acid rain. Although we can now buy fuels that have a low sulphur content, cars give off **oxides of nitrogen**. These oxides react in the atmosphere to form nitric acid.

Humans are making rain water even more acidic by releasing acidic gases into the atmosphere

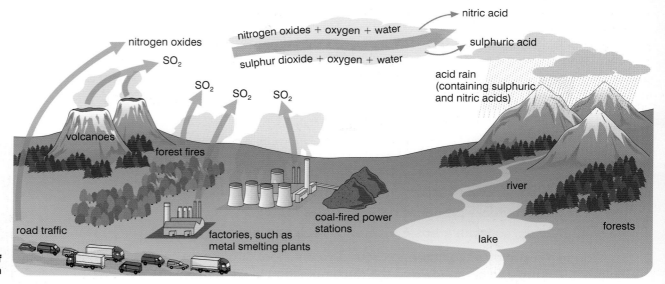

Causes of acid rain

Notice the sulphur dioxide in our atmosphere from **volcanic activity**. It is about 15% of the total made by human activity.

● The effects of acid rain

Effects on building materials: You have already seen how dilute acids react with some rocks and metals, dissolving them away. Over time, statues lose their fine features as carbonate rock (such as marble) is broken down.

Other stonework is also attacked. Metal structures need protecting so that corrosion does not weaken them.

Effects on plants: Some soils can cope well with acid rain. Alkaline soils will neutralise the acid rain. However, thin soil layers cannot neutralise much acid and essential nutrients get washed from the soil. This affects the growth of plants.

Acid rain also attacks the waxy coating that protects leaves. The plants then lose water too easily and are more prone to diseases and pests.

Effects on wildlife: Some animals that live in lakes and rivers, such as mayfly, are very sensitive to changes in pH. They cannot survive in water whose pH value drops even slightly.

Other animals further down the food chain may be more resistant to changes in pH. However the loss of food sources does affect them. If the pH drops below 5, fish eggs will not hatch. Once the pH falls below 4.5, no animal life survives.

Fighting the effects of acid rain: Acidic lakes can be neutralised by dropping powdered limestone into the water. This reacts with the acid and raises the pH of the water. Acidic soil can be neutralised by farmers. They use powdered limestone or slaked lime (calcium hydroxide) on their fields.

However, it is better to stop acidic gases reaching the atmosphere. Here are four ways to do this:

● use less fossil fuels
● remove the sulphur from a fossil fuel before you burn it
● prevent the acidic gases given off as a fuel burns from escaping into the air; you can use basic substances to neutralise the gases
● use cars that have catalytic converters to remove oxides of nitrogen.

ICT CHALLENGE

Do some research to find more information about acid rain. Each member of your group can research a different aspect of the problem. Then collate your reports into a display to share with the rest of your class.

Rain isn't that acidic yet, Mike!

Q1 Name a basic substance used in industry to neutralise acidic gases.

SUMMARY QUESTIONS

1 ☆ Copy these sentences. Complete them by filling in the gaps.
Sulphur . . . gas is the main cause of . . . rain. It affects buildings, . . . and animals.
We can . . . acidic lakes and soils. However, the best option is to stop acidic gases escaping into the . . . by using less . . . fuels.

2 ☆☆☆ **a)** Summarise the information in the diagram on page 104 as a flow diagram.
b) Nitrogen dioxide reacts with oxygen and water in the air to make nitric acid (HNO_3). Write a word equation and a symbol equation to show this reaction.

Key words
acid rain
fossil fuels
oxides of nitrogen
sulphur dioxide
sulphuric acid
volcanic activity

9G3 Monitoring pollution

LEARN ABOUT
- how we monitor and control pollution
- collecting evidence to answer a question
- judging the quality of evidence

Gruesome science

A report by the World Health Organisation in 2004 estimated that more than 10 000 children in Eastern Europe die each year as a result of air pollution. The figure for 2001 in Western Europe was much lower, at 178.

Air pollution in the past

Q1 Do you think that air pollution is worse now than it was 50 years ago? Think of some reasons to support your opinion.

The industrial revolution in the 19th century resulted in lots of coal being burned. People flocked into towns for the new jobs created.

Coal fires were the main source of heat in the workers' homes. The smoke and sulphur dioxide gas released from factories and houses became intolerable.

Robert Angus Smith was the scientist who first used the term 'acid rain' in 1856.

It was exactly a century later that the first Clean Air Act was passed in response to the Great London Smog of 1952. Other smoke reduction acts had been necessary in 1875 and 1926. But the smog (combination of smoke and fog) that clung to London in the winter of 1952 caused about 4000 extra deaths that year.

Look at the graph below:

The Great London Smog of 1952. London had become famous for its terrible smogs, or 'pea-soupers' as Londoners called them.

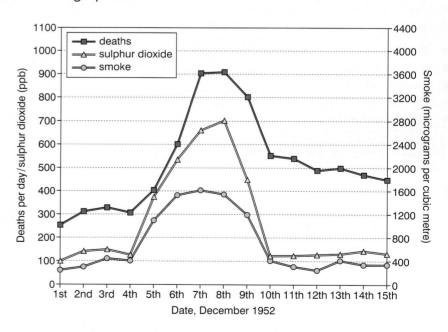

Q2 Look at the graph showing the deaths in London during the first half of December 1952. What pattern can you see?

Improving air quality

The Clean Air Act, passed in 1956, forced people to use 'smokeless' forms of coal. A later Clean Air Act in 1968 also made industry discharge its gases from tall chimneys. However, this just passes the pollutants on to another place.

Further pollution control measures followed these Acts, and the quality of our air has improved in many respects. But the massive increase in cars that started in the 1980s remains a problem.

Local Authorities are now responsible for monitoring air and water quality in their areas. You can find the data on local and national environmental websites.

Nowadays, we **monitor** air quality at about 1500 sites across the UK, using ever more sensitive equipment. The Environment Agency also uses sophisticated computer modelling to predict future pollution levels.

Water pollution

Rivers and lakes can get polluted by soluble substances leached from the land. Fertilisers get into the rivers and lakes causing **eutrophication**.

Water is also used as a coolant in power stations. This can cause **thermal pollution** if water is put back into the river at a higher temperature. Oxygen gas is less soluble in warmer water, and the delicate balance of ecosystems is disturbed.

There are 7000 sites in rivers and canals that are monitored by the UK Environmental Agency for water quality. The good news is that tighter controls and monitoring are improving the quality of most of our waterways.

Careful monitoring using sensitive instruments is improving the quality of rivers

LINK UP TO GEOGRAPHY

You will learn more about the effects of human activity on our environment in Geography.

Air pollution is monitored constantly in our cities

Eutrophication: Algae flourish, cutting off light to plants on the riverbed. Bacteria multiply as they feed on dead algae. The bacteria use up the dissolved oxygen in the water. This causes fish and other aquatic animals to effectively suffocate.

ICT CHALLENGE

Think of a question that you would like to ask about the quality of air or water. Use books and the Internet to find information. Look out for any bias in reports from particular sources and report on this, as well as other findings, to the rest of your class.

SUMMARY QUESTIONS

1 ✭ Copy these sentences. Complete them by filling in the gaps.

Air p. . . causes many deaths every year.

However, careful m. . . of pollutants in air and w. . . helps local authorities c. . . the levels and improve our environment.

2 ✭✭✭ a) Explain how eutrophication causes the deaths of aquatic animals in rivers.

b) How can farmers help to reduce this problem?

Key words

eutrophication
monitor
thermal pollution

LEARN ABOUT

- using secondary sources to answer scientific questions
- evaluating evidence put forward by others
- considering conflicting evidence to form your own opinion

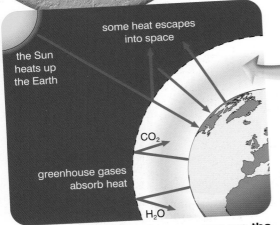

Carbon dioxide and water vapour are the main 'greenhouse gases'

The greenhouse effect

You've probably heard of the greenhouse effect and global warming. Carbon dioxide, along with water vapour, are the main **'greenhouse' gases**. The molecules of a 'greenhouse' gas absorb the heat given off by the Earth as it cools down at night. This traps the heat in the atmosphere and warms the Earth.

In the last 200 years we have burned more fossil fuels than ever before.

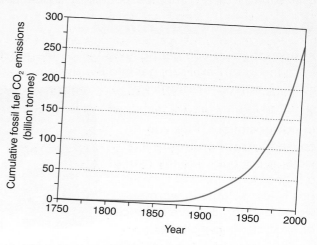

Fossil fuels are made up of carbon compounds. They react with oxygen to produce carbon dioxide as one of the products when they burn. For example, when we burn natural gas in plenty of air:

$$\text{methane} + \text{oxygen} \rightarrow \text{carbon dioxide} + \text{water}$$
$$CH_4 + 2\,O_2 \rightarrow CO_2 + 2\,H_2O$$

Not surprisingly, the proportion of carbon dioxide in the air has increased.

AMAZING SCIENCE!

The gases that have caused a hole to appear in our **ozone layer** – CFCs or chlorofluorocarbons – are also very effective 'greenhouse' gases. Fortunately their levels are now decreasing, so ozone depletion is slowing down and the latest reports from Antarctica suggest the hole is actually shrinking.

AMAZING SCIENCE!

Without carbon dioxide in our atmosphere, the average temperature on Earth would be about −19 °C!

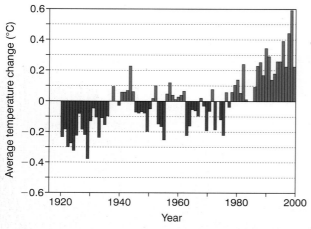

Look at the graph:

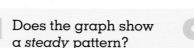
Q1 Does the graph show a *steady* pattern?

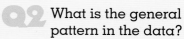
Q2 What is the general pattern in the data?

Q3 Are these data enough to be certain that the Earth's average temperature is rising and will continue to do so? Explain your answer.

Fuelling the debate!

Many scientists agree that we are now seeing the start of **global warming**. For example, six of the ten warmest years ever recorded were in the 1990s. The other four were in the 1980s. But even on this point there is some disagreement.

The main opponent of current theories on global warming is an American scientist called Richard S. Lindzen. He argues that the recent rises are due to natural variations in temperature. These have happened throughout the long history of the Earth. The last major change was the Ice Age, about 12 000 years ago.

We cannot predict with certainty the effects of increasing carbon dioxide levels – even with the aid of our most powerful computers. Lindzen thinks that the computer models used are incorrect. He argues that data gathered on climate change over the last one thousand years are not reliable.

However, other leading scientists are confident in their data. They have deduced temperatures from before records began. They do this by analysing tree rings and samples of ice from deep within ice caps. These scientists agree that global warming is a serious problem and is caused by human activity. Its effects could be:

- increased sea levels and flooding of low-lying areas
- changing weather patterns all over the world, affecting crops
- the extinction of some species of animals.

LINK UP TO
BIOLOGY

You can read more about the balance of carbon dioxide in the air in 9C5.

I don't fancy turkey this year!

DECEMBER 25TH

Global warming... it's not all bad, you know!

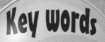
ICT CHALLENGE

What's your opinion?
- Use books, ROMs and the Internet to gather more information about global warming. Here are some questions to investigate, and think up some of your own questions too.
  – Which other gases, besides carbon dioxide and water vapour, are 'greenhouse' gases?
  – How are governments tackling the problem of global warming?
  – How can we help reduce the levels of carbon dioxide in the air in our own lives?
  – What temperature rise would a doubling of carbon dioxide in the air bring with it?
  – Which pollutants might produce a cooling effect in our atmosphere?
- Consider to which questions you can be certain of the answers you find, and which are open to debate.
- Listen to feedback from others in your group. Then form your own conclusions about global warming.

SUMMARY QUESTIONS

1 ☆ Copy these sentences. Complete them by filling in the gaps.
People are growing more and more concerned about . . . levels of . . . . . . gas in the air. The gas is given off when we burn . . . fuels.
They believe it is causing . . . warming.

2 ☆☆☆ a) What do we mean by 'a greenhouse gas'?
   b) Discuss the effects of planting more trees on the amount of greenhouse gases in our atmosphere.

Key words
global warming
greenhouse gases
ozone layer

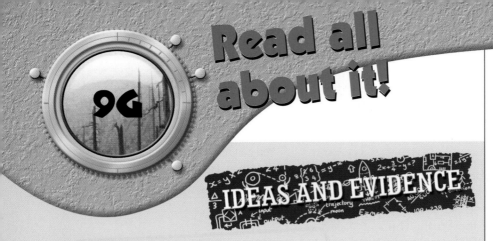

9G Read all about it!

IDEAS AND EVIDENCE

Looking for clues

Imagine having a time machine that could transport you back in time to almost 800 000 years ago. Scientists in Greenland think they have the next best thing. They have spent seven years drilling a hollow pipe down into the ice. On reaching the rock beneath the ice sheet in 2004, they had drilled out a cylinder of ice over three kilometres long!

When you shine light on the ice core sample, you see bands of light and dark. The dark bands are from winter snowfall, the light from summer snowfall. So it's a bit like looking at tree rings. The scientists are excited because each band tells a story about the conditions on Earth at the time the snow fell.

There are tiny bubbles of air trapped in the ice core. Scientists can analyse the air to find how the composition of the gases in the atmosphere has changed over time. This is one factor that influences climate on Earth. The amounts of greenhouse gases, such as carbon dioxide and methane, are particularly interesting. By following these we can see if the gases are linked to the temperature on Earth.

Initial analysis has shown that our current levels of carbon dioxide are higher than at any time in the last 440 000 years.

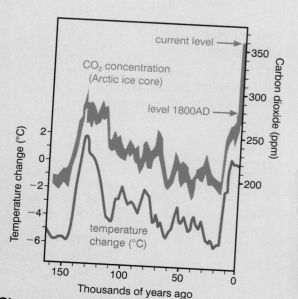

Changes in temperature and the concentration of CO_2 in the atmosphere in the last 150 000 years

SCIENTIFIC PEOPLE

'It was wonderful to reach the bottom and see frozen mud rising to the surface,' said Danish scientist Dorthe Dahl-Jensen, who was supervising the drilling of the ice core in Greenland. The professor from Copenhagen added, 'We wept with emotion. It was quite incredible to reach the end. I will never forget it!'

Evidence like this is used to argue against those who think that our current warm phase is not the result of increased levels of greenhouse gases. However, although a link can be established, it does not show which came first. Does the carbon dioxide level rise because the temperature rises (for some other reason)? Or does the increased carbon dioxide cause the temperature to rise?

By studying these results, the scientists hope that they will be able to predict the effect of human influences on climate in the future.

We know that in the last 800 000 years there have been 12 ice ages and that the periods of warmer conditions between them are relatively short. The good news is that current predictions say that the next ice age will be due in about 15 000 years time!

- Acid rain is caused mainly by **sulphur dioxide** gas from burning fossil fuels, and from natural sources. In fossil fuels, sulphur is an impurity. This burns to give sulphur dioxide:

  sulphur + oxygen → sulphur dioxide

  This reacts in the air with oxygen and water to form **sulphuric acid**. We can reduce the problem by removing sulphur before burning fossil fuels. We can also stop sulphur dioxide gas escaping (by neutralising the acidic gas) or by burning less fuel.
- **Nitrogen oxides** from cars also cause acid rain (forming **nitric acid**). Catalytic converters on exhausts help remove these gases.
- **Global warming** is caused by 'greenhouse' gases, such as carbon dioxide (from burning fossil fuels).
- There is some debate about whether the higher temperatures in the last few decades are just natural variations. However, most people agree that it is sensible to reduce the carbon dioxide we produce. Careful monitoring and controls on pollutants are helping to fight the effects of pollution.

Dissolved CO_2 does make even the purest rain water slightly acidic though.

You can blame greenhouse gases for global warming, Pete.

Even the Victorians were worried about air pollution... think of all the dirty smoke from coal fires.

DANGER! AVOID THESE COMMON ERRORS

Ozone protects us from harmful ultra-violet radiation from the Sun. If ozone levels fall, the cases of skin cancer will increase. But the hole in the ozone layer is not responsible for global warming. However, the gases, called CFCs, which caused the hole are also greenhouse gases. So they have helped to trap heat energy in our atmosphere as well as destroying ozone.

Key words

acid rain
biased
eutrophication
global warming
greenhouse gas
reliable
thermal pollution

REVIEW QUESTIONS
Understanding and applying concepts

1   If you have a chalky soil, you will find that its pH is 7.5 or above. This is often a stony soil that drains well. It is usually found above beds of chalk or limestone rock. This soil cannot absorb some essential elements needed for plant growth, such as manganese and iron.

    a   Is chalky soil acidic, neutral or alkaline?

    b   Suggest *two* ways to help plants grow in this soil.

    c   Chalky soil contains calcium carbonate. Name the salt formed when calcium carbonate reacts with a dilute solution of:
       i)   sulphuric acid
       ii)   nitric acid.

    d   What will be the effect of acid rain on a sandstone held together by a 'cement' of carbonate mineral?

    e   Give *two* factors that would make chemical weathering happen more rapidly.

2   In the USA, air quality is monitored and standards are set by the Environmental Protection Agency. They check six major pollutants:
- carbon monoxide
- lead
- ozone
- nitrogen dioxide
- sulphur dioxide
- particulate matter (tiny solid particles suspended in the air).

They have reported improvements in air quality from 1982 to 2001. For example, sulphur dioxide has decreased by 52%, carbon monoxide by 62%, nitrogen dioxide by 24%, and lead by 94%.

    a   Look at the figures above and comment on how such improvements could have been brought about.

    b   What problems do you think we have in looking at long-term trends in pollution? What can you say about the data we have nowadays compared to that available 20, 50 or 100 years ago?

    c   How can scientists today get clues about the composition of the air and our climate as it was thousands of years ago?

    d   Particulate matter in the atmosphere stops sunlight from reaching the surface of the Earth. How does this affect global temperatures?

3   **a**   Give two industries that produce sulphur dioxide gas as a pollutant.

    b   How is sulphur dioxide formed when we burn fossil fuels?

    c   Find out how nitrogen oxides are formed as air pollutants.

    d   Summarise the effects that acid rain has on the environment.

4   **a**   Gases that cause global warming are called 'greenhouse' gases. Name two of these gases and explain how they cause the temperature of the Earth to rise.

    b   Why are some scientists not convinced that the global warming observed in recent years is a result of human pollution?

    c   List some of the consequences that global warming could bring about. Why are these difficult to predict accurately?

5   Draw a concept map linking the following terms. Don't forget to label your links.

    **acid rain   global warming
    carbon dioxide   sulphur dioxide
    nitrogen oxides   fossil fuels**

Ways with words

6 We find that it is not always the countries that produce the largest amounts of acidic gases that suffer most from acid rain. The oxides of sulphur and nitrogen can travel hundreds of miles in the atmosphere, blown by prevailing winds, so the acid rain affects neighbouring countries.

For example, much of the pollution in the forests and lakes in Scandinavia comes from Britain. Pollutants from the USA affect large areas of Canada, and Japan suffers acid rain from gases given off by Chinese industry.

Write a letter to a British newspaper from a Scandinavian who owns a hotel on the shores of a Swedish lake affected by acid rain.

Making more of maths

7 In March 2002, a huge ice shelf collapsed into the sea from Antarctica. The iceberg formed was 200 metres thick and had an area of 3200 square kilometres. What was the volume of the iceberg?

Extension question

8 This question is about the gas ozone.

Find out the answers to the following questions:
a What is the chemical formula of ozone?
b Why has a hole appeared in the ozone layer around the Earth?
c Where is the hole in the ozone layer?
d Why is ozone in the stratosphere important for life on Earth?
e Ozone at ground level is considered a pollutant. Where does it come from?

SAT-STYLE QUESTIONS

1 Look at the table. It shows the results of pH tests on five soil samples.

Soil	A	B	C	D	E
pH of soil	8.0	4.5	7.5	6.0	7.0

a Which soil was neutral? (1)
b i) Camellia bushes grow well in acidic soils. Which soils would be good for growing camellias? (2)
   ii) Lilac trees prefer alkaline conditions. Which soils could be used to grow lilac trees? (2)
c Farmers and gardeners sometimes add slaked lime to acidic soil.
   i) What is the chemical name for slaked lime? (1)
   ii) Does slaked lime raise or lower the pH of soil? (1)
   iii) What type of reaction takes place between slaked lime and the acids in soil? (1)

2 Petrol contains a compound called octane, C_8H_{18}.
a Write a word equation for the complete combustion of octane. (1)
b Other gases are given off from a car's exhaust. Compounds of nitrogen are formed in an engine and these contribute to acid rain. Which compounds of nitrogen are released into the air? (1)
c Toxic carbon monoxide gas is also given off from cars. Some cars are fitted with catalytic converters. A catalytic converter, once it has warmed up, can change the toxic gas into carbon dioxide. With which environmental problem is carbon dioxide associated? (1)
d Give *two* ways that we can reduce the level of carbon dioxide in the air. (2)

Key words

Unscramble these:
loutlipon
idac iran
ballog gnawrim

9H

Using chemistry

You can thank chemistry for that... and that... and that... and that.

But not that on your head, surely!

What's it all about?

In this unit, you can remind yourself about different chemical reactions. You will look at chemical reactions as sources of energy and of new materials.

This will help your understanding of chemical equations. You will also see how important chemistry is in our everyday lives.

What do you remember?

You already know about:

- the test for carbon dioxide.
- how burning involves a reaction with oxygen in which oxides are formed.
- new materials forming when chemical reactions take place.
- identifying evidence for chemical reactions.
- representing chemical reactions by word equations and symbol equations.
- how we place metals in the Reactivity Series.

1 Which of these is formed in the combustion of magnesium?

magnesium nitrate
magnesium sulphide
magnesium oxide
magnesium hydroxide

2 Which one of these is a chemical reaction?

distilling crude oil
neutralising acid with alkali
condensing water vapour
melting sulphur

3 Finish off this balanced symbol equation:

$$2\,Ca + O_2 \rightarrow ?$$

CaO
$4\,CaO_2$
$2\,CaO_2$
$2\,CaO$

4 Which is the most reactive of these metals?

sodium   potassium
aluminium   magnesium

Ideas about reactions

Look at the cartoon above and discuss these questions with your partner.

a) Are the reactants and the products of a reaction always a different colour? How can you tell when a reaction takes place? What signs can you look for?

b) Do you think that chemical reactions always need the reactants to be heated before the reaction starts? Think of some examples to illustrate your answer.

c) Can atoms be created or destroyed in chemical reactions? What does happen? How can we make new substances without making new atoms?

LEARN ABOUT

- fuels burning and releasing energy
- the products formed when fuels burn
- evaluating advantages and disadvantages of a fuel

Q1 The chemical formula of ethanol is C_2H_5OH. Is ethanol a hydrocarbon? Explain your answer.

Q2 Write a word and symbol equation for burning methane.

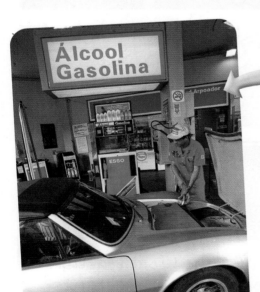

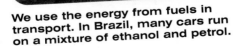

We use the energy from fuels in transport. In Brazil, many cars run on a mixture of ethanol and petrol.

Gruesome science

Fine particles of carbon are given off from diesel engines. These are harmful when breathed into our lungs. They can cause cancer.

● Complete combustion

In 7F5, you saw what happens when we burn natural gas that contains methane, CH_4. Methane is called a **hydrocarbon** – it is a compound made up of only hydrogen and carbon atoms.

Many fuels are hydrocarbons. Some of the energy released when fuels burn can be transferred into useful energy.

When a hydrocarbon burns in plenty of air (so that it gets enough oxygen to burn completely), we get carbon dioxide and water formed. For example, propane gas, C_3H_8, from crude oil is used in some household gas heaters:

propane + oxygen → carbon dioxide + water
$$C_3H_8 + 5\,O_2 \rightarrow 3\,CO_2 + 4\,H_2O$$

Reactions that give out heat are called **exothermic** reactions.

So the combustion of a fuel is an example of an exothermic reaction.

Another fuel is ethanol. This is the compound found in all alcoholic drinks.

Burning ethanol

SAFETY

a) Predict the word equation for the combustion of ethanol.

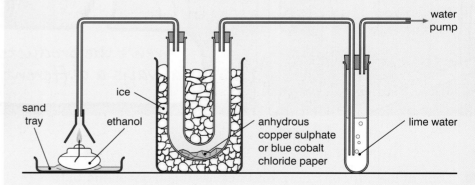

b) What happens in the U tube? Why is the U tube surrounded by ice?

c) What happens to the lime water? Which product do we test for with lime water?

d) Write a word equation and a symbol equation for the combustion of ethanol.

e) How could you run a 'control experiment'? (A control experiment checks that the products came from the burning ethanol and were not just present in the air anyway.)

● Incomplete combustion

Hydrocarbon fuels can produce some black smoke as they burn. The smoke is made up of small particles of solid carbon from the fuel. Not all the carbon in the fuel is converted completely into carbon dioxide. We call this **incomplete combustion**.

In a car engine, petrol or diesel is ignited in a small space. There is not much oxygen inside the engine with which the fuel can react. So we get incomplete combustion of the fuel.

As well as carbon dioxide and water vapour, we also get
● a toxic gas called **carbon monoxide**, CO
● unburnt hydrocarbon fuel
● carbon particles.

Carbon monoxide gas is very dangerous because it has no smell. It starves your cells of oxygen. (See 'Gruesome science'.)

Cars release a variety of pollutants into the air. Catalytic converters (once they are warmed up) inside exhausts can help. They can turn carbon monoxide into carbon dioxide, nitrogen oxides into nitrogen, and unburnt hydrocarbons into carbon dioxide and water vapour.

● Burning matches

Have you ever wondered how matches ignite when you strike them?
Look at the match head:

● When you strike the match on a rough surface, friction causes heat energy. This starts a chemical reaction in the head of the match.

● The phosphorus sulphide decomposes and starts to burn.

● This sets off the combustion reaction of antimony sulphide.

● This is made more vigorous by potassium chlorate(V), which provides oxygen for the combustion.

● The temperature is now hot enough to set fire to the wooden matchstick.

contents of match head:
• phosphorus sulphide, P_4S_3
• potassium chlorate(V), $KClO_3$
• antimony sulphide, Sb_2S_3
• glue

Gruesome science

Carbon monoxide bonds to haemoglobin, the molecule that carries oxygen around our bloodstream. The oxygen–haemoglobin bond breaks easily, releasing the oxygen to cells. However, the carbon monoxide–haemoglobin bond is much stronger. After breathing in the toxic gas for a while, the carbon monoxide takes up most of the haemoglobin molecules so you suffer from a lack of oxygen. Drowsiness is followed by unconsciousness and death.

SUMMARY QUESTIONS

1 ☆ Copy these sentences. Complete them by filling in the blanks.

The complete combustion of a hydrocarbon produces … … and …
If there is not enough oxygen, we get … combustion and the toxic gas …
… is also made.

2 ☆☆☆ Look at the diagram of the match above:
a) How many atoms are in a molecule of phosphorus sulphide?
b) How many elements are there in antimony sulphide?
c) Potassium chlorate(V) decomposes on heating to form potassium chloride and oxygen. Write a word equation and a balanced symbol equation for this thermal decomposition reaction.

3 ☆☆☆ Find out and note the advantages and disadvantages of using hydrogen as a fuel.

Key words

carbon monoxide
exothermic
hydrocarbon
incomplete combustion

Energy from reactions

9H2

LEARN ABOUT
- the energy released in displacement reactions
- how we can use energy from reactions as sources of energy

Chemical energy into heat energy

In unit 9F you looked at the Reactivity Series of metals. On page 92 you saw how a more reactive metal can displace a less reactive metal from its compounds. You used metals and solutions of their salts.

These **displacement** reactions are **exothermic**. They release stored chemical energy as heat. For example:

zinc sulphate + magnesium → magnesium sulphate + zinc
$ZnSO_4$ + Mg → $MgSO_4$ + Zn

Heat energy from displacement reactions

You can investigate the energy given out during these reactions in this enquiry.

- Use the same metals and solutions as in the experiment 'Predicting displacement from solution' on page 93.

- Plan an investigation to find out which reactions give out most energy.

Your teacher might give you a sheet to help.

Do not start any experiments before your teacher has checked your plan.

Chemical energy into electrical energy

We can use the energy from displacement reactions to make **electrical cells**. The chemical energy stored can be transferred directly to electrical energy.

Measuring differences in reactivity

- Using the apparatus above, measure the voltage between different pairs of metals from the previous investigation.

- Record your results in a table.
  a) Were your results as expected?

- You know the position of lead in the Reactivity Series. Predict the voltage you will get by testing lead with each of the other four metals.

- Check your predictions by experiment.

The displacement reaction between iron oxide and aluminium is very exothermic. It gives out so much heat that the temperature rises to over 1500°C and the iron produced melts (see page 93).

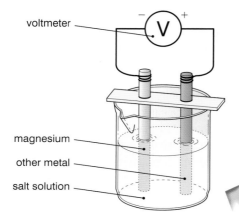

voltmeter

magnesium
other metal
salt solution

LINK UP TO
PHYSICS

You can find out more about making electrical cells in unit 9I.

We find that:

The greater the difference in reactivity between two metals, the larger the voltage produced.

Other useful exothermic reactions

Do you watch any outdoor sporting events in winter? If you do, you will know that spectators can get painfully cold. And that's when chemical hand and body warmers can be very useful. These products use exothermic reactions to warm you up.

Read the information provided by one distributor about how hand warmers work:

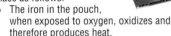

Warmers operate by a chemical reaction with air, similar to rusting. The warmer contains iron, water, cellulose, vermiculite, activated carbon and salt. The heating process takes place as follows:
- The iron in the pouch, when exposed to oxygen, oxidizes and therefore produces heat.
- When iron oxidizes it produces iron(III) oxide, more commonly referred to as rust.

- The salt acts as a catalyst.
- The carbon helps disperse the heat.
- The vermiculite is used as an insulator for the purposes of retaining the heat, and cellulose is added as a filler.
- All of these ingredients are surrounded by a polypropylene bag.
- Polypropylene allows air to permeate the ingredients while holding in moisture.

(from Grabber Performance Group)

Using the information above and reference books, answer the following questions:

Q1 Write a word equation for the exothermic reaction that produces the heat.

Q2 How do you think the exothermic reaction is started?

Hot stuff!

Mountaineers and explorers can take 'self-heating' foods with them on their adventures. One product uses the energy given out when calcium oxide reacts with water to heat the food.

- Design a self-heating, disposable food container for stew. Consider any safety issues involved in using your product.

Endothermic reactions

Not all reactions are exothermic ones that give out energy. Some reactions take in energy from their surroundings and the temperature falls. These are called **endothermic** reactions.

SUMMARY QUESTIONS

1 ☆ Copy the sentences. Complete them by filling in the gaps.

The ... energy ... in substances can be released during ... reactions. Reactions that give out heat energy are called ... reactions.

2 ☆☆☆ Using your design for a food-warmer in 'Hot stuff!' above,
   a) write a technical specification describing how to manufacture your container
   b) write an advert for a mountaineering magazine to publicise your invention.

Key words

displacement
electrical cells
endothermic
exothermic

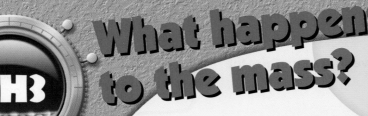

What happens to the mass?

LEARN ABOUT
- what happens to the mass in chemical reactions and in physical changes
- atoms combining in different ways as a result of chemical reactions

● Particles and reactions

In unit 9E you saw how atoms swap partners in chemical reactions. You used this to balance symbol equations. Let's look at another example.

You know the test for hydrogen gas. There is a POP! as hydrogen and oxygen from the air react together to form water. The reaction starts when you ignite the mixture of gases.

We can model the reaction in a **particle diagram**:

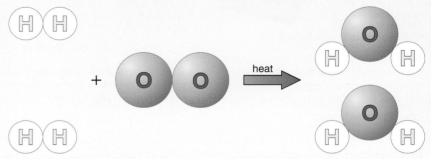

Q1 Think about the mass of H_2O formed in the reaction opposite. Compare this with the total mass of hydrogen and oxygen we started with. Explain your reasoning.

The word equation and balanced symbol equation are:

$$\text{hydrogen} + \text{oxygen} \rightarrow \text{water}$$
$$2\,H_2 + O_2 \rightarrow 2\,H_2O$$

You can check out your ideas by investigating a **precipitation** reaction. In a precipitation reaction, solutions react to form an insoluble solid.

Investigating the mass of reactants and products

You are given solutions of magnesium sulphate and barium chloride.

Barium chloride is toxic.

- Find out what happens when a small volume of each solution is added together in a test tube.
  a) What do you see happen?

  The formula of magnesium sulphate is $MgSO_4$ and barium chloride is $BaCl_2$. The precipitate formed in the reaction is barium sulphate, $BaSO_4$.
  b) Write a word equation and a symbol equation for the reaction.
  c) How do you think the mass of reactants compares with the mass of the products?

- Now plan an experiment to test your answer to question **c)**.
  Show your plan to your teacher before you do the experiment, or watch a teacher demonstration.

● Conservation of mass

As no new atoms are ever created or destroyed in a chemical reaction, we can say:

mass of reactants = mass of products

My dad suffers from 'conservation of mass'... his diets never seem to work!

What happens when gases are given off?

SAFETY

● This apparatus will be used to investigate the reaction between small pieces of marble chips, containing calcium carbonate, and dilute hydrochloric acid.

a) What are the word equation and the symbol equation for the reaction?

b) Predict what will happen to the mass readings on the balance as the reaction takes place. Explain your answer.

Check your prediction as you observe the experiment.

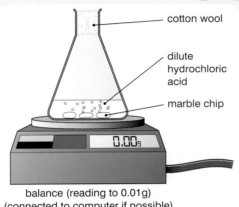

cotton wool

dilute hydrochloric acid

marble chip

0.00 g

balance (reading to 0.01g)
(connected to computer if possible)

Q2 What would happen to the mass if the gas could be contained within the apparatus?

Q3 What piece of apparatus could we use to measure a small volume of gas given off?

Investigating melting

a) Do you think that a substance changes mass when it melts? Why?

● Plan an investigation to see if crushed ice changes mass as it melts. Remember to prevent any water evaporating from your apparatus.

b) Was your prediction in question a) supported by your results?

● Evaluate your method.

● Conservation of mass in physical changes

So far you have seen how mass is conserved when atoms 'swap partners' in chemical reactions. In unit 7H you also saw how mass does not change when solids dissolve in water. But what happens in other physical changes, such as changes of state? Try 'Investigating melting'.

SUMMARY QUESTIONS

1 ☆ Copy these sentences. Complete them by filling in the gaps.
The mass of the . . . and the . . . is the same before and after a chemical or a . . . change. There are no new . . . made or . . . in the changes.

2 ☆☆☆ Read the following statements and correct them:
When paper burns, lots of mass is lost in the reaction – the ashes are really light.
I've seen some gunpowder burn. It disappears to nothing.

Key words

conservation of mass
particle diagram
precipitation

LEARN ABOUT

- plotting a graph and using it to obtain quantitative data
- the conservation of mass when materials burn
- new evidence sometimes requiring changes to theories

⬤ Gathering quantitative data

In Book 8, you looked at making compounds from elements.

One of the reactions was:

$$\text{magnesium} + \text{oxygen} \rightarrow \text{magnesium oxide}$$
$$2\,\text{Mg} + \text{O}_2 \rightarrow 2\,\text{MgO}$$

You can think of the particles reacting as shown below (although the Mg atoms and the particles in MgO would really be arranged in giant structures):

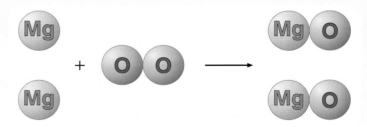

In the following experiment you can find the mass before and after the reaction.

LINK UP TO MATHS

You can use your skills from maths to draw and interpret graphs.

How much magnesium oxide forms?

- You will need to weigh some magnesium ribbon before it is heated in a crucible. You will also need to weigh the empty crucible and its lid.
  Your teacher will give you a sheet to guide you.

We know that the formula of magnesium oxide is MgO. This tells us that the ratio of magnesium particles to oxygen particles is always 1 : 1. Therefore we should get a straight line when we plot a series of points from experiments like the one above.

Here are some sample data:

Q1 How much magnesium oxide can be made from 1.8 g of magnesium?

Q2 How much magnesium is contained in 5.0 g of magnesium oxide?

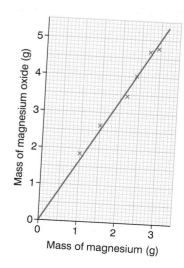

Changing our ideas about burning

Scientists in the 1700s believed that materials burned if they contained a substance called **phlogiston**. When something burns, they thought the phlogiston was given off. Then the true substance, the ash, was left behind. This was a good theory, as it explained many of the observations about burning known at that time. For example,

- Hardly anything was left when charcoal (carbon) burns ('That's because it contains so much phlogiston,' said the scientists of the time.)
- We can turn the ash from a metal back into the metal by heating it with charcoal ('That's because the phlogiston from the charcoal is transferred to the ash' – they thought that a metal is its ash plus phlogiston.)
- Flames go out in a fixed volume of air ('That's because the air gets saturated in phlogiston and can't hold any more.')

Q3 What would we call a 'metal ash'?

This theory was defended and survived even after Joseph Priestley had discovered oxygen gas. Priestley heated mercury oxide and collected a gas.

$$\text{mercury oxide} \rightarrow \text{mercury} + \text{oxygen}$$
$$2\,\text{HgO} \rightarrow 2\,\text{Hg} + \text{O}_2$$

This gas would let candles burn more brightly in it. Mice could survive longer in a jar of the new gas.

He shared his discovery with a French scientist called Antoine Lavoisier. Lavoisier set about investigating burning and came up with a new theory. His theory could explain the one big flaw in the phlogiston theory. The mass of a metal actually *increases* when it burns. This doesn't seem likely if it is *losing* phlogiston.

Lavoisier proposed that there was a reactive gas in the air, which he named oxygen. This gas added on to metals when they burned. It explained why their mass increased. This theory of **oxidation** could then explain more observations than the old theory, and was eventually accepted.

Burning wax

You saw on page 116 what forms when hydrocarbons (compounds containing hydrogen and carbon only) burn in plenty of oxygen.

Candle wax contains a mixture of large hydrocarbon molecules.

- What do you see happen when a candle burns?
- Explain why there appears to be a loss in mass during the reaction. Include a word equation in your answer.

Joseph Priestley (1733–1804)

Even though Joseph Priestley discovered oxygen, he died still believing the phlogiston theory!

SUMMARY QUESTIONS

1 ☆ Copy this sentence. Complete it by filling in the gaps.

The mass of a metal before its reaction with . . . is . . . than the mass of its oxide formed.

2 ☆☆☆ **a)** How do our ideas about particles help to explain what happens when a substance burns?

b) Why would the phlogiston theory fail to explain what happens when a metal 'ash', such as sodium oxide, is heated with charcoal?

Key words

oxidation
phlogiston

SCIENTIFIC PEOPLE

Stephanie Louise Kwolek was born in 1923

Making new materials – developing a revolutionary fibre

Not many people can claim to have invented a new material – let alone one that has literally saved thousands of lives. But in 1965 Stephanie Kwolek discovered a new fibre with properties that even she found hard to believe.

Stephanie had been working for almost 30 years in a team of research chemists for DuPont, a chemical company based in the USA. Their job was to research new **polymers** (very large molecules made of thousands of repeating units).

In the 1960s, people started to worry about a shortage of crude oil, and DuPont wanted to make a new material for lightweight but durable car tyres. Their theory was that the new lighter tyres would help save fuel.

One day in the lab, the chemicals Stephanie mixed formed a milky liquid, unlike the clear liquid she was expecting. Instead of throwing the liquid away and starting again, her experience and intuition told her to test the liquid. This would involve 'spinning' the liquid into fibres by forcing it through narrow jets in a machine called a spinneret.

She sent her discovery to the test lab, but they were reluctant to 'spin' it into a fibre, arguing that it would probably block up their spinneret. Eventually, they gave in and sent the results of their tests on the fibre back to Stephanie.

This stuff was incredible! It was nine times stronger than a similar mass of steel, but was only half as dense as fibreglass. Stephanie insisted on re-tests until she was absolutely sure no mistake had been made.

She and her team then had to work out how to scale up the process. Finally in 1971, the new fibre was launched under the name of Kevlar. It is used to reinforce tyres, but research continued and it is now used in hundreds of ways. Some of these are called composites, in which Kevlar fibres are mixed with other materials to give new products with improved properties. For example, it is used extensively in commuter aircraft to reduce weight but maintain strength. The work to develop new composites continues today.

But perhaps Kevlar's most famous use is in bullet-proof vests – and that is why Stephanie Kwolek can be proud that she has helped to save thousands of lives.

Sheets of Kevlar fibre are compressed together to make body armour

The synthetic racing 'leathers' of this rider contain Kevlar to protect against abrasion in case of an accident

Developing new products

- Draw a flow diagram outlining the processes involved in developing a new polymer, such as Kevlar.

- Conduct some research to find out about the development of another product. It might be a pharmaceutical drug, a plastic, or a foodstuff. Present the stages in its development as a flow diagram.

- Some **hydrocarbons** (compounds containing hydrogen and carbon only) are used as fuels. When a hydrocarbon burns in a good supply of oxygen we get:

hydrocarbon + oxygen → carbon dioxide + water

However, if there is **incomplete combustion**, we also get carbon monoxide (a toxic gas) and tiny particles of carbon (smoke or soot) formed.

- Combustion is an example of an **exothermic** reaction – one that gives out energy and the temperature of the surroundings increases. Some reactions are **endothermic** – one that takes in energy from the surroundings, resulting in a decrease in temperature.

- In any chemical reaction, the mass of the reactants is the same as the mass of the products formed. This is because atoms just 'swap partners' in reactions – no new atoms are created or destroyed. This is called **conservation of mass**. It also applies to physical changes, such as melting or dissolving.

No new atoms in a reaction, Pete... they just swap around to make new substances.

We don't see a colour change in every reaction, Benson.

Sometimes we need to supply some energy to start a reaction off... but some need no help at all.

DANGER! AVOID THESE COMMON ERRORS

The pictures we draw to help us balance equations are models. For example,

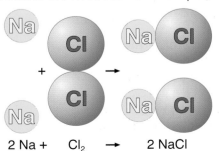

$$2\ Na + Cl_2 \rightarrow 2\ NaCl$$

You can see that the equation is balanced. However, we know that Na atoms are arranged in giant structures in sodium metal. We also know that NaCl is not a molecule made of just two atoms, as our model opposite suggests. This also has a giant structure, but we use the model to help us 'see' the numbers of atoms before and after a reaction.

Key words

combustion
conservation of mass
endothermic
exothermic
hydrocarbon
polymer

REVIEW QUESTIONS
Understanding and applying concepts

1 Match each of the following equations to a word from the list which best describes the type of reaction:

> **displacement**   **combustion**
> **photosynthesis**   **precipitation**

a $CH_4 + 2 O_2 \rightarrow CO_2 + 2 H_2O$
b $Na_2SO_4 + BaCl_2 \rightarrow 2 NaCl + BaSO_4$
c $2 AgNO_3 + Cu \rightarrow Cu(NO_3)_2 + 2 Ag$
d $6 CO_2 + 6 H_2O \rightarrow C_6H_{12}O_6 + 6 O_2$

2 Look at the experiment below:

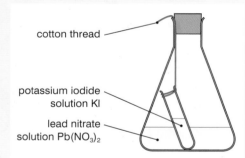

cotton thread

potassium iodide solution KI

lead nitrate solution $Pb(NO_3)_2$

A yellow precipitate of lead iodide forms when the solutions come into contact with each other.
a How could you use this reaction to demonstrate the conservation of mass?
b Explain conservation of mass using this reaction.

3 Read the information below, then answer the questions:

'Safety' matches work by separating some of the reactants in the match-making mixture between the match head and the striking board on the side of the box.

A mixture of red phosphorus and powdered glass is glued to the side of the box. The match head contains a mixture of sulphur, antimony sulphide and potassium chlorate.

The red phosphorus turns into the more reactive white phosphorus in the heat from the friction as the match is struck. This white phosphorus ignites spontaneously as it reacts with oxygen in the air, setting off the combustion reaction in the match head.

a Why is powdered glass used in the manufacture of safety matches?
b Which two *elements* are used in safety matches?
c White phosphorus, P_4, burns in air to form phosphorus pentoxide, P_2O_5. Write a word equation and a balanced symbol equation for this reaction.

4

a i) Why does a candle *appear* to lose mass as it burns?
  ii) Write a word equation for the complete combustion of wax.
b i) Name one other gas that is formed when you extinguish a candle under a beaker.
  ii) Why is this gas dangerous?

Ways with words

5 Write a letter from Antoine Lavoisier to Joseph Priestley that tries to persuade him to change his views on the phlogiston theory.

Extension question

6 Balance the following equations:
a $Fe + O_2 \rightarrow Fe_2O_3$
b $NaNO_3 \rightarrow NaNO_2 + O_2$
c $K + H_2O \rightarrow KOH + H_2$
d $W_2O_3 + H_2 \rightarrow H_2O + W$
e $MgSO_4 + NaOH \rightarrow Mg(OH)_2 + Na_2SO_4$
f $C_4H_{10} + O_2 \rightarrow CO_2 + H_2O$

SAT-STYLE QUESTIONS

1 Pip and Mike heated some magnesium ribbon in a crucible, fitted with a lid. They made sure they did not let any of the magnesium oxide formed escape.

Look at their results below:

crucible
mass = 60.00 g

crucible and magnesium
mass = 60.24 g

crucible and magnesium oxide
mass = 60.40 g

a How much magnesium did Pip and Mike start with? (1)

b How much magnesium oxide was formed in the reaction? (1)

c Explain why the mass of the crucible and its contents increased after the reaction. (1)

d Write a word equation for the reaction. (1)

e Balance this symbol equation for the reaction:

$$Mg + O_2 \rightarrow MgO \qquad (1)$$

f What is this type of chemical reaction called? (1)

2 Reese and Benson did six experiments making magnesium oxide from magnesium in a crucible. They measured the mass of magnesium before the reaction and the mass of magnesium oxide formed afterwards.

Here is a graph of their results:

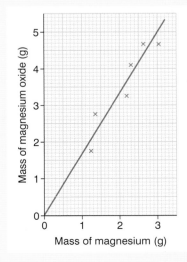

a Finish this sentence:
Reese drew a line of ... ... through the points on the graph. (1)

b How much magnesium oxide would be formed from 2.0 g of magnesium? (1)

c Reese and Benson made sure they had a lid on their crucible during their experiment. They lifted the lid slightly several times before they stopped heating.

i) Why did they need to lift the lid? (1)

ii) Why does the crucible need a lid in this experiment? (1)

iii) What piece of equipment could they use to lift the lid? (1)

3 Molly and Pete heated some copper carbonate powder in a crucible. They made sure no powder was lost during their experiment. They used an electric balance to find the mass before and after the experiment. Here are their results:

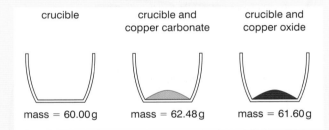

crucible
mass = 60.00 g

crucible and copper carbonate
mass = 62.48 g

crucible and copper oxide
mass = 61.60 g

a What mass of copper carbonate did Molly and Pete start with? (1)

b This is the word equation for the reaction:

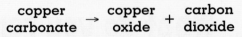

copper carbonate → copper oxide + carbon dioxide

i) Why did the crucible and its contents lose mass after the reaction? (1)

ii) How much copper oxide was formed in the reaction? (1)

c What do we call this type of reaction? Choose from the list:
thermal decomposition
combustion
displacement
reduction
precipitation (1)

Key words

Unscramble these:
logintshop
chonobdarry
toxichemer

9I Energy and electricity

Mum told me to wash my hands.

What's it all about?

In unit 7J, you learned about electrical circuits. We use electricity a lot in our lives, and each generation uses more than the one before. We use it because electricity is a good way of transferring energy from one place to another. For example, most people in the UK use a washing machine to wash their clothes. It's much more convenient than washing by hand. But remember, the electricity the machine uses comes from somewhere. In a power station somewhere, someone is burning coal or oil – fossil fuels – to release their energy. That energy heats the water, spins the drum in your washing machine and makes your life much easier.

In this unit, you will learn more about both electricity and energy. You will find out about devices that transform energy from one form to another, and about how electricity transfers energy from place to place.

What do you remember?

You already know about:
- different forms of energy.
- electrical circuits and current.
- measuring current.

1   You can connect electrical cells together to make a:

    battery   current   tissue   voltage

2   What quantity tells us about the push of a cell?

    ammeter   current   energy   voltage

3   What meter is used to measure current?

    ammeter   current meter
    electricity meter   voltmeter

4   As current flows round a circuit, it:

    gets weaker   gets stronger
    leaks out   stays the same

5   What do we call the energy of a moving object?

    force   kinetic   speed   stored

6   Which two types of energy reach us from the Sun?

    electrical   heat   kinetic   light

Ideas about energy and electricity

The Scientifica crew need to revise what they learned about electricity and energy in Year 7. Once they've answered these questions, they should realise that their experiment is not a very good idea.

a) What do we call the energy carried by an electric current?

b) What's the difference between connecting things in series and in parallel?

c) How does current flow in a parallel circuit?

d) What is the purpose of a fuse in a circuit?

e) What will happen if they turn up the voltage control?

◉ Playing with energy

Imagine blowing up a toy balloon. It's hard work, for two reasons: you are **stretching** the rubber of the balloon, and you are **compressing** (squashing) the air that you blow into it.

Let go of the balloon and see what happens. It flies round the room as the air rushes out of it. Perhaps you have seen how a blown-up balloon can be used to make a toy aeroplane fly, or a toy hovercraft glide across the floor.

Q1 What name do we give to the energy of the moving balloon?

◉ Energy stores

In science, we often use the idea of **energy** to help us describe what is going on. The blown-up balloon is a store of energy. This type of stored energy is called **potential energy**. The stretched rubber and the compressed air are stores of potential energy. When you let go of the balloon, that energy can be used to do something useful, like making the toy aeroplane fly.

Stretching and squashing aren't the only ways of storing energy. Think of using a hammer to hit a nail. You lift the hammer up high. Then you bring it down hard on the nail. The raised hammer has potential energy. When it hits the nail, it makes it move. So objects that have been lifted up are stores of potential energy.

Looking for energy

Scientists like to keep track of energy changes – it helps them to explain what's going on. Your teacher will show you some toys and other devices. You have to say:

● How do you know that energy is being used to do something useful?

● Where did that energy come from?

Keep an eye out for stores of potential energy!

!SAFETY! Some devices may be for teacher demonstration only.

The hands move slowly round... that's useful.

The weights start off high up, with potential energy. Then they slowly fall.

Transforming energy

chemical energy (of petrol) → kinetic energy (of car)

We need energy because it allows us to do useful things. We use many different things that **transform** energy from one form to another. For example, you get in a car and drive off. The petrol in the tank is a store of chemical energy. When the car starts off, some of that chemical energy is transformed to kinetic energy. We can represent this using an arrow diagram.

Q2 Draw an arrow diagram to show this: You burn some charcoal on a barbecue to release heat energy.

Using electricity

Why do we use electricity for so many things these days? The answer is in two parts:

- Firstly, electricity is a very convenient way of **transferring** energy from place to place. If you connect up a circuit, an electric current flows, carrying **electrical energy** from a battery or a power station to the different components in the circuit.
- The second good thing about electricity is that people have invented lots of different electrical devices, which do something useful. For example, light bulbs and light-emitting diodes (LEDs) produce light; an electromagnet can lift things up; heaters get hot and give out heat.

Q3 Name some devices that use electricity to make sounds.

SUMMARY QUESTIONS

1 ☆ **a)** Give another name for 'stored energy'.
   b) Give another name for 'movement energy'.

2 ☆☆ A wind-up alarm clock is an example of a device that makes use of the potential energy of a stretched or compressed spring. Give two other examples. Draw an arrow diagram for one of them, to show how it transforms energy.

3 ☆ Draw an arrow diagram to represent how an electric heater transforms electrical energy to heat energy.

4 ☆☆☆ Draw an arrow diagram for a light bulb. Take care! Light bulbs give out heat energy as well as light.

Key words

compressing
electrical energy
potential energy
stretching
transferring
transform

Battery power

912

LEARN ABOUT

- what's inside electrical cells
- measuring voltages

 CHALLENGE

Do you just throw your old batteries in the bin? Use the Internet to find out how to dispose of used batteries safely, and why it is important to do this.

Using batteries

Many of the electrical devices we use work with batteries. Think of a torch. Its batteries contain chemical substances which store energy – we call this **chemical energy**.

Switch on the torch, and the bulb lights up. The light we get out is useful. A chemical reaction is going on inside the batteries, and this slowly releases the energy which was stored in the chemicals. An electric current carries **electrical energy** to the bulb, where it is transformed to light energy. Eventually the batteries go flat, and the torch goes out. The chemicals are used up.

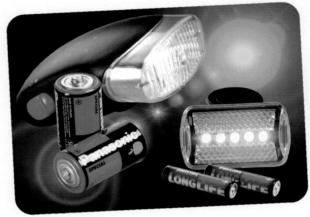

A modern cycle lamp needs less electricity to give the same amount of light as the old lamp. The old lamp needs a big battery or it would soon run down.

Q1 Explain why a bigger battery (e.g. AA) lasts longer than a smaller one (e.g. AAA).

More than 500 million batteries are sold in the UK each year. That's ten batteries for each person!

Inside a cell

- Your teacher will show you the inside of an electrical cell. Look for the chemical substances inside it.
  (If you have forgotten the difference between a cell and a battery, check it out at the top of page 136.)

!SAFETY! Never open a cell or battery yourself. The chemical substances inside are poisonous and corrosive.

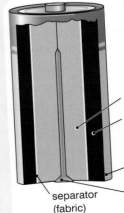

Both the anode and the cathode are soaked in an electrolyte solution of potassium hydroxide in water.

anode (powdered zinc)

cathode (mixture of manganese dioxide and carbon)

steel can

collector (brass pin)

separator (fabric)

● Measuring the voltage of a battery

When you buy a battery, it is usually marked with its **voltage**. The greater the voltage, the greater the 'push' it gives to make a current flow round the circuit.

You can measure the voltage of a cell or battery using a **voltmeter**. A voltmeter needs two leads, one coming out of each terminal. When the ends of the two leads are touched onto the two terminals of the battery, the meter shows the value of the voltage.

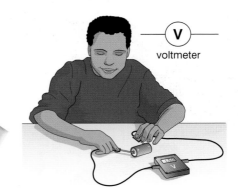
voltmeter

Investigating a vegetable cell

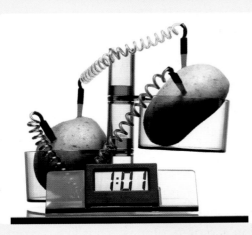

!SAFETY! Do not eat the vegetable or fruit used for this investigation.

The photo shows how a potato can act as the cell in a circuit, to make an electric clock work.

Two pieces of metal are stuck into the vegetable to act as the terminals of the cell. (They have to be different metals.) If you connect a voltmeter to the terminals, you can measure the voltage produced.

● Your task is to investigate the different factors that affect the voltage of a fruit or vegetable cell.

LINK UP TO
CHEMISTRY

If you have studied unit 9F, it may help you in your investigation to think about the reactivity of different metals.

SUMMARY QUESTIONS

1 ⭐ a) What energy transformation happens in an electrical cell?
   b) Draw an arrow diagram to represent this.

2 ⭐⭐ The chemical substances inside a flat battery are different from those inside a brand new battery. Why is this?

3 ⭐⭐⭐ When an electric current flows through a light bulb, it produces light. Name a device which makes an electric current flow when light falls on it. Where might you find one of these? Draw an arrow diagram to represent the energy transformation of this device.

Key words
chemical energy
electrical energy
voltage
voltmeter

Generating electricity

LEARN ABOUT
- dynamos and generators
- fossil fuels and nuclear fuels
- paying for electricity

On your bike

We don't just get electricity from batteries. Most of the electricity we use comes from the mains. How does this work?

Cyclists used to use a **dynamo** to generate the electricity for their lights, but these are becoming less common. The dynamo was turned by the rear wheel, and wires took the electric current to the lights.

Q1 With the dynamo working, the cyclist had to pedal a bit harder. Can you explain why? (Use the idea of energy.)

The picture shows another type of **generator**. You turn the handle and the lamps light up. Turn it slowly, and the lights are dim. The more lamps you connect, the harder it is to turn the generator to keep all the lights bright.

Mains electricity

You would get very tired if you had to generate all of the electricity for your home by pedalling a bicycle or turning a generator by hand. We get our mains electricity from power stations.

At the heart of any power station is a generator, which is like a giant version of a bicycle dynamo. The photo shows the generator in a large power station. It provides enough electricity for hundreds of thousands of homes.

Wind power

A small electric motor can work as a generator.

- Connect its two terminals to a voltmeter, and try turning the spindle. Does the voltmeter give a reading?
- Make windmill blades – this is called a **turbine** – and fix it to the spindle. Blow the turbine round, and watch the voltmeter. Describe how your energy is eventually transformed to electrical energy.

Oh no, they've converted us to hydroelectricity!

◉ Paying for electricity

Most of our power stations burn **fossil fuels** (gas and coal) to provide the energy we need. Some use uranium, which is a **nuclear fuel**. A small amount of our electricity comes from wind farms and hydroelectric power stations. The electricity they produce is all the same, though.

When we pay for our electricity, we are paying for the fuel used at the power stations. So it costs money to use any electrical appliance. You can tell which appliances use the most electricity by comparing their **power rating** labels. For example, a 100 W (watt) light bulb uses electricity faster than a 60 W bulb. A 2000 W heater uses electricity four times as fast as a 500 W kettle.

Look at the labels on different appliances to find out how quickly they use electricity. The power ratings are shown in watts (W) or kilowatts (kW).

Q2 Which costs more to run for an hour, a 100 W lamp or two 60 W lamps?

SUMMARY QUESTIONS

1 ☆ In a power station, which bit of machinery produces the electricity?

battery   dynamo   fuel   generator

2 ☆ Which of these is a nuclear fuel?

coal   gas   oil   uranium

3 ☆☆ Draw a diagram to represent this – include the names of the different forms of energy:

In many power stations, gas is burned. Its energy is used to turn a turbine, which turns a generator. Current from the generator carries electrical energy to people's homes. The electricity is used for heating and lighting.

Key words

dynamo
fossil fuel
generator
nuclear fuel
power rating
turbine

LEARN ABOUT
- measuring voltage and current
- voltages around circuits

Battery voltages

Cells are usually marked with the **voltage** they provide. On page 133, you learned how to use a **voltmeter** to measure the voltage of a cell.

To make a battery, you need to connect two or more cells end-to-end. Then their voltages add up.

Q1 You studied cells and batteries in unit 7J. Are cells connected in series or in parallel to make a battery?

Although you can't see them from the outside, there are six 1.5 V cells connected together inside this 9 V battery

Battery rules

- Use a voltmeter to measure the voltages of two or three cells. Are they marked with their correct values? Check the rule that their voltages add up when they are connected together.

- Make a prediction. What will happen to the voltage if one of the cells is turned round the other way? Test your prediction.

Using a voltmeter

You can use a voltmeter to find the voltage across any component in a circuit. It's important to know the correct way to use a voltmeter.

- Plug a lead into each of its terminals.

- Then touch the other ends of the leads on to two points in a circuit.

The voltmeter tells you the voltage between the two points. Now you can disconnect the voltmeter and use it to find the voltage between two other points in the circuit.

Gruesome science

Early investigators of electricity gave themselves shocks to find out how big a voltage they had generated – the bigger the shock, the bigger the voltage!

Around a circuit

In this activity, you can practise using a voltmeter. You can also learn an important fact about electric circuits.

● Connect up a circuit with a battery, a switch and two lamps. Use a voltmeter to measure the voltage across each lamp. You will have to think of a way to record your results.

● With the switch open, measure the voltage across each of the four components in the circuit. Repeat this with the switch closed.

a) What do you notice about the voltages you have measured?

● Repeat the experiment using a battery with a different voltage, or using a power supply.

b) What rule have you discovered?

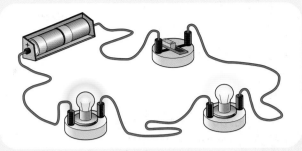

● Sharing out the volts

The cell or power supply in a circuit provides the push to make a current flow around a circuit. The volts it provides are *shared out* between the different components in the circuit. A bright lamp is getting a bigger share of the voltage than a dim lamp.

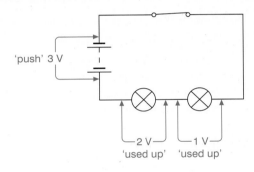

'push' 3 V

2 V 'used up'   1 V 'used up'

● Amps and volts

Don't get mixed up between ammeters and voltmeters.

An *ammeter* measures the current, in amps (A), flowing around a circuit. You have to break into the circuit to connect an ammeter, so that the current will flow through it. It is connected in series.

A *voltmeter* measures the voltage, in volts (V), between two points in a circuit. It needs two leads. You don't have to break into the circuit to connect it.

Q2 Is a voltmeter connected in series or in parallel?

SUMMARY QUESTIONS

1 ☆ Copy and complete the table:

Quantity	Meter	Symbol for meter	Connected in ...
current			
voltage			

2 ☆☆ A power supply provides 6 V for a circuit. There are two lamps, A and B, in the circuit.
   a) The voltage across lamp A is 4 V. What is the voltage across lamp B?
   b) Which lamp is brighter, A or B?

3 ☆☆☆ The diagram shows a simple circuit which includes a motor.
   a) Copy the diagram, and add an ammeter to the circuit. Add a voltmeter to measure the voltage across the motor.
   b) Use your diagram to explain why you only need one extra lead when you add an ammeter to a circuit, but two when you add a voltmeter.

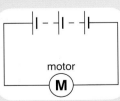

motor
M

Key words

ammeter
current
voltage
voltmeter

Voltage and energy

915

LEARN ABOUT
- energy in electric circuits
- scientific models

The battery provides 3 V ...

... and there's 3 V across the bulb.

So that makes 6 V altogether.

No, it's the same 3 V across each of them.

It all adds up

If you have a 3 V battery in a circuit, then the voltage across the other components must add up to 3 V. Another way to say this is that the voltage of the supply is *shared out* between the other components. This is the rule that you should have discovered in your experiment on the previous page.

There are two types of **component** in a circuit.

- There are the cells, power supplies, etc. that provide the voltage to push the current round the circuit.
- There are the bulbs, buzzers, heaters, etc. that 'share out' or 'use up' the voltage provided by the cells.

We can think about these two types of component in a different way:

- The cells, power supplies, etc. provide energy.
- The bulbs, buzzers, heaters, etc. transform the energy they receive into other forms.

Q1 In what form is the energy transferred from the cells to the other components?

High voltage

Perhaps you have guessed that voltage tells us about energy in a circuit. (Voltage is sometimes called **potential difference** because it tells you about the potential energy of the current.) That helps to explain why you have to be careful never to touch the electricity mains. The voltage is about 230 V, much higher than the voltage of a battery. It could push a large current through you, and transfer lots of energy to your body. That energy could literally cause your insides to boil and your skin to burn!

Even higher voltages than this are used to send electricity around the country.

- The generators in a power station produce 25 000 V.
- Some of the cables of the National Grid are at 500 000 V.

Stand well back!

Gruesome science

A teenager in Yorkshire died when the kite he was flying touched a 330 000 V overhead power line. Don't let it happen to you!

A model for current and energy

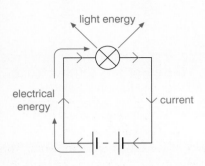

In unit 7J, you learned a bit about electricity and energy. You should recall that:

- Electric current goes all the way round a circuit.
- Electrical energy is transferred from the cells or power supply to the other components in the circuit.

In science, we often use **models** to help us picture ideas like this. Here's a model to explain circuits.

When you ride a bicycle, you turn the pedals, which then turn a big toothed cog-wheel. That wheel drags the chain round, and the chain turns the back wheel. So energy is transferred from your legs to the bicycle wheel.

About models

In science, a model isn't an exact replica of the thing we are thinking about. An electric circuit doesn't have a long, thin bicycle chain going around in its wires. A model is something we can understand relatively easily, and which in some ways is like the thing we are thinking about, so that it helps us to understand it a bit better.

Thinking about the model

- With a partner, discuss the bicycle chain model.
  a) What corresponds to:
    i) the power supply in a circuit
    ii) the current?
  b) How can you tell that energy is being transferred?

SUMMARY QUESTIONS

1 ☆ a) Name two components that can provide the voltage which makes current flow round a circuit.
   b) Name three components which can use up that voltage.

2 ☆☆ Draw energy arrow diagrams for:
   a) a cell
   b) a motor.

3 ☆☆ A milkman drives from the dairy and delivers milk all round an estate, before returning to the dairy at the end of his round. Explain how this could be a model for the way in which an electric circuit transfers energy.

Key words

component
model
potential difference

IDEAS AND EVIDENCE

New words for science

We use the word 'cell' a lot in science. In biology, it means the tiny building blocks from which living things are made. In physics and chemistry, it means an electrical device, which can make a current flow.

The first person to use the word 'cell' in a scientific sense was Robert Hooke. He had an early microscope, and he used it to look at all sorts of things. The picture shows his drawing of what he saw when he looked at a piece of cork. He noticed that it was made up of lots of tiny repeating units, and he called these 'cells', because they reminded him of the small rooms in monasteries, called cells, which monks lived in. At the time, he didn't realise that all plants and animals are made up of large numbers of these units.

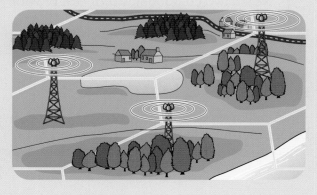

Robert Hooke looked down his microscope at a thin piece of cork and noticed that it was made of small compartments

A battery of cells

The first electrical cells were invented in Italy at the end of the 18th century. They were called 'cells' because it was necessary to join several together to get a big enough current to flow.

Several cells together were called a 'battery'. This is another word which scientists borrowed. A battery was the name for a row of cannons, used to defend a fortress or naval ship. So a row of cells came to be known as a battery.

The first cells were bigger than most of the ones we use today. The picture shows a battery of cells constructed at the Royal Institution in 1807 for Sir Humphry Davy. He needed a good electricity supply for his experiments in physics and chemistry.

Sir Humphry Davy's battery of cells. The man on the left is holding up the insides of one cell.

Moving around

When new mobile phone systems are invented, new masts must be set up around the country to send out and receive messages from nearby phones. The whole country is divided up into areas with a mast at the centre. The area around a mast is called a 'cell', and that's why mobile phones are sometimes called 'cellphones'.

Scientists often have to make up words for new inventions or ideas. They borrow words from all over the place; sometimes they use an old language, such as ancient Greek or Latin ('microscope' comes from the Greek), and sometimes they use a modern language ('tsunami' is a Japanese word).

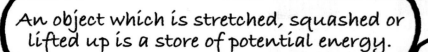

An object which is stretched, squashed or lifted up is a store of potential energy.

Energy can be transformed from one form to another.

Electrical energy is carried around a circuit from cells or power supplies to other components, which transform it into other forms.

Electricity is a useful way of transferring energy from place to place.

4·5V

3·0V
1·5V
4·5V

The voltage across a component in a circuit is measured using a voltmeter connected in parallel with it.

The voltages across components in a series circuit add up to the voltage of the supply.

DANGER! AVOID THESE COMMON ERRORS

You have to be careful with scientific terminology. The word 'electricity' is a bit vague. People may not know if you mean current, voltage or energy. So, don't say 'Electricity goes round the circuit'; it's better to say, 'An electric current flows round the circuit.'

Key words

biology
chemistry
physics

REVIEW QUESTIONS
Understanding and applying concepts

1   Electricity is a good way of transferring energy from place to place. Imagine that you live on a remote island, and that your electricity comes from a wind turbine. You switch on the television.

Draw a diagram to show how the energy of the wind allows you to see TV programmes. Show the different forms of the energy as it is transferred from place to place.

2   Seagulls sometimes pick up snails on the beach, and then fly high up where they drop them on the rocks below to smash their shells.

What form of energy do the snails have
i)   before they are dropped
ii) as they are about to hit the rocks?

3   You can't store electricity, but there are other ways of storing energy. For each of the examples below:
i)   say what form the energy is stored in
ii) give an example of a way in which we could use the stored energy.
a   a stretched rubber band
b   a 9 V battery
c   water stored behind a dam.

Ways with words

4   We say that a wound-up spring is a store of potential energy. Explain what your teacher might mean if your science report said: 'You could make more of your potential in this subject.'

Making more of maths

5   If you read your electricity meter, you can find out how much electricity you are using and work out how much it will cost.

The pictures show the meter in Benson's house on two different days.

a   How many days passed between the two readings?
b   How many units of electricity were used? (Work out the difference between the two readings.)
c   If one unit costs 8 p, what was the total cost of the electricity used?

6   A 1000-watt electric fire uses 1 unit of electricity if it is switched on for an hour.
a   How much electricity is used if a 2000-watt fire is switched on for 3 hours?
b   If one unit costs 8 p, how much would this cost?

Thinking skills

7   The box below shows some forms of energy and some devices. (Make sure you know which are which.)

Think up a way of re-organising these to show the connections between them.

electrical energy	alarm clock
kinetic energy	battery
heat energy	light energy
chemical energy	light bulb
solar cell buzzer	sound energy
electromagnet	heater
potential energy	

SAT-STYLE QUESTIONS

1 Pete went on a ride at the theme park. The picture shows the car at different points on the ride.

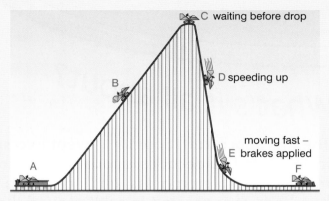

a At which point did the car have most potential energy? Explain how you know. (2)

b Name two points at which the car had no kinetic energy. (2)

c At which point did the car have most kinetic energy? Explain how you know. (2)

2 Pip set up an electric circuit as shown.

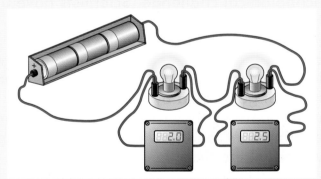

a Were the lamps connected in series or in parallel? (1)

b How many volts did the battery supply? (1)

Pip wanted to check the voltage of the battery. The picture shows the circuit diagram.

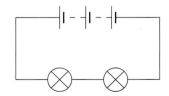

c Copy the diagram, and add a voltmeter to show how Pip could measure the voltage of the battery. (1)

Pip also wanted to measure the current flowing around the circuit.

d On your diagram, mark with an **A** a point in the circuit where she should include an ammeter to do this. (1)

3 Before he went camping, Mike charged up his rechargeable torch.

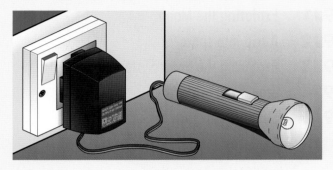

a What energy change took place in the torch as the batteries were recharged? Choose from:

> **chemical to electrical**
> **light to electrical**
> **electrical to light**
> **electrical to chemical**

(1)

b What energy change took place when Mike used the torch in his tent at night? Choose from:

> **electrical to chemical to light**
> **electrical to potential to light**
> **chemical to electrical to light**
> **chemical to heat to light**

(1)

Key words

Unscramble these:
at pet lion
buntier
chin gretts
melt voter
ret orange

Gravity and space

Don't forget the can opener!

We'll need it to get out of these suits!

What's it all about?

The first spacecraft, *Sputnik 1*, went into space in 1957. In five decades, space science has made incredible progress, and now there are hundreds of spacecraft in orbit around the Earth. It's getting quite crowded up there!

Other spacecraft have travelled around the Solar System, sending back detailed information about the other planets and the Sun. They have even taken a close look at comets.

Space travel has been a great scientific and technological challenge. Scientists have used their understanding of forces, particularly gravity, to work out the best way to send tonnes of metal into space. Engineers have designed and built spacecraft that can survive the heat generated by friction with the atmosphere as they return to Earth. It's an exciting story, and new chapters are being written all the time.

 # What do you remember?

You already know about:
- how the Moon orbits the Earth.
- all the things that make up the Solar System.

1 The Earth is . . .

    flat   an asteroid   a planet   a star

2 The Moon is . . .

    an asteroid   a planet
    a satellite   made of cheese

3 What force keeps us on the Earth?

    atmospheric pressure   glue
    gravity   magnetism

4 Space is full of . . .

    air   alien life-forms   gas   nothing

Lost in space

Once we are above the atmosphere, we'll be free of gravity.

We'll need to take a lot of fuel if we are going to orbit for a few months

Our spaceship has a streamlined shape to reduce drag in space.

On the Moon, we'll be able to float about in mid-air.

I vote we explore a planet in another Solar System.

I think I might stay at home.

FUEL

QUESTIONS

The Scientifica crew have built their own spacecraft. Unfortunately, they have forgotten some of the things they learned in Year 7 about space travel and the Solar System.

a) How would you launch a spacecraft like this into space?

b) Can you suggest improvements to its design?

c) Why does a spacecraft need a supply of energy?

d) What would it be like to visit the Moon?

e) Would you like to join the Scientifica crew on their maiden voyage? Explain why.

LAUNCH

LEARN ABOUT
- gravity
- mass and weight

● Quarter of a million miles from home

In 1969, Neil Armstrong and Buzz Aldrin became the first people to step on the Moon. This was an extraordinary achievement. We are all stuck to the Earth and held here by its gravity. Armstrong and Aldrin had broken free of the Earth's **gravitational pull**, the first human beings ever to do so.

Far-from-home movies

- Watch a video of astronauts on the Moon. You can find out a lot about what the Moon is like. Think about how the astronauts move, what they wear, the ground and the sky.
What can you deduce about the following?
  i) The surface of the Moon
  ii) Gravity on the Moon
  iii) The Moon's atmosphere, and the weather.

Oh no! Time to hide, folks!

They won't stay long!

You can tell a lot about the Moon just from a photo like this. Why does the flag need a rod along the top to stiffen it?

AMAZING SCIENCE!

The Moon turns just once on its axis each time it orbits the Earth. That's why we always see the same side. No-one saw the other side until the first spacecraft went round the back of the Moon.

● Loony fun

Astronauts have played games on the Moon. One hit a golf ball – it went farther than on Earth, because the Moon's gravity is weak. Of course, the ball landed back on the ground, because it was pulled down by gravity, but it travelled much farther before it landed.

The weak gravity meant that the astronauts were lighter, too. Their **weight** was less than on Earth. If it hadn't been for their cumbersome suits, they would have been able to jump much higher than on Earth.

Q1 What unit do we measure weight in?

Planet	Weight of 1 kg object (N)
Mercury	3.7
Venus	8.8
Earth	9.8
(Moon)	1.6
Mars	3.7
Jupiter	25.9
Saturn	9.1
Uranus	7.7
Neptune	11.3
Pluto	0.4

One day, perhaps in your lifetime, astronauts may visit another planet. Mars is the most likely one to receive visitors from Earth. The strength of gravity is different on each planet. The table shows you how much a 1 kg object weighs on each planet of the Solar System (and on the Moon).

It gets you down

The **force** of gravity pulls on you, wherever you go on the Earth. It doesn't matter where you go. Australia may be on the other side of the Earth, but gravity still works there.

Weight is a force, so we can represent it by an arrow. The arrow always points downwards, towards the centre of the Earth. 'Down' is always the direction of gravity, towards the centre of the Earth – unless you've made it to the Moon or another planet.

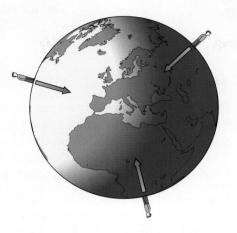

When scientists first discovered how to measure the mass of the Earth, they found it was 6000 000 000 000 000 000 000 000 kg.

Gravity, weak and strong

Why is the Moon's gravity so much weaker than the Earth's? We have to think about how the Earth and the Moon compare. The Earth is bigger, and has a much greater **mass** than the Moon. It's the mass of an object that gives it a gravitational pull.

Q2 What unit do we measure mass in?

So we all have mass, but our masses are much smaller than the mass of the Earth or Moon. We too have a gravitational pull, but it is very, very weak. If you find yourself attracted to another person, it's not because of their gravity (unless their mass is unusually high!).

- Your *mass* tells you something about yourself – how much matter you are made from.
- Your *weight* tells you about the pull of something else on you – if that something has a lot of mass, like the Earth, its pull will be strong.

The Earth's mass is 40 times the Moon's mass. Its gravity is 6 times as strong.

SUMMARY QUESTIONS

1 ☆ In which direction does the force of gravity act?
upwards   downwards   sideways   depends where you are

2 ☆☆ Which of these gets less, if you go to the Moon?
**your height   your mass   your weight
the amount of matter you are made from**

3 ☆☆ Calculate the weight of a 50 kg person on Earth, on the Moon and on Mars. (Use information from the table on the opposite page.)

4 ☆☆ Draw a circle to represent the Moon. Around the edge, draw three astronauts. Add a force arrow to each to show the direction of his weight.

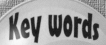

Key words
force
gravitational pull
mass
weight

A trip into space

9J2

LEARN ABOUT

■ gravity and space
■ forces on spacecraft

● Above the atmosphere

Imagine that you are in a spacecraft on top of a rocket, ready for blast-off. Ten, nine, eight, . . . A few minutes after lift-off, you are in space. That means that you are beyond the Earth's **atmosphere**, the thin layer of air that surrounds our planet. All around you, the sky is black and you can see stars in all directions.

Don't switch off your rocket motor just yet! 'Space' is where there is no air, but that doesn't mean there is no gravity. If your motor stops now, you will fall back to Earth, pulled downwards by its **gravitational attraction**. (Some people imagine that it's the atmosphere that makes the Earth have gravity. They're wrong – it's the other way round. Gravity keeps the atmosphere in place. It's the Earth's large mass that causes its strong gravity.)

Q1 What would happen to the atmosphere if the Earth's gravity stopped working?

● Keeping moving

To fly to the Moon, you will need to keep your motors burning for a few more hours. As you move away from the Earth, its gravity gets weaker and weaker. Gravity gets weaker as the distance between two objects gets bigger.

Watch out! As you get closer to the Moon, you begin to feel the pull of its gravity. Soon the Moon's pull is stronger than the Earth's. Your craft goes faster and faster as it falls towards the Moon.

If the two forces on your spacecraft are balanced, you will come down at a steady speed

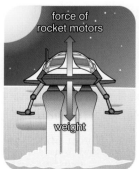

Put your motor control into the 'reverse thrust' position, so that it pushes upwards on you, slowing your fall. With any luck, you will land gently on the Moon's surface.

The Apollo 11 spacecraft was the first to land men on the Moon

● Taking off

A spacecraft is quite small; its mass is a few tonnes, less than a double-decker bus. The rocket that puts it into space is massive, because it has to burn a lot of fuel very quickly to provide the force needed to push the spacecraft into space.

There are two forces at work when a spacecraft is launched:

- the upward push of the rocket
- the downward pull of gravity (the weight of the rocket).

The upward push must be greater than the rocket's weight, or it will never get off the ground.

Q2 Are the forces on the rocket **balanced** or **unbalanced,** as it lifts off the ground?

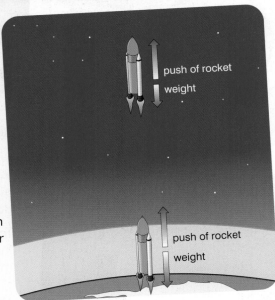

push of rocket
weight

push of rocket
weight

 Out in space

Once the rocket is high above the Earth, its weight is less for two reasons. Its mass is less because it has burned a lot of its fuel; and the Earth's gravitational pull is less, because the rocket is further from the centre of the Earth. That makes it easier for the rocket to go faster and faster. Eventually, when all the fuel is used up, the spacecraft separates from the rocket and continues on its speedy journey. The discarded rocket falls back to Earth.

Q3 What force pulls the rocket back to Earth?

Mapping a journey to the Moon

- On a large piece of paper, draw a picture to represent a trip to the Moon. Show:
  - the rocket as it lifts off from Earth
  - the rocket just before the spacecraft separates from it
  - the spacecraft half-way to the Moon
  - the spacecraft landing on the Moon.
  Use force arrows to show the forces acting at each stage of the journey.
  Write a commentary to go with your picture.

AMAZING SCIENCE!

The rocket motors that launch NASA's Space Shuttle provide a force of over 2 million newtons.

SUMMARY QUESTIONS

1 ☆ The Earth's gravitational attraction is caused by its . . .
   atmosphere   mass   Moon   surface

2 ☆☆ The Moon has no atmosphere because . . .
   its mass is small   its gravity is weak   both of these

3 ☆☆ Draw a diagram to show a rocket as it has just left the ground. Add force arrows to show the two forces acting on it. Label them with their names.

4 ☆☆☆ There is a point between Earth and Moon where their gravitational attractions cancel out. It is nearer the Moon than the Earth. A spacecraft could 'hover' at this point, without falling to the Earth or the Moon.
   Draw a diagram to show the Earth, Moon and a hovering spacecraft. Show the forces on the spacecraft. Are they balanced or unbalanced?

Key words

atmosphere
balanced forces
gravitational attraction
unbalanced forces

Exploring the Solar System

9J3

LEARN ABOUT

- exploring the Solar System
- models of the Solar System

Orbiting Saturn

In 2004, the Cassini spacecraft reached Saturn. It wasn't the first craft from Earth to reach this planet, hundreds of millions of kilometres away, but it was the first to go into orbit around Saturn. It has sent us back lots of fascinating photographs.

Today, we have many photographs of the nine planets that make up the Solar System, together with their moons. This means that we are much more familiar with the planets than anyone was fifty years ago.

Around we all go

We are also quite used to imagining the Sun at the centre of the system, with the planets orbiting around it. This is the **heliocentric model** of the Solar System. 'Heliocentric' means 'Sun-centred'.

In this model, the Sun is at the centre. The planets all travel around the Sun in the same direction, and their orbits are all roughly in the same plane – that's why we can draw it easily on a flat piece of paper.

A view of Saturn taken by the Cassini spacecraft

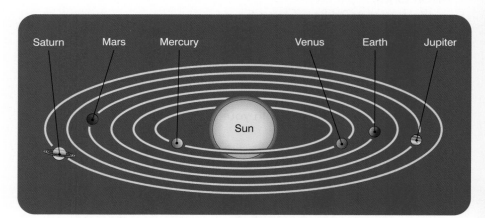

The heliocentric model

Gruesome science

Giordano Bruno was burned at the stake in 1600. He suggested that there might be other planets orbiting other stars, populated by people who were just as important as human beings.

- Discuss this model of the Solar System. You may have to do a bit of research to answer some of these points:
  a) Is the Sun really as big as shown here in the picture (compared to the planets' orbits)? Are the planets shown correctly?
  b) What shape are the planets' orbits? Are they circles? Do they all orbit at the same speed?
  c) Has the Solar System always looked like this? Is the Sun changing? Are the planets' orbits changing?

Saturn   Mars   Mercury   Venus   Earth   Jupiter

Sun

More models

It is increasingly difficult to see the stars in the night sky. Street lighting in our towns and cities is blotting out our view. However, it is important to remember that, in the past, people only had their view of the sky at night to tell them what the Universe was like. They were familiar with the patterns of the stars, which remained the same from year to year.

Planets are different. Their positions change gradually, night-by-night. You have to watch the sky carefully to notice this.

People thought that their lives were governed by gods, and that the movements of the planets could tell them about how the gods were behaving. That's why some of the planets have names like Mars (god of war) and Venus (goddess of love).

Because the stars, Sun and planets all move across the sky, it seems that they must be travelling around the Earth. That's a very sensible guess – after all, we can't feel the Earth turning on its axis. A model of the Solar System with the Earth at its centre is called a **geocentric model** (Earth-centred).

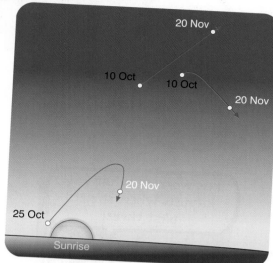

This diagram shows how the positions at dawn of three planets change in 2007

Two astronomers

In the 16th and 17th centuries, two scientists made the big step of realising that the geocentric model was wrong.

- **Nicholas Copernicus** suggested that the Earth orbited the Sun, and gave the correct order of the planets. However, he didn't have scientific proof.
- **Johannes Kepler** analysed data about the motion of Mars across the sky. He was able to explain these data by saying that both Mars and Earth orbit the Sun, following elliptical paths.

Other people, including some of the ancient Greeks, had previously suggested that the Earth orbited the Sun, but they didn't have the necessary data to prove it. At the same time, some religious leaders felt that it was blasphemous to suggest that the Earth wasn't at the centre of everything, so both Copernicus and Kepler suffered discrimination. Copernicus didn't dare to publish his ideas until he was on his deathbed.

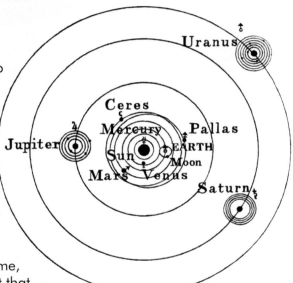

This drawing shows Copernicus's heliocentric model of the Solar System. It was drawn in the 19th century, and the artist added in Uranus and the moons of three planets.

SUMMARY QUESTIONS

1 ⋆ Which word means 'Sun-centred'?

egocentric   geocentric   heliocentric   solarcentric

2 ⋆⋆ Describe how the Sun moves across the sky in the course of a day. How do the stars move at night? What is different about the way the planets appear to move?

3 ⋆⋆ Find out about Pallas and Ceres, two objects shown in the drawing of Copernicus's model of the Solar System.

Key words

Nicholas Copernicus
geocentric model
heliocentric model
Johannes Kepler

LEARN ABOUT
- forces on orbiting objects
- the orbiting planets

Orbiting around

Lots of things go around:

- The planets **orbit** the Sun, the Moon orbits the Earth.
- The Earth **spins** (or **revolves**) on its axis.

And there are lots more: the hands of a clock, a cyclist on a track, the washing during the spin cycle.

Q1 What is the difference between orbiting and spinning?

I'm worried what will happen when it gets past three!

Around on a string

- Watch – or join in – a demonstration as a rubber bung is swung around in a circle.
  a) How does the bung move if the string breaks or is released?
  b) Why must the bung be attached to a string?

- Watch as the bung orbits on different lengths of string. Suggest how you could find out how its speed depends on the length of the string. Does it go faster when the string is longer, or more slowly?

!SAFETY! Take great care with the moving bung. Keep it well away from other people and from anything it could break.

What the string does

As the bung goes round, the string is taut. The bung is trying to get away, but the string keeps pulling on it. It's that pulling force that stops the bung from escaping, and keeps it in its orbit around you. The pulling force always points towards the centre of the circle.

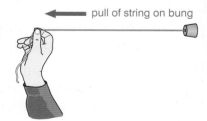

pull of string on bung

If the string breaks, the bung flies off in a straight line. That's how things move when they don't have a force pulling on them, making them go round in a circle.

Gruesome science

A black hole has a very strong gravitational pull. If an astronaut went near one, they would be stretched out like a long thin strand of spaghetti.

● Around the Sun

What has all this to do with gravity and space? The Earth orbits the Sun. There must be a force holding it in its orbit. Otherwise, the Earth would disappear off into the dark, cold depths of space and that would be the end of us.

What is the force that does the trick for us? Of course, it's gravity. The Sun's gravity pulls on the Earth, keeping it in its orbit. The Sun is 150 million kilometres away, but it's a very massive object and its gravitational pull reaches all the way to the Earth, and onwards, even beyond the edge of the Solar System.

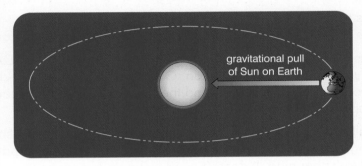

gravitational pull of Sun on Earth

In the same way, it is gravity that keeps the Moon in its orbit around the Earth. We say that the Moon is the Earth's natural **satellite**. A satellite is any object which orbits around another.

● Long years, short years

A year is the time it takes for the Earth to complete one orbit around the Sun. Mercury is much closer to the Sun, and its year is much shorter than ours.

The table shows the speeds of the planets in their orbits around the Sun.

Q2 What pattern can you see in the data?

Planet	Speed in orbit (km/s)
Mercury	48
Venus	35
Earth	30
Mars	24
Jupiter	13
Saturn	9.6
Uranus	6.8
Neptune	5.4
Pluto	4.7

SUMMARY QUESTIONS

1 ☆ An object which orbits another object is called a . . .

   bung   moon   satellite   spacecraft

2 ☆☆ Copy this sentence, choosing the correct word from each pair.

   The further a planet is from the Sun, the *faster/slower* it orbits, and the *weaker/stronger* the pull of the Sun's gravity on it.

3 ☆☆ Copy and complete this sentence:

   To make an object move round in a circle, there must always be a . . . pulling it towards the . . . of the circle.

4 ☆☆ Draw a diagram showing the Moon in its orbit around the Earth. Draw and label a force arrow to show the force that keeps the Moon in its orbit.

Key words

orbit
revolve
satellite
spin

Satellites at work

LEARN ABOUT
- putting satellites into orbit
- how satellites can help us

Into orbit

A **satellite** is a spacecraft that is in orbit around the Earth. It is a tricky job putting a satellite into the correct orbit. A big rocket carries the spacecraft into space; the satellite must be travelling at the right speed and in the right direction if it is to stay in orbit.

- If it is travelling too fast, it will disappear off into space.
- If it is travelling too slowly, gravity will pull it back down to Earth.

Satellites have small rocket motors so that their controllers on Earth can adjust their speed and position. Once they are in the correct orbit, the motors can be switched off and the satellite will orbit for years at a steady speed. It doesn't need to use any fuel to keep orbiting.

If a satellite is travelling at a steady speed, its **kinetic energy** isn't changing. It stays at a constant height above the Earth, so its **potential energy** isn't changing. It doesn't need a supply of energy.

> **Q1** If a satellite fell towards the Earth, how would its potential energy change? How would its kinetic energy change?

The Space Shuttle must get a piggy-back ride up to its orbit

Keeping an eye on Earth

There are thousands of satellites orbiting the Earth. There is almost certainly one passing across the sky this very second, but you won't see it during daylight. Occasionally you might see a satellite at dusk or at dawn. What are satellites used for?

- *Weather satellites* take photographs and make other measurements to help weather forecasters.
- *Environmental satellites* monitor conditions on Earth – they can help spot the effects of climate change, for example.
- *Communications satellites* send telephone messages around the world, and beam down satellite TV programmes.
- *Scientific satellites* carry instruments to make observations of features, such as the Earth's magnetic field. Some carry telescopes that have a clear view of space from above the atmosphere.

In fact, more than half of all satellites are used for military purposes. They spy on targets around the world, control military aircraft, and so on.

The International Space Station is a manned science lab in space. New sections are added from time to time, and crew members come and go by shuttle.

Where on Earth?

The Global Positioning System (GPS) is an important network of satellites. Each satellite sends out radio waves giving information about its position. On Earth, a GPS detector receives these radio waves from four or more satellites, and can work out its position.

Airliners use GPS detectors to follow their routes in the sky. GPS is useful for people looking for new natural resources to exploit. Many modern cars are fitted with GPS, so you can't get lost.

 ICT **CHALLENGE**

Search the Internet for a diagram showing how the GPS satellites are arranged around the Earth. How many are there altogether?

The satellite kit

There are certain things that every satellite needs:

- A **power supply**: Most satellites have solar panels to convert sunlight to the electricity needed to make all the instruments work. Batteries are charged up to give the satellite an energy supply if its orbit takes it into the Earth's shadow.
- A **communications system**: All satellites have to communicate with Earth. Look for the 'dish' aerials used to receive and send messages.

The Magellan space probe has two solar panels and a very large dish aerial

UK in space

The UK has many scientists working on projects that use satellites. These projects are often organised by the European Space Agency (ESA).

- Search the ESA website (www.esa.int) to find out about a recently launched satellite, which involved UK scientists. Make an illustration of the satellite. Label it with information about all of the different parts which you can identify.

Scientists have to pay for their experiments to be carried into space

SUMMARY QUESTIONS

1 ☆ If you watch satellite TV, the weather forecaster is orbiting the Earth in a satellite. True or false? Explain your answer.

2 ☆☆ The *Apollo 11* spacecraft went to the Moon. Would it be correct to call it a satellite?

3 ☆☆☆ There is no friction in space – that's why a satellite keeps moving at a steady speed. Imagine that there was friction up there, so that a satellite gradually slowed down. Draw a diagram to show how you think its orbit would change.

Key words

communications system
kinetic energy
potential energy
power supply
satellite

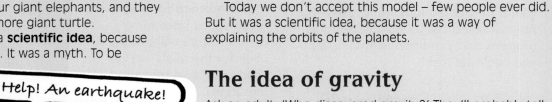

IDEAS AND EVIDENCE

Ideas of the Universe

People have believed all sorts of things about the **Universe**. One ancient Indian idea was that the Earth was flat; it was supported at the corners by four giant elephants, and they stood on the back of an even more giant turtle.

This doesn't really count as a **scientific idea**, because they never tried to check it out. It was a myth. To be scientific, an idea must try to explain our observations. In 1596, Johannes Kepler published his scientific idea of the Universe. He believed that the Sun was at the centre of the Universe, and he knew the order of the planets. But how could he explain the different sizes of their orbits?

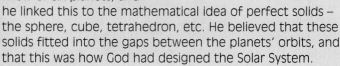

Help! An earthquake!

Sorry, I just burped!

His **model** is shown in the picture. He knew of six planets, and he linked this to the mathematical idea of perfect solids – the sphere, cube, tetrahedron, etc. He believed that these solids fitted into the gaps between the planets' orbits, and that this was how God had designed the Solar System.

Today we don't accept this model – few people ever did. But it was a scientific idea, because it was a way of explaining the orbits of the planets.

The idea of gravity

Ask an adult, 'Who discovered gravity?' They'll probably tell you it was Isaac Newton, but they're wrong. No-one can say who 'discovered' **gravity**. It's the force that makes things fall, and we all know that things fall. So what part did Newton play in our understanding of gravity?

Before Newton had his big idea, people thought that the Universe was divided into two 'spheres'. Down here on Earth, things fell to the ground, friction stopped things moving, and so on. Beyond the Earth was the sphere of the gods. Different rules applied out there, and we shouldn't expect the scientific laws we discovered here to apply out there.

Isaac Newton realised that the Earth's gravity does two things: it makes things fall to the ground, but it also keeps the Moon in its orbit around the Earth. By investigating gravity here on Earth, we could find out about gravity on the Moon, or anywhere else. The same laws apply in space as on Earth. He also worked out a formula for calculating the size of gravitational forces.

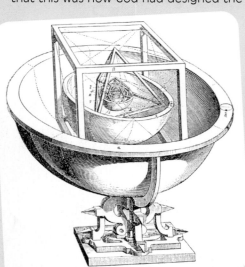

A model of Kepler's idea of the Solar System. Saturn orbits outside the cube, Jupiter is between the cube and the tetrahedron, and so on.

Legend has it that Isaac Newton was hit on the head by a falling apple. It was then that he realised that gravity affected the Moon in the same way that it affects objects on Earth.

Gravity is a force caused by an object which has mass.

The further apart two objects are, the weaker the gravitational attraction between them.

A satellite is an object which orbits another.

The force of gravity is needed to hold a satellite in its orbit.

Spacecraft have many different uses.

Today, we use a heliocentric model of the Solar System with the Sun at its centre.

DANGER! AVOID THESE COMMON ERRORS

Remember that an orbiting satellite doesn't need a source of energy to keep it going. If it was far off, away from the Earth's gravitational attraction, it would travel at a steady speed in a straight line. Close to the Earth, it can travel round in a circle at a steady speed. The Earth's gravitational pull keeps it in its orbit.

In the same way, the planets don't need rocket motors to keep them orbiting the Sun. That would be very odd!

Key words

gravity
model
scientific idea
Universe

REVIEW QUESTIONS
Understanding and applying concepts

1 As a rocket shoots up into space, it rapidly burns its stores of fuel. Give *two* reasons why the Earth's gravitational pull on the rocket decreases as it goes upwards.

2 Galileo used the newly-invented telescope to look at Jupiter. He discovered that it had four moons. The table shows the time each of these moons takes to orbit the planet.
  a What force keeps the moons in their orbits?
  b Use what you know about satellites to decide which of these moons is closest to Jupiter, and which is farthest away.

Moon	Time for orbit (days)
Callisto	16.7
Europa	3.6
Ganymede	7.2
Io	1.8

Ways with words

3 'Gravity' is the force which pulls us down towards the Earth. Two centuries ago, people started flying in hot-air balloons. They believed that hot air had a property called 'levity', the opposite of gravity. We don't believe this any more.

Find out the non-scientific meanings of gravity and levity, and write sentences to show these meanings.

There wasn't much levity when my parents came to the Parents' Evening!

You must have under-estimated the gravity of the situation!

Thinking skills

4 Which is the odd-one-out in each group? Give a reason for each choice. (There could be more than one choice in each case.)
  a   Sun   Moon   Earth   Jupiter
  b   mass   weight   friction

Extension question

5 Saturn is a planet famous for its rings. For centuries, astronomers weren't sure what they were made of.
  ● Were they solid rings, or made of dust and rocks?
  ● Were they stationary, or did they orbit around the planet?

Now we know that they are made of orbiting particles of dust.

Use what you have learned in this unit to answer these questions:
  a What would happen to these dust particles if they didn't orbit the planet (if they were stationary)?
  b Do you think that all of the particles travel around at the same speed? Or do some orbit faster than others?

SAT-STYLE QUESTIONS

1 The picture shows two astronauts on the Moon. One is lifting up a Moon rock.

a Which arrow shows the correct direction of the force of the Moon's gravity on the rock? (1)

b Which arrow shows the direction of the force of the astronaut's hand on the rock? (1)

The astronauts weigh their Moon rocks using a newtonmeter, and pack them into the spaceship. They climb aboard and set off for the return trip to Earth.

c What happens to the pull of the Moon's gravity on the spaceship as it travels away? (1)

d What happens to the pull of the Earth's gravity on the spaceship as it gets closer to Earth? (1)

e The scientists weigh their Moon rocks when they get back to Earth. What difference will they notice? (1)

f Explain why the rocks have a different weight on Earth than on the Moon. (1)

2 The picture shows a spacecraft in orbit around the Earth. Its rocket motors are switched off.

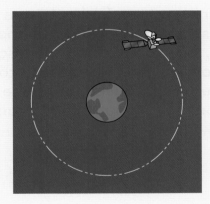

a Copy the drawing and add an arrow to show the direction of the force of the Earth's gravity on the spacecraft. (1)

b Describe how the spacecraft would move if the Earth's gravity was not pulling on it. (1)

c Give *two* uses of spacecraft orbiting the Earth. (2)

3 The photograph shows the Hubble Space Telescope.

Astronomers have used the space telescope to find out more about distant stars and galaxies.

a Which method do these astronomers use to gain new information? (1)
Choose from:
– They carry out experiments in their laboratories.
– They ask what other scientists think.
– They make observations of the environment.
– They find data on the Internet.

b Astronomers have benefited a lot by using spacecraft. Suggest one way that spacecraft have helped astronomers gather new information about the Solar System. (1)

c Astronomers have found that there are many planets orbiting distant stars, far beyond the Sun. What does this suggest about our knowledge of space? (1)

d Give one reason why scientists might reject an old idea and replace it with a new one. (1)

Key words

Unscramble these:
eric c the lion
he eats prom
till tease
viagra tonit

Speeding up

What's it all about?

How do we talk about how fast we move? In the past, people might have said: 'It's a day's walk to reach London'; or 'It's ten miles or so to the village – you'll be there by mid-day.'

Today, we might say, 'It takes 10 minutes in the car.' We are more concerned with how far and how fast we travel, and how long it will take us. We have speed limits to obey, because we have to take account of other people on the road.

In this unit, you can find out more about how we measure speed – which is important for athletes, for example. You will also find out about how we can use forces to control how we move. You will need to use the ideas about forces that you studied in unit 7K.

 # What do you remember?

You already know about:
- how to measure forces.
- how friction affects movement.
- how to represent forces.
- using graphs to represent movement.

1 Which of these is the unit of force?

gravity   kilogram   newton   pound

2 Which of these is *not* a unit of speed?

m/s   mph   km/h   s

3 We can represent forces using:

bows   arrows   crosses   dots

4 Which of these is *not* a force?

friction   speed   upthrust   weight

5 An object is stationary. An unbalanced force pushes on it. What will happen?

6 When Archimedes jumped out of his bath, he shouted:

Towels, please!   Wow, that's hot!
Eureka!   You rotter!

What was he so excited about?

Ideas about forces and movement

Speech bubbles in the cartoon:

"I'll fire the starting gun..."

"...and I'll start the stopwatch."

"Then you run down the track and give the watch to Reese..."

"...and she'll stop it."

"If you run 100m in 20 s..."

"...that's 2000 metres per second."

"A steady force will keep you moving at a steady speed."

"It's cool how these baggy clothes flap in the wind and make you go faster."

LAUNCH

QUESTIONS

Look at the cartoons – it's sports day at Scientifica High.
Discuss these questions:

a) How accurately will Molly and Mike be able to time the races? How could you improve their method?

b) Reese and Benson seem to think that the further you run and the longer it takes, the greater your speed. Do you agree? How would you calculate a runner's speed?

c) What force makes a skateboard go? What force slows it down?

d) What clothes can help a runner or cyclist to go faster?

9K1 Measuring speed

LEARN ABOUT

- measuring speed
- calculating speed
- thinking about precision

Two legs are better than three

The Scientifica crew have organised a three-legged race. Their teacher fired the starting pistol and recorded the time each pair took to run 100 metres. They ran more slowly than if they had not been tied together.

Molly + Mike 20.0 s

Pip + Benson 25.0 s

Reese + Pete 20.2 s

Q1 Which pair ran the fastest? How can you tell? How can you tell that Pip and Benson were far behind the others?

Start and stop

The car in the picture runs down the slope and along the table to the finishing line. How can you tell how fast it is going?

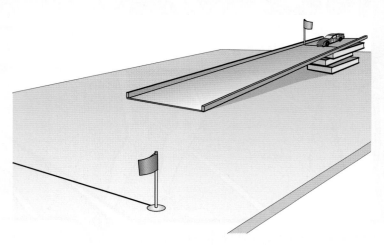

In a race like this, the winner may be only a fraction of a second ahead

- Start the stopwatch when you let go of the car.
- Stop the stopwatch when it crosses the line. This tells you the **time taken**.
- Measure the **distance travelled** by the car.
- Now you can calculate the car's **average speed**:

$$\text{average speed} = \frac{\text{distance travelled}}{\text{time taken}}$$

Timing the car for the complete run will only tell you its average speed. This is because the car's speed changes. It speeds up as it runs down the ramp. It slows down as it runs along the flat table.

Q2 At which point is the car's speed greatest?

AMAZING SCIENCE!

Light is the fastest thing around. In a vacuum, it travels exactly 299 792 458 metres every second. That's a very precise figure!

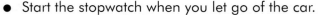

Calculating speed

In July 2004, Philip Rabinowitz ran 100 m in 28.7 s, beating the world record for a 100-year-old. Unfortunately, the electronic timer broke down and his record didn't count!

$$\text{His average speed} = \frac{100\,\text{m}}{28.7\,\text{s}} = 3.5\,\text{m/s}$$

You will probably need a calculator for sums like this.

Speed check

- Make a car run down a long, gently-sloping ramp. Use a stopwatch to find the time it takes to travel 1 m.

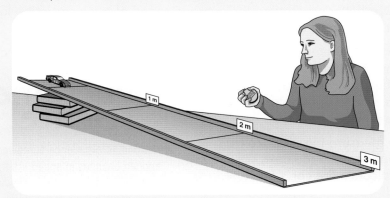

Make sure that you repeat the measurement several times. Why is this important?

- Repeat for 2 m and 3 m.
- Look at your results. Do you think this is a good way to find the car's speed? Can you suggest a better way?

Thinking about precision

In athletics championships, runners are timed electronically. The starter's pistol sets the clock running, and it stops exactly as the winner crosses the line. The length of the track must be measured very accurately, too.

- In July 1988, Florence Griffith Joyner became the first woman to run 100 m in under 10.5 seconds. Her time of 10.49 s was the world record for many years.
- In April 2003, Paula Radcliffe set a new record by running the marathon in 2 hours 15 minutes 25 seconds. The next woman runner was more than a minute behind.

Florence's time was measured with great **precision**, to the nearest one-hundredth of a second (0.01 s). Paula ran a much longer race (over 42 km), and her time was measured less precisely, to the nearest second.

Q3 Why was it important to measure Florence's time so precisely?

SUMMARY QUESTIONS

1. ☆ A snail crawls 10 cm in 2 minutes. A slug creeps 6 cm in 1 minute. Which slithers most quickly?

   both the same   slug   snail   can't say

2. ☆☆ Work out the speed for each pair in the three-legged race (opposite page).

3. ☆☆ A police speed camera takes two photographs of a car which it detects speeding. Why does it need to take two pictures? How can the car's speed be found from the photos?

Key words

average speed
distance
precision
time

Speeding up

LEARN ABOUT
- using light gates
- improving precision

● Electronic speed measurements

There are problems with using a stopwatch to time a toy car or a runner. When you see the car pass the mark, it takes a little time for your brain to react and for your finger to press the button. It's the same if someone shouts 'Start!' and 'Stop!' as the car travels along.

This means that you won't get the same measurement each time. You only get a rough idea of the time taken by the car. Your answer is not very **precise**.

Here's a better way to find the average speed of a toy car in the lab. Use a **light gate**, connected to a computer.

- When you release the car, it passes through the first light gate and starts the timer.
- When the car passes through the second light gate, it stops the timer.

If you measure the distance from one light gate to the next, you can calculate the car's average speed.

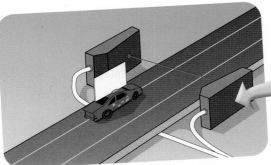

A light gate has a beam of light; when the beam is broken, it starts the timer

Astronauts experience some very sudden changes in speed. As they come in to land, the force slowing them down is four or five times their weight – heavy, man!

LOOK-ALIKE CONTEST

I'm going as Elvis Precisely!

Speed check again

- Repeat your experiment with the car running down the gently-sloping ramp. Use two light gates to find its average speed over 1 m, 2 m, and so on. If you're lucky, the computer will calculate the speed for you!

- Repeat each measurement, to get an idea of how precise your measurements are. Are they more precise than when you used a stopwatch?

- Use your results to draw a graph to show the distance travelled by the car at different times.

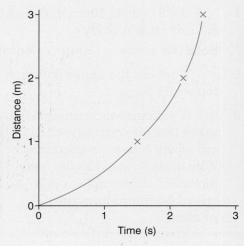

● Speed at a point

How can you find the speed of a car as it goes along? Here's one way using a light gate.

A car's speedometer tells you the car's speed at any moment as you go along. It doesn't tell you the average speed.

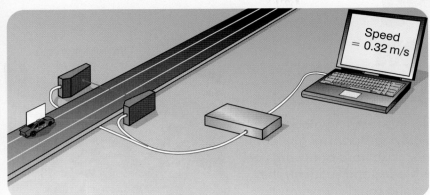

The car has a card attached to the top. The car passes through the light gate, which is connected to a timer or data logger. The card breaks the light beam.

● The front edge of the card breaks the beam and starts the timer.
● When the back edge of the card passes the gate, the beam is no longer broken, and the timer stops.

In this way, you can measure the time for the card to pass through the light gate.

Q1 What other quantity do you need to know, to find the car's speed?

A single light gate

You can find out a lot more about how things move if you use a light gate instead of a stopwatch.

● Cut a card 5 cm long. Fix it to a toy car or lab trolley, and run it down a ramp and along the bench. Your task is to measure the speed of the car, using a light gate, as it runs along the bench.
  a) Does the car's speed change as it gets further from the ramp?

● Think up your own questions to investigate.

SUMMARY QUESTIONS

1 ☆ A car takes 0.45 s to travel through the first light gate, and 0.54 s to travel through the next light gate. Is it speeding up or slowing down?

2 ☆☆ A toy car is 10 cm long. It takes 0.2 s to pass through a light gate. Calculate its speed.

3 ☆☆☆ Benson used a stop clock to time a toy train as it travelled 2 m along the track. The table shows his results when he repeated the measurement five times.

His teacher asked him if he could really be sure that his answer was correct. What do you think? What would you have deduced from Benson's results? Explain your ideas.

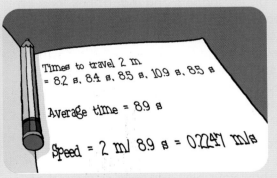

Times to travel 2 m
= 8.2 s, 8.4 s, 8.5 s, 10.9 s, 8.5 s

Average time = 8.9 s

Speed = 2 m / 8.9 s = 0.2247 m/s

Key words

average speed
light gate
precise

9K3 Changing speed, changing direction

LEARN ABOUT
- how forces affect movement
- accelerating – going faster

On your marks

Sprinters use starting blocks to get off to a flying start. The gun goes off, they push hard backwards on to the blocks, and suddenly they are moving rapidly forward. It takes a big forward **force** to get them moving.

Ice skaters can move even faster than sprinters. How do they do it? Ice skating is easy – once you've got moving. There is almost no friction to slow you down, so you go sailing along at almost **constant speed** in a straight line.

Getting started is harder. You have to turn your skates sideways and push back against the ice. (Roller blades are similar.) And if an ice-skater wants to change direction, they have to push sideways on the ice.

You need a force to make you go faster. The scientific word for 'going faster' is '**accelerating**'.

Q1 How would you slow down if you were an ice-skater?

Forces and sports

- Think about how forces are important in sports. Find photographs – look on the sports' pages of newspapers and magazines, and on the Internet – showing sports in action. Sort them out as follows:
  - Find examples where someone or something is moving at a steady speed, because there is no force to slow them down.
  - Find examples where someone or something (e.g. a ball) is speeding up or slowing down, because of a force.
  - Find examples where someone or something is changing direction, because of a force.
- Prepare a presentation. For each example, name the force that is causing the movement to change (e.g. the force of the racket on the ball). Be prepared to show your best examples to the rest of the class.

Disabled athletes are very fit – they need to be, to score at netball

● Force arrows

If you are setting off on a bicycle, you have to turn the pedals quite hard. Then there is a force, which starts you moving. The diagram shows how to represent the force with a labelled arrow. (You should recall how to draw force arrows from unit 7K.)

To slow down, you apply the brakes. Now there is a backwards force, slowing you down.

Often, there are several forces at work. The rocket in the diagram will go faster and faster as it takes off, because the forces on it are **unbalanced**. The thrust is greater than its weight.

Q2 What would happen to the rocket if the upward thrust was less than its weight? Draw a diagram to show this situation.

● Getting away from it all

Some spacecraft fly far from Earth. When they are in deep space, they are free from the Earth's gravitational pull. Then there is no force acting on them, and they move steadily ahead, without needing to fire their rockets. (In fact, the Sun's gravity may affect them slightly.)

It is very unusual for us to experience what it is like to move without any forces acting on us. It helps if we can avoid friction. An ice-skater is almost free of friction, so that they carry on moving at a steady speed in a straight line.

Sometimes we imagine that we need a force to keep something moving. However, that is usually because we need a force to balance friction, which is trying to slow things down.

In the sport of curling, team members sweep the ice with brushes to make it smooth, so that the puck will travel further

SUMMARY QUESTIONS

1 ☆ An unbalanced force is needed to make an object:
speed up   slow down   change direction   all of these

2 ☆ If the forces on an object are balanced, it will:
**come to a halt   move at constant speed in a straight line
change direction   none of these**

3 ☆☆ Use the idea of forces to explain why it would be very difficult for a runner to sprint on an ice-rink.

4 ☆☆ Draw a diagram to show the forces acting on the powerboat in the picture. Include its weight, the upthrust of the water, drag, and the forward thrust of its motor. If the boat is going at a steady speed in a straight line, which pairs of forces must be balanced? How could the rider change direction?

Key words

accelerating
constant speed
force
unbalanced forces

It's a drag

9K4

LEARN ABOUT
- air resistance and drag
- streamlined shapes
- saving fuel and energy

● Smooth legs

It's said that racing cyclists often shave their legs so that they will travel faster. Hairy legs mean more **air resistance**, which slows you down. Today's top cyclists usually wear body-hugging Lycra outfits to help them slip through the air with less resistance.

Even sprinters wear tight clothing, for the same reason. Although they move much more slowly than cyclists, they are still concerned about the effects of air resistance.

Q1 Does air resistance increase or decrease as you move faster?

● Efficient driving

Motorists should be concerned about the efficiency of their cars. They want to travel as many kilometres as possible for each litre of fuel they use. Manufacturers may advertise information about the fuel consumption of their cars, and the Government publishes data for all makes of car.

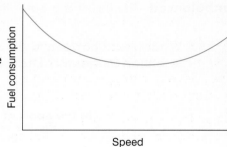

The graph shows how much fuel a typical car uses at different speeds.

- At high speeds, it uses a lot of fuel for each kilometre travelled, because air resistance is greater.
- At low speeds, it uses a lot of fuel, because car engines don't work very efficiently at low speeds.

You can see that the car uses less fuel at in-between speeds, when the engine is working well and there isn't too much air resistance.

ICT CHALLENGE

Use the Internet to find fuel consumption figures for some popular cars. Are 4×4s worse than other cars?

● Better design

Cars with a **streamlined** shape are designed to reduce the effects of air resistance. You may have seen lorries with wind deflectors on top of the cab. These help to push air up over the top of the lorry so that it uses less fuel.

In unit 7C, you studied how some animals have a streamlined shape, as an adaptation to their way of life and the environment they live in.

Q2 Give an example of a streamlined animal, and explain why streamlining is important for it.

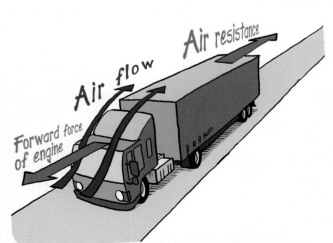

The cost of air resistance

As a car or lorry travels along the road, it has to push air out of the way. A lorry travelling at 70 mph (31 m/s) pushes aside as much as 1 tonne of air every second. Pushing that much air around takes a lot of energy, and that's why cars and lorries use more fuel at top speed. And fuel costs money.

Increasing air resistance

You can use what you know about air resistance to make a car go more slowly.

- Make a small toy car run down a slope.
- Now change the shape of your car by sticking pieces of card or other materials to it, so that there is more resistance to its movement.
  How can you show that the modified car moves more slowly?

The resistance of water

People with damaged limbs may be encouraged to take exercise in water, to help build up their muscles. They have to struggle against the resistance of water, a force which is known as **drag**.

If you try to move through water, you will experience more resistance than when moving through air. Water is much denser than air, so you have to push many more kilograms of mass out of the way when you wade or swim through water.

SUMMARY QUESTIONS

1. ☆ The force that tends to slow things down as they move through water is called:

   air resistance   drag   streamlining   upthrust

2. ☆☆ Explain why a racehorse can increase its strength more effectively by swimming than by galloping around.

3. ☆☆ A century ago, cars didn't travel very fast. How can you tell this from the shape of the car in the picture?

4. ☆☆☆ The resistance of water slows you down when you are swimming. However, you wouldn't be able to swim at all without drag. Explain why not. (Hint: Think about why it is impossible to swim through air.)

AMAZING SCIENCE!

There are special swimming pools in which racehorses can swim, to build up their strength.

Key words

air resistance
drag
streamlining

LEARN ABOUT
- moving up and down
- air resistance and speed

Up in a balloon

If you want to go up in a balloon, you will have to understand about forces. The balloon rises up because it is filled with hot air that is lighter than the cooler air surrounding it. This means that the **upthrust** is greater than the **weight** of the balloon.

When the balloon reaches the right height, the forces on it must be balanced. Let some of the hot air out of the balloon, so that the upthrust and weight are equal.

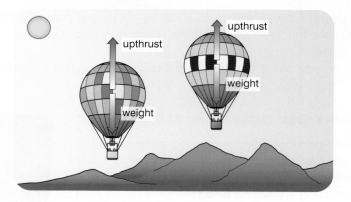

Q1 Which of these forces changes when air is let out of the balloon?

Parachuting down

Now is the time to jump out of your balloon, but don't forget your parachute! At first, you go faster and faster as you accelerate towards the ground. Then you pull the cord, and your parachute opens. A big force slows you down to a safe speed for landing.

What is that big force? It's **air resistance**, of course. The parachute has a big area, and you are moving very fast; both of these factors mean that there's a lot of air resistance, which is what you need if you aren't going to hit the ground at high speed.

The graph shows your journey down to the ground.

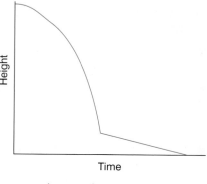

Q2 At which point on the graph are you falling fastest?

Q3 What other creatures can you name that make use of air resistance? Why is air resistance important for the dispersal of some plant seeds?

Many spiders have hairy legs. They are natural parachutists. If they fall from a high point, they spread their legs out. The hairs greatly increase their air resistance, and they fall gently to the ground.

Air resistance, more or less

There's more air resistance when something moves faster, and when it has a big area. These are two **factors** that affect the force.

- Devise a way of showing that faster movement and bigger area both give more air resistance. (It might help you to think about parachutes.) Can you measure the force?

!SAFETY! Follow your school safety rules if working outside the classroom or with heavy weights.

Many insects can fall thousands of metres through the atmosphere. They don't need a parachute to survive – air resistance is enough to make sure that they fall slowly. Remember that the next time you throw a spider out of the window.

● The big drop

Free-fall parachutists don't open their parachutes until they are quite close to the ground. At first, they fall faster and faster, until they reach their top speed. When they open their parachutes, they slow down to a safe speed.

The graph shows how a parachutist's speed changes as he/she falls. A **speed–time graph** is like a story which you can interpret using your knowledge of forces, and how they affect the way things move.

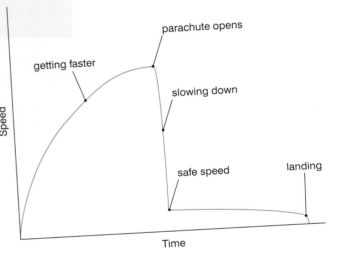

SUMMARY QUESTIONS

1 ☆ The force of upthrust always pushes:

   **upwards   downwards   sideways
   depends which way you're moving**

2 ☆☆ The force of air resistance always pushes:

   **upwards   downwards   sideways
   depends which way you're moving**

3 ☆☆ Imagine that you are up in a balloon, floating at a steady height. How could you change the forces acting on your balloon to make it go
   a) higher
   b) down to the ground?
   Draw force diagrams to illustrate your answers.

4 ☆☆☆ Look at the graph on this page, showing the free-fall parachutist's drop. At which of the points marked on the graph:
   a) is the parachutist moving fastest
   b) does the parachute open
   c) are the forces on the parachutist balanced?

Key words

air resistance
factors
speed–time graph
upthrust
weight

9K Read all about it!

IDEAS AND EVIDENCE

The table shows how the women's marathon record has been broken over and over again. Because it's a long race, the times are measured to the nearest second, not to 0.01 s. The timings don't have to be so precise.

Apr 2003	Paula Radcliffe	2 h 15 m 25 s
Oct 2002	Paula Radcliffe	2:17:18
Oct 2001	Catherine Ndereba	2:18:47
Sept 2001	Naoko Takahashi	2:19:46
Sept 1999	Tegla Loroupe	2:20:43
Apr 1998	Tegla Loroupe	2:20:47
Apr 1985	Ingrid Kristiansen	2:21:06

Runaway successes

At the Barcelona Olympics in 1992, Linford Christie (UK) won the men's 100 m sprint race. He broke the 10 s barrier, so his average speed was more than 10 m/s. Each runner's time was measured to the nearest one-hundredth of a second (0.01 s). The table shows the time it took for Linford to run the race at each 20 m section.

Distance (m)	0	20	40	60	80	100
Time (s)	0.00	2.93	4.74	6.48	8.22	9.96

Athletes and their coaches analyse data like this, to work out how they can scrape another fraction of a second off their times. You can see that Linford took nearly 3 s for the first 20 m, but only 1.74 s for the last 20 m. At the end of the race, he was running at 11.5 m/s – that's over 25 miles per hour!

In the longer run

Paula Radcliffe is a marathon runner. She beat the World Record in 2002, and then beat her own record in 2003.

Precision timing

Scientists and engineers often want to measure times to very great **precision** – much more precisely than in sprint races. For example, astronomers measure the distances to other planets using radar. They have to time the radar waves as they travel to the planet and back again. They need to be sure that their **measurements** are precise enough to send a spacecraft to the planet.

For such precise measurements, physicists have developed the **atomic clock**. This uses the fact that atoms vibrate at very steady rates. The vibrations happen trillions of times a second. By counting the vibrations, they can make measurements to the nearest trillionth of a second. Of course, they have an electronic machine to do the counting for them! The photo shows one of these atomic clocks, at the Greenwich Observatory in London. (That's an ordinary clock on the wall!)

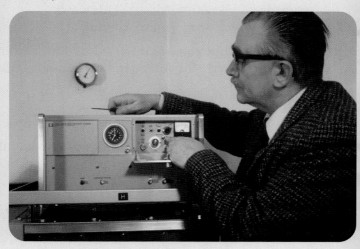

- Speed can be found by measuring distance travelled and time taken.

- Average speed = distance travelled/time taken.

- If any object's speed increases, we say that it accelerates.

- If no forces act on an object, it will move at a steady speed in a straight line.

- The greater the force acting on an object, the more it accelerates.

- Streamlined shapes reduce friction (air resistance and drag).

DANGER! AVOID THESE COMMON ERRORS

It's easy to think that an object needs a force to keep it moving. That's because there's usually friction at work, trying to slow it down. So you need a force to balance out friction.

But, when there's no friction, you don't need a force to keep you moving. You just keep moving along at a steady speed in a straight line – provided the forces on you are balanced.

Key words

atomic clock
measurements
precision

REVIEW QUESTIONS
Understanding and applying concepts

1   Joe was driving along the seafront on a summer's day. He drove faster and faster, until a police officer flagged him down, and said: 'My radar gun shows that you were going at 15 m/s. The speed limit is just 10 m/s!'

In court, Joe's lawyer said: 'Joe travelled 800 m in 100 s. He didn't exceed the speed limit.'

   a   Calculate Joe's average speed along the seafront.
   b   Explain how the police officer could have been correct, even if Joe's average speed was less than the speed limit.
   c   Copy the graph. Add to it to show how you think Joe's speed might have changed as he drove.

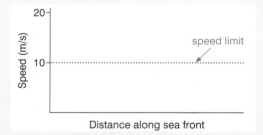

2   The force diagrams show a car going at different speeds. Decide which diagram matches each description, and explain your choice.

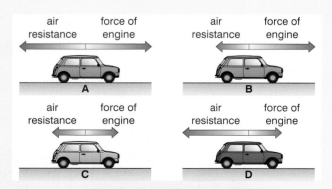

   a   The car is travelling slowly at a steady speed.
   b   The car is travelling quickly at a steady speed.
   c   The car is speeding up.
   d   The car is slowing down.

Ways with words

3   There's a difference between being *accurate* and being *precise*; see if you can work it out from this example:

The Scientifica crew were looking at the clock, waiting for the bell to ring.

Benson said, 'It's 2.57 pm.'
Reese said, 'It's nearly four o'clock.'
Molly said, 'It's two minutes and 40 seconds to three.'

   a   Who was more precise, Molly or Benson?
   b   Whose statement was the least accurate?
   c   Now make up another example that shows the difference between being accurate and being precise.

Making more of maths

4   Graphs are a useful way of showing information about how things move.

A distance–time graph shows how far an object has moved at different times.
A speed–time graph shows how fast it is moving at different times.

Draw two graphs, one of each type, to show this motion:

A car drove down the road at a steady speed. When it reached the countryside, it accelerated to a higher speed. It continued at this speed for a while, until it had to slow down and stop at a level crossing.

Thinking skills

5 Is air resistance a good thing or a bad thing? Prepare notes for a short presentation to show that air resistance and drag can be useful at some times and a problem at others.

Extension question

6 In science, we measure speeds in m/s, but in everyday life, we use mph (miles per hour). Here's how to find what 30 mph is in m/s:

There's 1600 m in 1 mile, so:
- Distance travelled in 1 h = 30 miles
  $$= 30 \times 1600$$
  $$= 48\,000\,m$$
  There's 3600 s in one hour. So if you go 48 000 m in 1 h:
- Distance travelled in 1 s = 48 000/3600
  $$= 13.3\,m/s.$$

a Using the same procedure, work out what 70 mph is in m/s.

b A sprinter runs at 10 m/s. How much is this in mph?

SAT-STYLE QUESTIONS

1 The picture shows Reese pushing a heavy box.

a Which arrow shows the direction of:
  i) the force of gravity on the box (1)
  ii) Reese's push on the box? (1)
b Reese pushes the box for 5 s. In this time, its average speed is 2 m/s. How far does it move? (2)
c Name a force which opposes Reese's push. (1)
d In which direction does this force act? (1)

2 The graph shows how Molly won the 100 m sprint race.

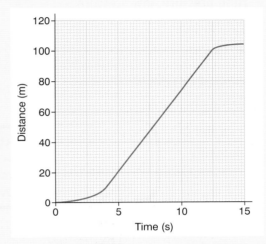

a Copy the graph. On your copy, add the following:
  i) Mark with an A, one point when Molly was running her fastest. (1)
  ii) Mark with a B, the point when Molly crossed the finishing line. (1)
b For most of the race, Molly ran at a steady speed. During this time, were the forces on her balanced or unbalanced? (1)
c After how many seconds did Molly cross the finishing line? (1)
d Work out Molly's average speed in the race. (2)

Key words

Unscramble these:
cofer
calace tree
scorpieni
dinel master
iris rat seance

Pressure and moments

Our teachers are putting us under pressure because the SATs start any moment now.

What's it all about?

It's all about forces. You can probably guess why 'pressure' has something to do with forces, but what about 'moments'? As you know, there are lots of words which have special meanings in science.

When scientists get new ideas, they look around for a handy word to use, to represent the idea. Sometimes they make up a new word, and sometimes they use a ready-made word, which means approximately what they are trying to say. So 'pressure' is a way of thinking about forces pressing on surfaces. 'Moments' is to do with using levers to change the effect of a force.

In this unit, you will find out about the scientific meaning of pressure, and a little bit about how pressure is used. You will also learn about levers and how they are used to make forces have useful effects.

 ## What do you remember?

You already know about:
- measuring forces.
- the particle model of matter.

1 Which of the following **cannot** be changed by a force?

    shape   speed
    direction   your mind

2 Which of these is a unit of area?

    metre   square metre
    cubic metre   electricity meter

3 In the particle model, the particles are furthest apart in a . . .

    solid   liquid   gas   crystal

4 In the particle model, the particles have fixed positions in a . . .

    solid   liquid   gas   vacuum

5 Which is most easily compressed (squashed)?

    solid   liquid   gas   kryptonite

Circus Scientifica

The Scientifica crew are trying out their circus skills –
but they haven't applied much scientific understanding.

a) Who is using a lever to make their friend fly through the air?
What's wrong about the way they are using it?

b) Why doesn't Pip, the human cannon-ball, fly very far?

c) What will happen when Molly drops the large weight?

High pressure, low pressure

LEARN ABOUT
- the meaning of pressure
- high and low pressure
- pressure in nature and technology

The pressure builds up

It would be fun to watch a volcano explode – wouldn't it? There are places in the world where tourists can do just that, but you need a reliable guide.

Inside a volcano, the **pressure** slowly builds up. Eventually, the pressure is so great that hot lava blows out into the air in a spectacular explosion. You will be safe if the volcano explodes at regular intervals, so that you can predict when its next blow-out will happen. It's not a good idea to hang around if the explosion is overdue.

'Pressure' in science

The word 'pressure' has a special meaning in science. Here's one way to understand it.

Imagine that your friend has been playing on a frozen pond. Suddenly the ice breaks and he falls through. You are on the bank – how can you save him? Very wisely, you dial 999 – if you run onto the ice, you will probably fall through, too.

Then you notice a ladder lying nearby. You lay the ladder across the ice, crawl to your friend, and pull him onto the ladder. You are both safe.

Please use your scientific knowledge to save me!

The problem with the thin ice is that it is likely to break if you stand on it. The force of your weight is too great when you are standing upright. However, if you spread your weight out over a bigger area (like the ladder on the ice), you should be safe.

Q1 Is your weight less when you use the ladder?

We say that the pressure is less when your weight is spread over a bigger area. A small **force** on a big **area** gives a small pressure. A big force on a small area gives a high pressure.

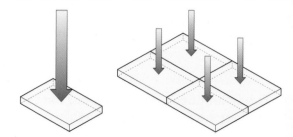

The same force spread over a bigger area gives lower pressure

Q2 When you stand upright on the ice, what is the 'small area' your weight is pushing on?

Pressure at work

By thinking about pressure, you can understand things from both the natural world and the technological world.

For example, a camel has big feet, with splayed-out toes. This is useful if it is walking on soft desert sand. Its weight is spread over a large area, so the pressure on the sand is less and the camel is less likely to sink in.

At some time in your life, you must have had an injection. (Perhaps you have had acupuncture.) Doctors use needles which are very thin and pointed. This means that the force pressing on your skin is concentrated on a tiny area. The pressure is high, and the needle pushes easily through your skin.

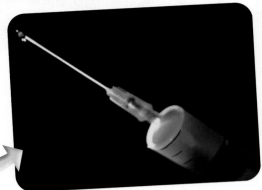

A sharply-pointed needle looks alarming, but it requires a smaller force to puncture your skin than a fatter needle

Snowshoes and shark's teeth

● Draw up a table like the one shown. Fill the four boxes with examples from the natural and technological worlds.

Here are some examples – but where do they belong in the table?

**snowshoes   pins and needles
ducks' feet   bee stings   skis
ice skates   sharks' teeth**

Be prepared to share your ideas with the rest of the class.

Natural world: force concentrated on small area	Technological world: force concentrated on small area
Natural world: force spread over large area	**Technological world: force spread over large area**

SUMMARY QUESTIONS

1 ☆ Copy the following sentence *twice* to give two different sentences about pressure:

A *big/small* force pressing on a *big/small* area gives a *high/low* pressure.

2 ☆ An ostrich can run as fast as a horse, up to 60 km/h. Its feet are wider than a horse's feet. What does this tell you about the places where ostriches live?

3 ☆☆ Explain why knives work best when they are sharp.

4 ☆☆ Look at a computer keyboard. Two of the keys (F and J, or D and K) have small raised dots sticking up from them. Why are they there? Use the idea of pressure to explain how they work.

An ostrich on the run

5 ☆☆ Draw pictures to show how you would position yourself to make the greatest pressure on the floor, and the least pressure. Explain your answers.

Key words

area
force
pressure

Holes in the floor

Some public buildings with high-quality wooden floors display notices saying 'No Stiletto Heels'. Pointed heels could press into the floor and damage it.

Each stiletto heel has a small area – about 1 square centimetre ($1\,cm^2$). As someone walks across the floor, their weight may be pressing down on just one heel. Their weight might be 800 N, and 800 N pressing on $1\,cm^2$ results in a high pressure.

The same buildings don't say 'No Elephants'. An elephant is much heavier than a person, but their feet are much bigger than stiletto heels. The area of an elephant's foot is about $1000\,cm^2$. But watch out for elephants wearing stiletto heels!

Q1 Find out another meaning for the word 'stiletto'.

Calculating pressure

To work out the **pressure** caused by a force, you need to know two quantities:

- the size of the **force** (in N)
- the **area** it is pressing on (in cm^2 or m^2).

Here's the **equation** to work out the pressure:

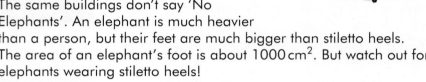

force

area

$$\text{pressure} = \frac{\text{force}}{\text{area}}$$

And here's how to work out the pressure of a person weighing 800 N standing on a $1\,cm^2$ stiletto heel:

$$\text{pressure} = \frac{\text{force}}{\text{area}} = \frac{800\ N}{1\ cm^2} = 800\,N/cm^2$$

We say that the pressure is 800 newtons per square centimetre.

Q2 What is the pressure of a 500 N force pressing on an area of $1\,cm^2$?

Body pressure

- If you stand on one foot on a small block of wood, what pressure do you cause on the floor? Decide what measurements you would need to make, and how to make them.

  !SAFETY! Take care that you cannot slip or fall from the block. Your teacher must check your plan for safety before you carry it out.

- What pressure is needed to push a drawing pin into a pinboard? Design an experiment to find out.

Pressure in liquids and gases

Blow up a balloon. You have to press hard on the air to push it into the balloon. When the balloon is blown up, you know that the air inside is under pressure – just pop it with a pin.

Does all that blowing make you feel faint? Have a lie-down and you'll feel better. Your heart has to pump blood all round your body, and it is harder to push the blood up to your head than down to your feet.

Q3 Why is it easier for your heart to pump blood to your head if you are lying down?

The air inside a balloon presses outwards in all directions so that the balloon is almost spherical. In the same way, the blood in your body pushes outwards in all directions. If you cut a major artery, the result can be both dramatic and dangerous. Try not to spring a leak!

Particles and pressure

Liquids and gases press outwards in all directions, and we can explain why if we think of the **particles** they are made of. In a liquid or gas, the particles can move about. In the air around you, they are moving at over 400 m/s – that's fast!

Think about the particles of air in a balloon. As they move, they bump into the inside surface of the balloon. Each little bump gives a little push, and billions and trillions of pushes each second on every square centimetre add up to the pressure of the air on the balloon.

In the same way, the air presses on you. You don't feel the individual particles as they collide with you, but the total effect is large.

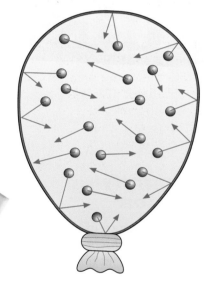

SUMMARY QUESTIONS

1. ☆ What quantities do you need to know in order to calculate pressure? Choose *two* from:
   area   force   newtons   speed

2. ☆ What are the units of pressure?
   N   m/s   cm^2 N/cm^2

3. ☆☆ Calculate the pressure when a force of 100 N presses on an area of 5 cm^2.

4. ☆☆ Which gives the greater pressure, a force of 400 N pressing on 20 cm^2, or a force of 1000 N pressing on 40 cm^2?

5. ☆☆☆ Use the idea of particles to explain why the air presses with a strong force on a glass windowpane. Why doesn't the window get pushed in by the air pressure?

Key words
area
equation
force
particles
pressure

Hydraulics

9L3

Big diggers

Many big digging and lifting machines (such as JCBs) work using **hydraulics**. Look for the shiny steel pistons, which move the different parts up and down.

How does this work? A liquid (oil) is pumped into a chamber, and this pushes a piston to operate the machine. Liquids are useful for this, because they can transmit pressure. The pump presses on the oil, and the oil presses on the piston. A hydraulic system can easily make forces go round corners.

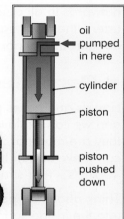

oil pumped in here

cylinder

piston

piston pushed down

Magnifying forces

Look at the picture of the model system. A small force pressing downwards can lift a much bigger weight. How does this work?

The small force presses on the liquid and increases its pressure. The pressure is the same everywhere in the liquid. It presses upwards on the bigger piston. Because the bigger piston has a bigger area, the force on it is greater.

This might seem like a cheat – perhaps you expected the force on the bigger piston to be smaller. Are we getting something for nothing? The thing to notice is that the small force must move down a long distance to lift the heavy weight a short distance.

Compressing materials

- In unit 7G, you may have tried to **compress** syringes containing air, water and wood. Try this again now. Use the particle model of matter to explain why air can be compressed but water cannot.

Q1 Why is it important for a hydraulic system to use a material which cannot be compressed?

- Your teacher will show you a model pneumatic system, like the one in the picture. What load can be lifted when a force of 10 N presses down on the smaller piston?

!SAFETY! Wet floors are slippery and dangerous. Mop up spilt water immediately.

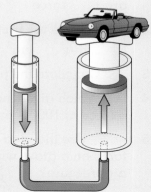

Pressing downwards on the smaller piston makes the bigger piston move upwards

● Getting higher

If you have ever climbed Mount Everest, or even a smaller mountain, you may have noticed your ears popping as you go upwards. You can experience the same thing in an aircraft as it goes up and down. What's happening?

The air gets thinner as you go upwards. (That's why many mountaineers take their own supplies of oxygen.) Thinner air means that the air is less dense, so its pressure is lower.

As you come down a mountain, the air pressure is increasing. It pushes into your ears, and makes them pop. On the way up, it's the air *inside* your ears that is at a higher pressure, and it pushes outwards – pop!

Q2 Use the particle model to explain why the pressure of air is less if its density is less.

● Atmospheric pressure

Air pressure is also known as **atmospheric pressure**. It's usually about $10\,\text{N/cm}^2$, which is the same as $100\,000\,\text{N/m}^2$ (newtons per square metre). This is also written as $100\,000\,\text{Pa}$ (**Pa** stands for **pascals**).

The air in a car's **pneumatic** tyre is compressed to about three times atmospheric pressure. Your ride would be a lot less comfortable if you didn't have four cushions of compressed air to ride on!

LINK UP TO TECHNOLOGY

In Design and Technology, you may have had the chance to make models or toys which work hydraulically or pneumatically.

AMAZING SCIENCE!

The pressure of the air around you results in a force of about $200\,000\,\text{N}$ on your body! Fortunately, the fluid inside your cells presses outwards with an equal force, to cancel out the effects. Otherwise, the air pressure would crush you!

SUMMARY QUESTIONS

1 ☆ Which of these is *not* a unit of pressure?
cm^2 N/m^2 Pa N/cm^2

2 ☆☆ Foam rubber appears to be a solid material, but it is easily compressed. Why is this?

3 ☆☆ The picture shows a tall container of water, with small holes in its sides. What pattern can you see in the jets of water? Use what you have learned about pressure to explain the pattern.

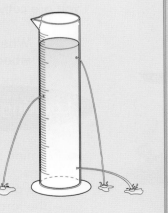

4 ☆☆ The word 'hydraulics' starts with hydra-, from you the Greek word for water. What other words do know that start with hydra- or hydro-? And what do they have to do with water?

5 ☆☆☆ Pneumatic machines are like hydraulic machines, but they work with compressed air instead of oil. Find out some examples of pneumatic machines.

Key words

atmospheric pressure

compress
hydraulic
pascal (Pa)
pneumatic

Levers everywhere

9L4

LEARN ABOUT

- levers, pivots and forces
- levers in your body

● Lifting the lid on levers

What is the easiest way to lift the lid of a tin of paint? The lid fits tightly (so that air cannot get in), so it can be very difficult to get the lid off. Use a screwdriver. Put the end of the screwdriver under the edge of the lid, and lever it upwards. Hey presto! It's off.

You are using the screwdriver as a **lever**. People have used levers for thousands of years – for example, the ancient Egyptians used levers to help in lifting some of the stones for the pyramids. A lever allows you to move something that, unaided, would require a bigger force.

Q1 A cyclist may have a set of tyre levers. What job is made easier by using tyre levers?

● Finding the pivot

How does the screwdriver-paint-tin-lid lever work? The diagram shows two forces:

- the force you exert, pushing down on the handle of the screwdriver
- the force exerted by the lid on the tip of the screwdriver, which the screwdriver has to overcome.

This wouldn't work if there wasn't something else: the rim of the paint tin. The lever touches the rim, and this point is the **pivot** of the lever. As you push down on one end, the other end moves up; the pivot is the point which doesn't move.

A wheelbarrow acts like a lever. You lift the handles, and the heavy load in the barrow is raised off the ground.

A pair of scissors is two levers in one. As you squeeze the handles together, the blades exert a force on the paper you are cutting.

Q2 Where is the pivot of a wheelbarrow-lever?

Surely there must be an easier way!

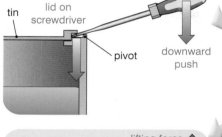

force of lid on screwdriver

tin

pivot

downward push

lifting force

weight

Looking at levers

- Examine some examples of levers. In each case, look for three things:
  - the pivot
  - the force that you apply when using the lever
  - the force that you are trying to overcome by using the lever.

LINK UP TO BIOLOGY

There's more about muscles in unit 9B.

Levers in your body

A lever is a tool or simple machine, a clever human invention. But there are plenty of natural levers, too. Some are inside your body.

Pick up a weight in your hand. Lift it up towards your shoulder. Your arm is acting like a lever, with your elbow as the pivot. Your **muscles** provide the force needed to lift the weight.

If you look at your upper arm, you will see your biceps muscle bulging impressively as it **contracts** to lift the weight. (The word 'muscle' means 'little mouse' because it looks as though a mouse is running up your arm, under the skin, when you contract your biceps.) The triceps muscle at the back of your upper arm pulls the opposite way, allowing you to lower the weight gently.

Your legs have muscles and joints, too. Your hip, knee and ankle are all joints, controlled by muscles. The big muscles at the back of your thigh (the hamstrings) help to straighten your leg when you stand upright. The smaller quadriceps muscle, at the front of the thigh, pulls in the opposite direction to bend your leg when you run, walk or sit.

Muscles can only provide pulling forces. They do this by contracting. When they **relax**, they simply stop exerting a force. That's why many of our muscles come in pairs, one pulling in one direction and the other pulling in the opposite direction. A pair of muscles like this is called an **antagonistic pair**. (If you're 'antagonistic' to someone, you're against them in some way.)

Q3 Name the two muscles of the antagonistic pair in your upper arm, and the two of the pair in your thigh.

I'm stronger than I thought!

200kg

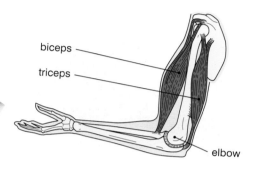

biceps
triceps
elbow

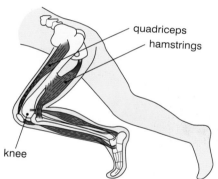

quadriceps
hamstrings
knee

SUMMARY QUESTIONS

1 ☆ What name is given to the point about which a lever turns?

2 ☆ Copy this sentence, choosing the correct word from each pair:
Muscles cannot *push/pull*; they can only *push/pull*.

3 ☆☆ Draw a diagram to show how an ancient (or modern) Egyptian could use a lever to lift a large block of stone. What would they use for the pivot? Add force arrows to your diagram. Which force is greater, the weight of the block or the push of the Egyptian?

4 ☆☆☆ Some hospital patients are given exercises by a physiotherapist to help build up their muscles after they have been in bed for a while. In one exercise, the patient puts a weight on their foot. If they then lift and lower the weight by wiggling their ankle, which muscles are being exercised? And if they lift the whole of their lower leg, with their knee as the pivot, which muscles are being exercised?

Key words

antagonistic pair
contract
lever
muscle
pivot
relax

LEARN ABOUT
- why levers are useful
- balancing a see-saw

● Lifting a load

Why do we use levers? They allow us to do things which we might be too weak to do without a lever. For example, you would find it hard to lift a paving slab, but it's much easier if you use a lever.

The picture shows how this works. You can see two things:

- Your **effort** force pushing downwards is smaller than the **load** you are trying to lift upwards.
- The effort is further from the pivot; the load is closer to the pivot.

That's why levers are so useful. They can allow us to use a smaller effort to move a bigger load. But this only works if our force is further from the pivot.

Q1 Check this idea by thinking about a wheelbarrow. Which is closer to the pivot, your lifting force or the weight of the load in the barrow? Which requires less force, lifting the load by hand, or lifting it in the wheelbarrow?

● Mighty muscles

Your hand and arm are a set of levers, operated by several pairs of antagonistic muscles. Your muscles may be stronger than you think.

What's the biggest load you can lift, using just your lower arm?

Q2 Do you recall how to find the weight of an object, if we know its mass? There's a clue in the picture. What is the weight of an object of mass 2 kg?

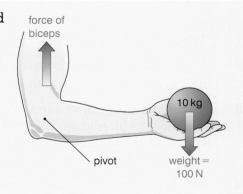

Scientists at Oxford University are studying the New Caledonian crow. This bird has taught itself to make levers and hooks from twigs. It uses them to extract insects from awkward cracks.

Suppose you can lift a load of 100 N. From the diagram, you can see that the force of your biceps muscle, pulling upwards, is much closer to the pivot than the load you are lifting. This means that your muscle force must be much greater than the 100 N weight. Your biceps has to provide hundreds of newtons of force!

See-saw balancing

If you are still young at heart, a see-saw is a fun way of using a lever. A single adult can balance two small children. Alternatively, a small person can balance a large one, if they sit further from the pivot.

Q3 Sketch a see-saw to show how a small child can balance a large adult.

A model see-saw

Use a ruler and a pivot to model a see-saw. Use a 500 g or 1 kg mass to represent an adult, and smaller masses to represent children.

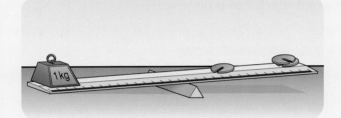

- Demonstrate different ways in which the see-saw can be balanced.
  a) How could you use a see-saw like this to find out if one child is heavier than the other, or if they have the same weight?
  b) How could you find out the weight of one child, if you know the weight of another? (Try to think up more than one way.)

!SAFETY! Keep fingers and feet well clear of falling weights. Use boxes to catch weights that fall, or fasten weights securely to the ruler.

Turning effect

A force makes a lever turn about the pivot. We say it has a **turning effect**. The bigger the force and the further away it is from the pivot, the greater its turning effect.

By moving a force so that it is twice as far from the pivot, you can double its turning effect.

SUMMARY QUESTIONS

1 ☆ What word means the force that you are trying to move with a lever? And what word means the force with which you push the lever?

burden   effort   load   weight

2 ☆☆ Copy these sentences, choosing the correct words from each pair:
  a) With a lever, we can use a force to lift a *smaller/larger* load. The load must be *closer to/further from* the pivot.
  b) The *bigger/smaller* the force, and the *greater/smaller* its distance from the pivot, the *greater/smaller* its turning effect.

3 ☆☆ Sketch a see-saw to show how a large adult can balance three small children.

4 ☆☆ Imagine that you had to lift a heavy brick in a wheelbarrow. Where in the barrow should you put the brick, to make it easiest to lift?

Key words

effort
load
turning effect

Moment of a force

A 3 N force, which acts 4 m from a pivot, has the same turning effect as a 6 N force acting 2 m from the pivot. That's because:

$$3\,N \times 4\,m = 6\,N \times 2\,m$$

We say that the **moment** of a force is the size of the force multiplied by its distance from the pivot.

Moment = force × distance from pivot

(The word 'moment' here means 'effect'; it's a bit like 'a momentous event', an event which has a big effect.)

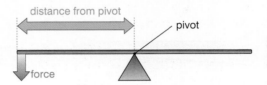

Calculating moments

If a force of 20 N presses down at a distance of 3 m from a pivot, its moment is:

moment = 20 N × 3 m = 60 N m

The unit of moment is the newton-metre (N m), because we are multiplying newtons by metres.

Q1 Calculate the moment of a 10 N force which acts 4 m from a pivot.

You can use this idea to see if a see-saw is **balanced**.

In the picture:

- the 30 N force is pressing down to the right of the pivot; it is trying to turn the see-saw clockwise
- the 20 N force is pressing down to the left of the pivot; it is trying to turn the see-saw anti-clockwise.

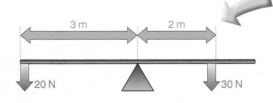

To work out if the see-saw is balanced, we calculate the moment of each force.

Moment of 30 N force = 30 N × 2 m = 60 N m
Moment of 20 N force = 20 N × 3 m = 60 N m

So the two forces have equal moments. They are trying to turn the see-saw in opposite directions, so their effects cancel out. The see-saw is balanced.

Testing the principle of moments

Set up a ruler on a pivot. Place a weight on either side, so that it balances. If you make suitable measurements, you can work out the moment of each force. They should be equal.

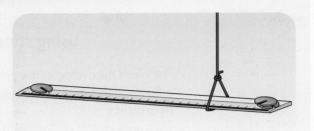

- Your task is to devise a **systematic** way of showing that the principle of moments is correct.
  Method 1: Move one of the weights in even steps, and find the balancing position of the other weight.
  Method 2: Change one of the weights, and find the weight which will balance it.
  For each method, draw up a table that will allow you to show whether your results support the principle of moments.

- Now extend your enquiry. Have a single weight on one side of the pivot, and two weights at different positions on the other. How can you work out the moment of two weights?

Balanced forces

If the turning effects of the forces on a lever cancel out, then the lever is balanced. In other words, the clockwise moments must equal the anti-clockwise moments. This is known as the **principle of moments**.

ICT **CHALLENGE**

Use a spreadsheet program to handle the results from your enquiry. It can do the calculations for you!

SUMMARY QUESTIONS

1 ☆ To calculate the moment of a force, which *two* quantities do we multiply together?

   distance   load   force   moment

2 ☆☆ Look at the diagram. Force *F* is pushing down on a beam.
   a) Is force *F* trying to turn the beam clockwise or anti-clockwise?
   b) Which arrow shows the correct distance used for calculating the moment of force *F*?

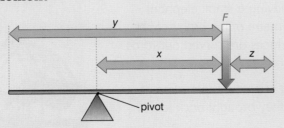

3 ☆☆ A force of 50 N pushes on a lever, 0.4 m from the pivot. What is the moment of the force?

4 ☆☆ Look at the diagram. The see-saw is balanced. What is the size of the force *X*?

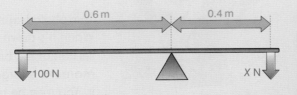

Key words

balanced
moment
principle of moments
systematic

Read all about it!

SCIENTIFIC PEOPLE

Auguste Piccard was a Swiss physicist. Switzerland is a country with no coastline, but that didn't stop Auguste thinking up ways to explore the oceans. In 1947, he invented a deep-sea diving submarine, which he called the bathyscaphe.

Submarines must have curved surfaces to withstand the great pressures they experience when they dive deep beneath the surface of the sea

Piccard's bathyscaphe went down to a depth of 4000 m, where the **pressure** of water is enormous – more than 4000 N/cm^2. A later version went to the bottom of the deepest known part of the ocean, the Mariana Trench, where the pressure is more than 10 000 N/cm^2 – 1000 times atmospheric pressure.

A pressure of that size is like having a small elephant standing on each square centimetre of the bathyscaphe, so all of the bathyscaphe's surfaces are curved outwards to withstand these enormous forces.

Piccard's vessels were used for scientific exploration of the deep oceans, from where they brought back lots of useful information. They were also used to look at submerged wrecks, including the US nuclear submarine *Thresher*.

Auguste Piccard also made lots of exciting balloon flights. He died in 1962, but he isn't forgotten: he lives on as Professor Calculus, the character he inspired in the *Tintin* books.

Auguste Piccard, aka Cuthbert Calculus

Using science today

The giant excavator in the photo is clearing up debris at a demolition site. It makes use of both **levers** and **hydraulics**.

You can see that the vertical arm (with the bucket on the end) is a lever. It is pivoted near the top. The top end of this arm is pushed and pulled by a hydraulic piston. It's a bit like a human arm, but it doesn't need a pair of antagonistic muscles to make it work. The hydraulic piston can move the arm in both directions.

This photograph shows a bridge that opens like a lever. When it's down, it acts as a roadway. Because the raised section of the bridge is so long and so heavy, its **moment** is large, and it takes a very strong force to lift it. You may be able to see a large counterweight, which helps to balance the weight of the bridge.

- A big force concentrated on a small area gives a high pressure.

- Pressure = force / area

- Pressure is measured in N/m^2 or pascals (Pa).

- The further a force acts from the pivot, the greater its turning effect.

- Moment of a force = force × distance from pivot

- Moment is measured N m.

- When an object is balanced, clockwise moments = anti-clockwise moments.

DANGER! AVOID THESE COMMON ERRORS

You need to remember how to calculate the pressure exerted by a force, and the moment of a force about a pivot.

Try to remember that the pressure caused by a force depends on the area it is spread over. If a force is spread over a large area, it gives a small pressure. That's why we calculate pressure = force/area. (Picture a force being spread over an area, and say to yourself, 'Pressure equals force over area.')

The moment of a force is bigger if the force gets bigger and if its distance from the pivot gets bigger. So moment = force × distance.

Key words

hydraulic
lever
moment
pressure

REVIEW QUESTIONS
Understanding and applying concepts

1 Some buildings have glass roofs. They may have a notice saying, "Use crawling boards". This means that anyone working on the roof must put a board on the roof and walk on the board, instead of walking on the roof itself. Explain how this helps to avoid damage to the roof.

2 We often use levers because a lever can increase the force we apply. Archimedes was an ancient Greek scientist. He said, "Give me a lever that is long enough, and I will move the Earth!" His idea was that even an enormously heavy object could be moved if you had a long enough lever.

 There is a problem with Archimedes' idea – what would he use as a pivot? Draw a picture of Archimedes trying to move the Earth with a long lever, and explain why he might find it impossible.

Ways with words

3 We use the word 'pressure' in science to mean the quantity force/area. We use the same word in everyday life, but its meaning is not quite the same.

 Write two sentences using the word pressure, one with its scientific meaning and the other with its everyday meaning.

 In what way is the scientific meaning similar to the everyday meaning?

Making more of maths

4 Here's a way to think about the moment of a force.

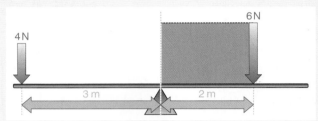

The diagram shows how to calculate the moment of a 6 N force, acting 2 m from the pivot; the force arrow is 6 units long, to represent 6 N. The rectangle has an area of $6 \times 2 = 2$ N m. This represents the moment of the force, because to calculate the moment of a force, you multiply the force by its distance from the pivot. The bigger the area of the rectangle, the greater the moment of the force.

 The 6 N force is balanced by a 4 N force, 3 m from the pivot.

a Copy the diagram carefully, making sure that you draw the distances and force arrows to scale.

b Draw the rectangle that represents the moment of the 4 N force.

c Show that it has the same area as the first rectangle.

5 Here's a way to think about pressure. The diagram shows a force of 20 N pressing down on an area of 5 m². We can divide the 20 N force arrow into 5 shorter arrows, each pressing down on 1 m².

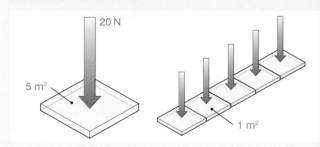

a What force does each of the shorter arrows represent?

b What is the *pressure* on the surface (what is the force acting on each square metre)?

c Draw similar diagrams to represent a force of 6 N pressing on an area of 4 m². What pressure does this give?

Thinking skills

6 Choose the odd-one-out from each list. In each case, explain your choice.

a	force	pressure	speed	moment
b	N	N/cm²	N/m²	Pa
c	weight	pressure	upthrust	drag
d	force	pressure	speed	density

Extension questions

7 Imagine climbing a high mountain. As you go higher, you are moving upwards through the atmosphere. The air gets colder and less dense.

a If the air is colder, what can you say about the speed of its molecules? How will this affect the pressure of the air? (Use the particle model.)

b If the air is less dense, how will this affect the pressure?

8 Use the principle of moments to work out the force that is needed to balance the beam shown in the diagram.

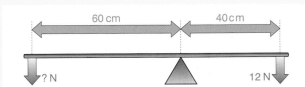

SAT-STYLE QUESTIONS

1 The table shows the weights of three of the Scientifica crew.

Molly	600 N
Benson	650 N
Reese	570 N

a Molly sat on one end of a see-saw. There was no-one on the other end. In which direction did Molly's end move? (1)

b Then Benson sat on the opposite end. He sat at the same distance from the pivot as Molly. How would the see-saw move? (1)

c Reese took Benson's place on the see-saw. She wanted the see-saw to be balanced. Who should sit closer to the pivot, Molly or Reese? (1)

2 Pete picked up a heavy metal block. It weighed 30 N. It covered 20 cm² of Pete's palm.

a What was the pressure of the weight on Pete's hand? Give the unit. (2)

b The diagram shows the muscles in Pete's arm.

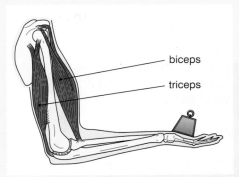

biceps

triceps

i) Which muscle must contract to lift the metal block? (1)

ii) What must the other muscle do? (1)

Key words

Unscramble these:

scumsle
claspa
serp user
tommen
rip pencil

9A Inheritance and selection

9A1 The quagga is an extinct horse-like animal that lived in Southern Africa until about 100 years ago. Its colouring was similar to a horse, but it had stripes like a zebra over its head and shoulders. Some people now think that it was not a separate species but a variation of zebra. Find out more about quaggas and how scientists are trying to solve the problem.

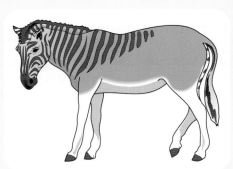

What a quagga looks like

9A3 Charles Darwin, who proposed ideas about how features are inherited, bred fancy pigeons – tumblers, fantails, and so on. Other people keep and breed fancy goldfish, such as veil tails, lion heads and comets. There are also fancy chickens, fancy rats and fancy guinea pigs. Find out and make a poster about fancy breeds of one animal.

A lion head goldfish bred for its unusual features. How is it different from a normal goldfish?

9A4 Gregor Mendel was a scientist who explored how features are inherited. He used peas as his experimental material and worked out the rules of inheritance. Find out about the work Mendel did and write a short biography suitable for use in a wall display.

9B Fit and healthy

9B1 Investigate how astronauts compensate for the lack of gravity to keep muscles and bones healthy. You could look at the NASA website: www.NASA.com.

An astronaut exercising

9B2 Find out about artificial joints such as those used to replace worn hip joints.

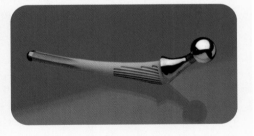

9B5 Find out how the law governs smoking, the sale and advertising of tobacco, and the portrayal of smoking on TV and films. What do you think about the government's proposal to ban smoking in public. How has this worked in other countries such as Ireland?

9B6 Write 'agony aunt' letters on problems linked with smoking, alcohol abuse and drug abuse. Swap letters with a friend and write replies.

Key words

Research these new words:
sickle-cell anaemia
genetically modified maize
ball-and-socket joint

9C Plants and photosynthesis

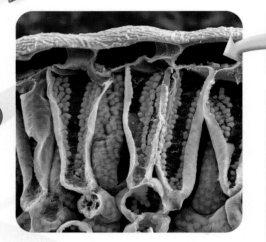

9C1 Make a collage or 3-D wall poster to show the structures inside a leaf.

9C2 Find out how changes in light intensity affect photosynthesis. Set up pondweed in a beaker with a lamp shining on it. The lamp should be as close to the beaker as possible.

- Measure the distance between the lamp and the pondweed.
- Measure the rate of photosynthesis by counting the number of oxygen bubbles given off in 5 minutes.
- Move the lamp 5 cm further away from the pondweed. This reduces the amount of light reaching the pondweed. After a few minutes measure the new bubble rate.
- Continue to move the lamp further away, 5 cm at a time. Each time measure the new rate of photosynthesis.
- Draw a graph of your results.

9C4 Desert plants need to make use of every scrap of soil moisture or rain water that is available. Some have very deep roots to reach water far down in bedrock. Others have roots that spread very widely to catch rain.
Find out more about how desert plants are adapted to obtain water and reduce water loss from their leaves.

9C5 Some species of animals and plants are facing extinction because they are losing the forest habitat in which they live. There are rescue and breeding programmes for orang-utans and lion-maned tamarin marmosets to try to conserve the species. Find out about what is being done to conserve these species or other species facing extinction through loss of forest habitat.

9D Plants for food

9D1 Rubber from the rubber tree revolutionised travel when it became available for making tyres. Rubber trees grew in the Amazonian jungle. Some young plant material was smuggled out to start rubber plantations in Malaya and other parts of the far East. Find out about the story of rubber and the products that are made from it.

A rubber tree being tapped for its latex

9D2 Different fertilisers are recommended for different plants. For example, fertilisers rich in nitrate salts encourage plants to make lots of lush leafy growth. Look at commercially available fertilisers to find out which ones are best for growing tomatoes, making flower bulbs flower again, and for growing vegetables. How does the mineral composition vary between them?

9D4 Find out more about the harmful effects pesticides can have on seals.

9D5 Crops grown in glasshouses (large greenhouses) are important commercially in Holland and Spain. Find out more about the types of crops grown in glasshouses.

Key words

Research these new words:
cellulose
DDT
aphids
compost
organic

9E Reactions of metals and their compounds

Copper has typical metallic properties

Sulphur is a typical non-metal

9E1 **a)** Compare and contrast the typical properties of metals and non-metals, using copper and sulphur as examples. Quote actual data on the two elements to illustrate your answer.
b) Write a paragraph about a metal that does not display the usual metallic properties.

9E2 Phosphoric(V) acid forms salts called phosphates.
a) Find out the formula of phosphoric(V) acid.
b) The 'combining power' of the phosphate group is 3. Use the table in Question 6 on page 82, to work out the chemical formula of:
  i) sodium phosphate(V)
  ii) aluminium phosphate(V)
  iii) magnesium phosphate(V).

9E3 Limestone and malachite are both rocks which contain metal carbonates.
Plan a safe investigation to see which rock is weathered more quickly by acid rain.

9E4 In 58.5 g of sodium chloride there are 6.02×10^{23} ions of sodium and the same number of chloride ions.
a) What is an 'ion'?
b) Using the information above, say why the formula of sodium chloride is NaCl.
c) A packet of salt contains 585 g of sodium chloride. How many sodium ions does it contain?
d) Find out why a sodium ion is positively charged and a chloride ion is negatively charged.

9E5 Ammonium nitrate is used as a fertiliser.
a) i) Find out the chemical formula of ammonium nitrate.
  ii) How many different elements does it contain?
  iii) Why is it used as a fertiliser?
b) Find out how ammonium nitrate is manufactured.

9F Patterns of reactivity

9F1 The hulls of ships have blocks of magnesium bolted to them. Explain this method of preventing rust forming on iron.

9F2 Iron reacts with steam. One of the products of the reaction is iron(III) oxide, Fe_2O_3.
a) Write a word equation for the reaction.
b) Write a balanced symbol equation for the reaction.
c) Design a set of apparatus that could be used to collect the gas that forms in this reaction.

9F3 Aluminium is protected from chemical attack by a layer of aluminium oxide on its surface. This protection can be further improved by a process called anodising.
Find out how you would anodise a piece of aluminium.

9F4 Make up your own model that can be used to explain the displacement of one metal by another more reactive metal.
You can present your answer as a cartoon strip or as a piece of explanatory text.

9F5 Francium is the metal at the bottom of Group 1 in the Periodic Table.
Write a short article on the metal for a teenage science magazine.

Key words

Research these new words:
barium
galvanise
verdigris
tungsten

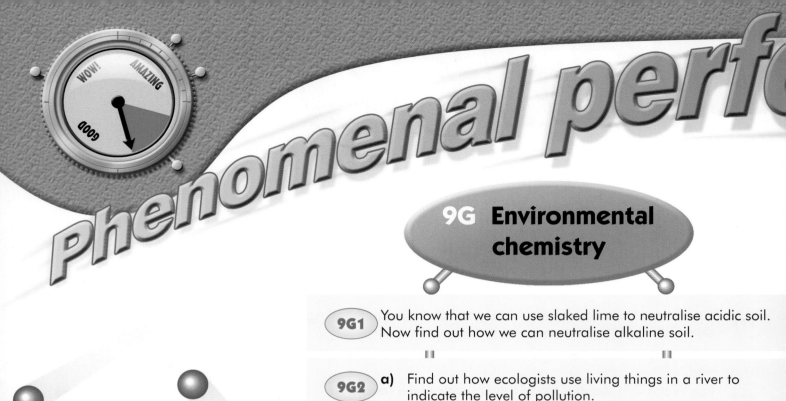

9G Environmental chemistry

9G1 You know that we can use slaked lime to neutralise acidic soil. Now find out how we can neutralise alkaline soil.

9G2
a) Find out how ecologists use living things in a river to indicate the level of pollution.
b) List five industrialised countries in order of their SO_2 emissions.
c) Find out how acid rain has affected the Black Forest in Germany.

9G3 Millions of tonnes of oil are spilt into our seas every year – sometimes deliberately.
Carry out a case study of a large oil spill. Include the measures taken to reduce the effects on the environment and wildlife.

9G4 Look at this graph produced from data taken from an ice core by Russian scientists in Antarctica.
Comment on the data collected and its significance.

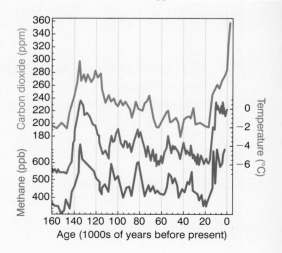

9H Using chemistry

9H1 Write a health and safety leaflet warning landlords about the dangers of fitting gas heaters without sufficient ventilation. You should explain how toxic gas can be produced when hydrocarbons burn, and the effects it has on the body.

9H2 Design a can for a drink that can be cooled using an endothermic reaction just before you open it.

9H3 Limestone is heated in a limekiln. The mass of lime you get from the kiln is always much less than the mass of limestone you put in. Explain this. Include a chemical equation in your answer.

9H4 When iron reacts with sulphur they combine in the ratio 7:4 by mass (Fe:S).
a) Draw a graph with the mass of iron you start with along the horizontal axis, from 0 g to 10 g of Fe, and plot the mass of iron sulphide formed up the vertical axis.
b) How many grams of iron sulphide can be formed from 2.8 g of iron?
c) The formula of iron sulphide is FeS. What can you say about the relative masses of iron and sulphur atoms?

Key words
Research these new words:
CFCs
gasohol
ozone
polymers
smart materials

91 Energy and electricity

911 At some theme parks, you can ride in a boat on a flume. You can shoot the rapids as the water flows downhill. Large electric pumps push the water back to the top of the ride, and electric motors haul the boats back to the top. Draw an illustration of a ride like this, and label it to show the energy changes that are involved.

912 Think of an idea for a computer game which would illustrate the ideas of voltage and energy in electric circuits. In your game, players must go round a circuit. How could you represent voltage, and how could you represent energy? Be ready to describe your game to others in the class.

913 The table shows the power ratings for some domestic appliances. Molly says this shows that things which heat up a lot use energy fastest. Do you agree with her?

Appliance	Power rating
heater	2 kW
microwave oven	350 W
computer	120 W
light bulbs	60 W, 100 W
electric stove (oven and 4 rings)	7 kW
hair dryer	1200 W

9J Gravity and space

9J1 The picture shows an artist's impression of the first human visitors to Mars.

Find out what plans there are for a manned trip to Mars.

● How long would the trip take?
● What dangers would the astronauts have to face?
● In what ways would a trip to Mars be different from a manned mission to the Moon?

9J3 When we look at the Moon and the Sun, they look almost exactly the same size as each other. If we went to the Moon, which would look bigger in the sky, the Earth or the Sun? Use a diagram to help you explain your answer.

(It may help you to think about eclipses to answer this question.)

9J5 Satellites can be very useful – they can help us with weather forecasts, broadcasting TV programmes, and prospecting for minerals. Some spacecraft – a small fraction of the total – are used for finding out more about the Solar System and the rest of the Universe.

This information is not very 'useful', and people might claim that these spacecraft are a waste of money.

A space probe visits Jupiter – is it worth the money?

a) What reasons do astronomers give to support their work?
b) Why should we fund this work? What do you think about this?

Key words

Research these new words:
electromotive force
gas turbine
exobiology
Sedna

9K Speeding up

9K2 Find out about how track events are timed at an athletics contest. How precise are the times and distances?

An electric cable connects the starting pistol to the electronic timer

9K3 Find out what it means to be 'weightless'. How can you tell that the astronauts in the picture are weightless? What can they do which we cannot do on Earth? Are they really free from gravity? What would you do if you could experience weightlessness?

9K5 Sketch a speed–time graph to show this story:
A car sets off from the traffic lights, and goes faster and faster. Then it travels at a steady speed, until the driver notices a blue flashing light. It's the police! The driver slows down and drives within the speed limit.

9L Pressure and moments

9L2 Pressure is measured in units of N/m². This unit is sometimes called a pascal (Pa).
Find out about Blaise Pascal, after whom the unit was named. (You may have studied 'Pascal's triangle' in maths.)

9L3 When you suck up a drink through a straw, your sucking reduces the pressure in your mouth. Atmospheric pressure pushed the drink up the straw.
Draw a diagram to show how this works (you may have to do some research), and explain it to another member of your class.

9L5 If you use a screwdriver to open a paint can, it is a lever with the pivot between the load and the effort. But not all levers have the pivot at the middle. Some have the load at the middle, and others have the effort (the force you apply to move the load) between the load and the pivot.
Find examples of levers of each of these two types.

9L6 Your jaw is a lever, pulled by muscles. Suggest how you could measure the force your jaw exerts when you bite something.
Find a diagram showing your jaw, skull and muscles. How could you estimate the force of the muscles?

Forceps are a pair of levers working together. Where's the pivot?

Key words

Research these new words:
accelerometer
odometer
dynamometer
equilibrium

Why do animals have funny shapes?

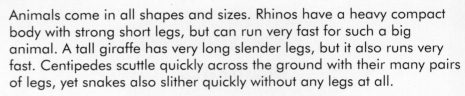

LEARN ABOUT
■ finding out more about animal adaptations

Animals come in all shapes and sizes. Rhinos have a heavy compact body with strong short legs, but can run very fast for such a big animal. A tall giraffe has very long slender legs, but it also runs very fast. Centipedes scuttle quickly across the ground with their many pairs of legs, yet snakes also slither quickly without any legs at all.

Each animal's shape is adapted perfectly for the environment it lives in. Scientists have to work out how an animal's shape is adapted for the life it leads.

The long and the short of it

Which legs are the strongest? Short like a rhino, long like a giraffe, wide like an elephant, or slender like a gazelle?

You will need to investigate this problem in stages because there are two factors (variables) that you can change. These two factors are 'length of leg' and 'thickness of leg'.

When you change one of these factors, it is important that you keep the other one the same during your experiment.

You could make model legs from many materials such as moulding clay, drinking straws, or modelling straws. You may need to use different materials for different parts of your activity.

- You will need to make model legs of different lengths. How can you do this? How will you keep the thickness the same?

- You will also need to make legs of different thicknesses. How can you do this? Remember to keep the length the same.

- Think of a way to measure the strength of your model legs.

- Test your sets of model legs.

- Present your data in the most suitable way.
  a) How did length affect the strength of your model legs? Did you find a pattern?
  b) How did thickness affect the strength of your model legs? Did you find a pattern?
  c) Can you compare your data from the two investigations?
     If you can – what can you say about how size of legs affects their strength?
     If you cannot – explain why can't you compare your data.

- Extend your thinking – Why do you think runners with longer legs can often run faster than runners with shorter legs?

Heat loss

It's hot on the African plains. Active mammals generate a lot of body heat as they move about. They have to transfer this heat to their surroundings or risk overheating. Lots of animals that live in this environment, for example elephants, have large ears. Scientists think that this helps them to keep cool. As blood passes through their large thin ears it loses heat to the air around.

- How could you find out if objects with a large surface area lose more heat than objects with a smaller surface?

- Use a temperature sensor to monitor the temperature inside your object.

Key words

adapt
heat loss
modelling
pattern

Who dunnit?

EXTRA LESSONS

LEARN ABOUT
- using chromatography
- identifying unknown substances

● Forensic science

The police rely on the help of forensic scientists to convict criminals. The scientists can analyse substances found at the scene of a crime. They also use their observational skills to match up fibres, fingerprints and plaster casts of footprints or tyre marks.

Spot the ink SAFETY

In this activity you can help to find out who forged a cheque.

A bank reported a suspicious cheque to the police. They have a suspect who could have tampered with the cheque. You have some of the black ink taken from the suspect's home and a sample from the cheque.

● Your task is to use chromatography to see if the suspect's ink matches the ink from the cheque.

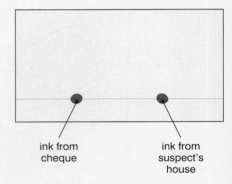

ink from   ink from
cheque   suspect's
                  house

● Analysing an unknown substance

We can use flame tests to identify some metals in compounds. Then we can use chemical tests to find out what else is in the compound.

To solve the problem in the next activity, you will need to know these tests.

Flame tests

Metal in compound	Colour of flame
potassium	lilac
sodium	yellow
copper	blue/green
calcium	brick red
barium	apple green

Chemical tests

Non-metal part of compound	Test and result
chloride	Dissolve in dilute nitric acid, then add silver nitrate solution → white precipitate
bromide	Dissolve in dilute nitric acid, then add silver nitrate solution → cream precipitate
iodide	Dissolve in dilute nitric acid, then add silver nitrate solution → yellow precipitate
sulphate	Dissolve in dilute nitric acid, then add barium nitrate solution → white precipitate

Which substance?

The police have found a suspicious white powder in someone's car. Your task is to use the tests above to identify the unknown powder.

● To carry out a flame test, you wet a clean nichrome wire and dip it into the powder to be tested. Then heat a small sample of powder in a transparent Bunsen flame.

● To carry out the chemical tests, you start with a small quantity of the powder to be tested in a test tube.

!SAFETY! Wash your hands after the tests.

a) What is the chemical name of the powder?
b) Was the powder anything illegal?
c) Write a word equation for the positive chemical test you carried out.

Key words

chromatography
flame test
forensic

Stretching rubber, stretching your mind

LEARN ABOUT
- stretching rubber
- the swing of a pendulum
- making careful measurements

Scientists always work with care, especially when they are making measurements. It's not like cooking; you can't say, 'This block weighs about a kilo, and its weight is nearly 10 N.' You might miss some interesting detail that could reveal something surprising and new. Here's an experiment where you have to work with great care to see what's going on.

Stretching with care

If you gently stretch a rubber band, it gets longer. Keep increasing the force with which you pull it, and eventually it becomes very difficult to stretch it any more. Now release the force and the band goes back to its original length – doesn't it?

- Hang a rubber band from a clamp. Put a weight hanger on it (to straighten it out).

- Measure its length.

- Add a weight to the hanger, and measure its length again. Record your results in a table.

- Add more weights, one at a time, and measure its length each time. Do this *very carefully*; don't let the band get any slacker as you add the weights, and don't overstretch it as you add weights.

- When you think the band is in danger of snapping, start removing the weights one by one. Record the length each time. Again, do this *very carefully*; don't let the band get slack as you remove a weight.

  !SAFETY! Wear eye protection in case the rubber band snaps. Use a box to catch falling weights, and keep feet and fingers well clear.

- Draw a graph to show your results (or use a spreadsheet to do this). Use different colours for points when the weight was increasing, and when it was decreasing. Do the points follow a nice straight line? What shape is your graph? Is there anything surprising about it?

People in the gym often stretch springy equipment to build up their muscles

● Galileo's clock idea

One day, late in the 16th century, Galileo was in church. Perhaps he was bored, or perhaps he just looked for scientific ideas wherever he went. Anyway, he noticed that one of the chandeliers was swinging gently to and fro. He looked at his wrist. He didn't have a watch there, because they hadn't been invented, but he did have his pulse. He counted his pulse, and he counted the swings of the chandelier. (That's pretty tricky!) He realised that they each had a regular rhythm.

Perhaps he could use his pulse as a 'timing machine'! Unfortunately, the idea was so exciting that it made his pulse speed up. OK, he thought, I'll use a swinging pendulum to keep regular time, just like the chandelier.

Galileo investigated pendulums, and eventually came up with a design for the first pendulum clock. By then, he was very old, but his son built the model shown in the picture.

Galileo's design for the first ever pendulum clock

Investigating a pendulum

- Set up a pendulum, using a length of string and a weight.

- Investigate the factors that affect the time it takes for a complete back-and-forth swing.

- Can you set up a pendulum that makes exactly 60 swings in one minute? Test your pendulum against others in the class.

Key words

experiment
investigate
measurement
record
spreadsheet

Investigating water

Water is essential to life on our planet. In Book 8, on pages 210 and 211, you saw a range of ways that scientists can investigate different types of problem. You can use some of these to investigate questions about water.

Generating questions

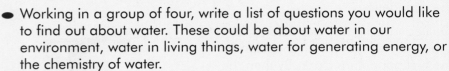

- Working in a group of four, write a list of questions you would like to find out about water. These could be about water in our environment, water in living things, water for generating energy, or the chemistry of water.
- Decide how you would set about answering each of your questions.
- After ten minutes, share your list with another group and discuss the methods you have chosen.

!SAFETY! Your teacher must check your plans before you carry out any practical work.

Why do elephants throw water over themselves?

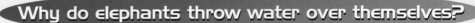

Elephants are very large mammals. They live in a hot environment in Africa and South East Asia. They enjoy visiting ponds, wading in and splashing water around with their trunks. They also lie down in mud and cover themselves.

- Where could you look to research elephant's habits and find out why they do this?

Biologists think elephants splash water over themselves to keep cool. Elephants lose heat energy when water evaporates from their skin.

- Test this idea by making a model elephant and wetting the surface. A round-bottomed flask of warm water makes a good model. You could cover it with a layer of fabric 'skin' to wet. You can use a thermometer in the flask to monitor the internal temperature.
  - Make a prediction about what you expect to happen.
  - What factors will you need to think about in your investigation?
  - What will be your control?
  - How much data should you collect?
  - How are you going to do your investigation safely?

!SAFETY! Your teacher must check your plans before you carry out any practical work.

- Carry out your investigation.
  Present your data in an appropriate graph.
  Compare your data with your prediction and comment on your results.
  a) Was your method good enough to tell you what you wanted to know? What could you change to make it better?
  b) Did you have enough data to draw a firm conclusion?

What affects the pH of rain water?

- Make a list of the factors that could affect the pH of rain water.
- Choose one to investigate.
  a) How do you think the factor chosen will affect the pH? Why?
  b) What problems would you face trying to collect enough data yourself to spot any patterns?
  c) What secondary sources of information can you use to gather evidence for your ideas?
- Make sure your teacher checks any practical plans you have made.
- Carry out your research and draw your conclusions.
  d) Evaluate the strength of your evidence and the conclusions you made.

Which contains more water, an orange or an apple?

Some questions seem easy to answer, but you may need careful experimental technique if you are going to be sure of the answer.

This is a simple enquiry, but you need to think carefully about how confident you are in your answer at the end of it.

- Cut up an apple and an orange. Find their masses.
- Put them on metal trays in a hot oven, and dry them out. Weigh them again.
- Which has lost a greater fraction of its mass?
- Now, think about the method you have used.
  a) Did the fruit lose all its water?
  b) Might it have lost anything other than water?
  c) Are all oranges the same, and all apples?

These questions will help you to evaluate the method you have used, so that you can decide whether or not your answer is valid.

Key words

conclusion
evaluate
evidence
secondary sources
factors
prediction
technique
valid

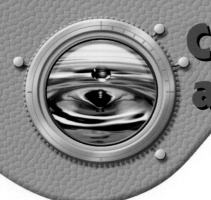

Coursework activities

What factors affect the time it takes for amylase to digest starch?

You can mix amylase enzyme with starch solution in a test tube. It will break down starch to glucose. You can test whether there is still starch in the mixture by adding a drop of mixture to a drop of iodine solution.

● You could try using starch solution at different temperatures and find out how long it takes amylase to break down the starch.
● You could try changing the pH of the starch solution.
● You could try changing the amount of starch.
● Make a prediction about what you expect to happen.
  – Can you use your scientific knowledge to explain why you think this will happen?
● You will have to think about making your method a fair test.
  – What other things will you need to keep the same?
  – What difference would it make to your results if you did not keep them the same?
  – What would be a suitable control experiment?
  – How many different, say, temperatures will you need to take?
  – How much data will you need to collect to be confident in your findings?
● How are you going to present your data.
● What pattern are you looking for?

Which mixture makes the loudest pop?

Calcium reacts with water to form a solution of calcium hydroxide and hydrogen gas. You can collect the hydrogen gas in a test tube.

● Your task is to vary the hydrogen/air mixture in the test tube to see which mixture gives the loudest pop with a lighted splint. You can do this by changing the amount of water you start with in your upturned test tube.
● How will you judge how loud each pop is?
● Make sure your teacher checks the plan before you start.

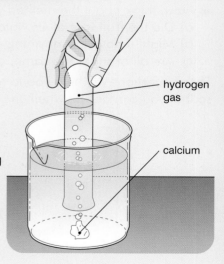

hydrogen gas

calcium

!SAFETY! Do not touch calcium metal or the solution formed in the reaction. Start with a fresh beaker of water for each test.

Which fuel gives out most energy?

You are given three spirit burners with a different alcohol in each one.

- Your task is to find out which of these fuels gives out most energy.
  - How will you make it a fair and safe test?
  - How will you measure how much energy is released when the fuels burn?
  - How will you measure how much fuel was used up in each test?
  - What apparatus will you need?

- Make sure your teacher checks the plan before you start.

!SAFETY! Never heat a thermometer directly with a flame.

What force is needed to pull a heavy object up a slope?

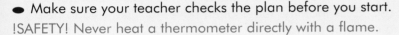

It's easier to push a heavy load up a slope, or to pull it up the slope using a rope, than to lift it straight up. 'Easier' means that you need a smaller force if you are using a ramp.

- Set up a sloping wooden plank or board as your ramp. Use a newtonmeter to pull an object up the ramp. Read the value for the force from the newtonmeter.

!SAFETY! Keep fingers and feet well clear of falling weights. Use boxes to catch weights that fall. Your teacher must check your plans before you carry out any practical work.

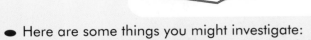

The steeper the slope, the harder it is to get to the top

- Here are some things you might investigate:
  - If you increase the weight of the load, what happens to the force you need?
  - How does the force depend on the steepness (angle) of the slope?
  - What is the effect of using different surfaces?

In each case, you will have to think about making your method a fair and safe test. It's often easiest to try out the experiment; then you will start to see some of the problems.

Key words

alcohol
amylase
control
data
factor
fair test
measure

Revision of Year 7 and Year 8 work

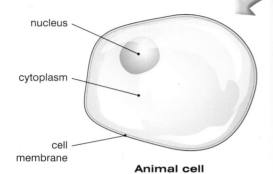

nucleus

cytoplasm

cell membrane

Animal cell

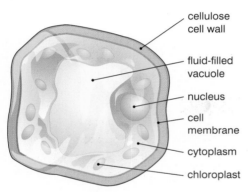

cellulose cell wall

fluid-filled vacuole

nucleus

cell membrane

cytoplasm

chloroplast

Plant cell

7A Cells

- Living things are made of cells. Cells can only be seen with a microscope. Cells contain cytoplasm and a nucleus surrounded by a cell membrane. Plant cells also have cell walls, chloroplasts for photosynthesis and a large vacuole.
- Cells are adapted for their function. For example, sperm cells have a tail for swimming so that they can deliver a package of genes to an egg cell. Cells that line tubes often have hair-like cilia to help move the contents along.
- Body organs work together in systems that carry out one of the life processes, such as obtaining nutrients, or responding to stimuli.
- New cells are made by cell division. A cell duplicates all its genetic information and divides into two. Bacteria and some plants can reproduce themselves using this process.

7B Reproduction

- Humans follow a typical growth pattern. Hormones control maturation into an adult and reproductive activity.
- Ovaries make egg cells and testes make sperm. The menstrual cycle produces eggs. During the first two weeks the uterus is prepared and the egg matures. In the second two weeks the egg is released and travels to the uterus. If it is not fertilised, it is discharged with the lining of the uterus.
- Fertilisation occurs when a sperm nucleus enters an egg in the oviduct. The embryo develops in the uterus. Nutrients and oxygen pass from the mother's blood through the placenta to a developing embryo, wastes pass in reverse. The placenta is a barrier to harmful things, such as bacteria. Chemicals from cigarette smoke, alcohol and some viruses pass from the mother's blood stream to the baby and cause harm.

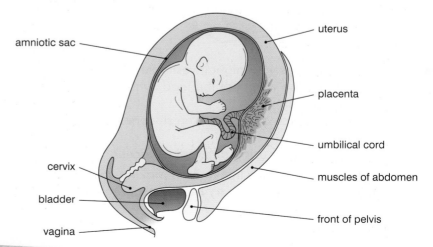

amniotic sac

cervix

bladder

vagina

uterus

placenta

umbilical cord

muscles of abdomen

front of pelvis

7C Environment and feeding relationships

This also covers 8D Ecological relationships.

- Environments vary in many ways. The key physical factors in an environment are temperature range, water availability, oxygen and light.
- Animals and plants are adapted to survive within their environment. Animals have adaptations that help them move through air or water, to find food, to be active at night or in unfavourable environments. Animals and plants are adapted to avoid being eaten. Herbivores are adapted for grazing on vegetation but carnivores are adapted for catching and killing prey.
- Animals and plants compete with each other for resources they need from their environment. This competition limits how many animals or plants can live in a habitat. The number of predators depends on how many prey there are for them to eat. The prey population is affected by how many predators there are.
- Animals and plants are part of food chains. Food chains start with plants. Plants are producers. They fix light energy in their biomass. Producers are eaten by consumers. The arrows show the way energy passes along a chain. A pyramid of numbers shows how many there are of each sort of plant and animal in a food chain.
- Animals eat different types of food and are involved in several food chains. Linked food chains form a food web. Anything that affects one organism in a food web will have an indirect effect on the others in the web.

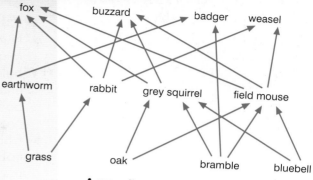

A woodland food web

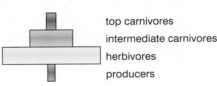

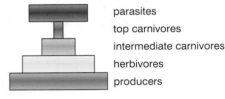

Pyramids of numbers

7D Variation and classification

- Individuals in a species are not identical. Some differences in their features are inherited, some are due to the environment. Inherited features are passed on. Inherited features are carried as genes on chromosomes in the nucleus of cells. They are passed on through sperm and eggs.
- Animals and plants are grouped together on the basis of their shared inherited features. There are five kingdoms – animals, plants, bacteria, fungi and single-celled organisms. Animals are separated into vertebrates, which have a backbone, and invertebrates, which do not. Plants are also divided into groups such as flowering plants and ferns.

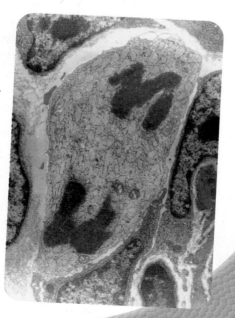

Key words

cell
food web
gene
organ
placenta
pyramid of numbers
vertebrate

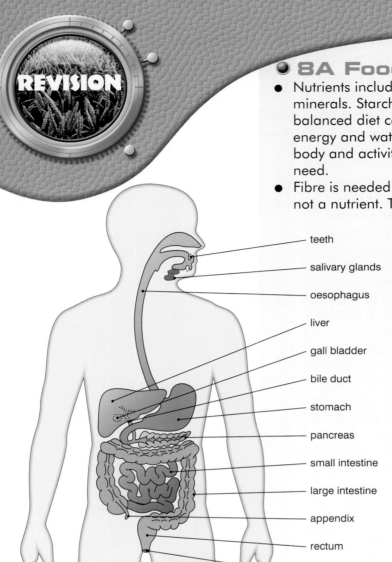

8A Food and digestion

- Nutrients include fats, proteins, carbohydrate, vitamins and minerals. Starch and sugar are two types of carbohydrate. A balanced diet contains nutrients in the correct proportions, enough energy and water. We need energy for growth, maintaining the body and activities. The more active we are, the more energy we need.
- Fibre is needed to keep food moving along the intestines, but it is not a nutrient. Too little fibre causes constipation.
- We need proteins for repair and growth. Carbohydrates are our main energy source. We need fat as a long-term energy store, to make new cells and for heat insulation. Vitamins and minerals are needed in small quantities each day. Calcium is used for bones, and iron is necessary for red blood cells.
- Food is digested into small soluble molecules that can be absorbed into the blood. Useful nutrients are absorbed from the small intestine. They are carried round the body by the blood.
- Enzymes carry out digestion. A different enzyme digests each type of food. Enzymes lose their activity if they become too hot. They also need the correct pH.
- Carbohydrates are digested into glucose. Protein is digested into amino acids.

teeth

salivary glands

oesophagus

liver

gall bladder

bile duct

stomach

pancreas

small intestine

large intestine

appendix

rectum

anus

8B Respiration

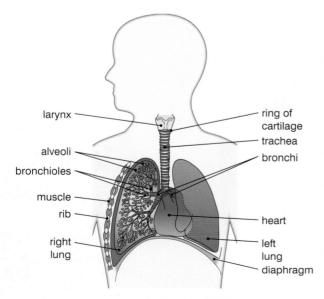

- All living things, including plants and bacteria, respire. Respiration is the process that releases energy from glucose. It takes place in every cell and is vital for life.
- The respiration process can be written as a word equation:

**glucose + oxygen → carbon + water   (energy is
                                   dioxide   released)**

- Carbon dioxide passes into the blood. It is taken to the lungs to be released.
- Breathing is the mechanism we use to get air into our lungs. In the lungs we absorb oxygen and release carbon dioxide. This exchange of gases takes place in alveoli, which are tiny air sacs.
- Oxygen passes into the blood. It is carried round the body by red blood cells. The heart pumps blood round the body through arteries, veins and capillaries.

larynx

ring of cartilage

trachea

alveoli

bronchi

bronchioles

muscle

rib

heart

right lung

left lung

diaphragm

8C Microbes and disease

- Bacteria, viruses and fungi are micro-organisms. They are generally too small to see without a microscope
- Bacteria and fungi make useful products, such as yoghurt, bread, cheese, antibiotics and washing powder enzymes. In a laboratory they are grown on nutrient agar jelly. Bacteria form colonies. Antibiotics, disinfectants and antiseptics kill micro-organisms or stop them growing.
- Some micro-organisms cause disease when they enter the body and multiply. Infectious micro-organisms can spread from one person to another through food, water, air and via wounds. We have defences against infections.
- White blood cells capture bacteria and digest them. Other white cells make antibodies against bacteria and viruses.
- Vaccination mimics this process. A vaccine contains harmless material made from microbes that provokes the body's defences.

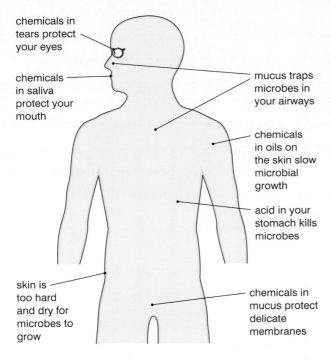

chemicals in tears protect your eyes

chemicals in saliva protect your mouth

mucus traps microbes in your airways

chemicals in oils on the skin slow microbial growth

acid in your stomach kills microbes

skin is too hard and dry for microbes to grow

chemicals in mucus protect delicate membranes

Protecting your body

8D Ecological Relationships

See 7C Environment and feeding relationships on page 217.

Key words

alveolus
antibody
enzyme
glucose
micro-organism
nutrient
respiration

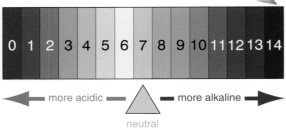

0 1 2 3 4 5 6 7 8 9 10 11 12 13 14

◄— more acidic —   — more alkaline —►

neutral

The pH scale

7E Acids and alkalis

- There are many useful **acids** and **alkalis**.
- Weak acids are often found in foods.
- You can make a corrosive acid or alkali safer by making it more dilute.
- **Indicators** are dyes that are different colours in acid and alkali. **Universal indicator** is a mixture of dyes. It has a range of colours. A liquid with a pH of 7 is neutral (neither acidic nor alkaline).
- When acids react with alkalis they **neutralise** each other.
- There are many useful neutralisation reactions, including indigestion remedies to get rid of excess acid in your stomach.

7F Simple chemical reactions

- In a chemical reaction, we get new substances formed. We can represent these using word equations, in which:

reactants → products

- Examples of general word equations include:

acid + a metal → a salt + hydrogen

Many (but not all) metals react with acid, giving off hydrogen gas. The hydrogen 'pops' when tested with a lighted splint.

acid + a carbonate → a salt + water + carbon dioxide

The carbon dioxide turns lime water milky.

metal + oxygen → metal oxide

When substances burn in air, they react with the oxygen present to form oxides.

- Fuels containing carbon and hydrogen burn in plenty of air as shown below:

fuel + oxygen → carbon dioxide + water

We can test the water formed by seeing if white anhydrous copper sulphate turns blue (or blue cobalt chloride paper turns pale pink). There are also other products formed if fuels burn in a limited supply of oxygen (see unit 9H, page 117).

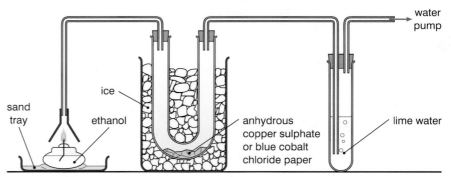

7G The particle model

- We can explain the properties of solids, liquids and gases using the **particle theory**.
- In a **solid** the particles are lined up next to each other. They are fixed in position but do vibrate.
- In a **liquid** the particles are still very close together, but can slip and slide over each other.
- In a **gas** the particles whiz around and there is lots of space within the gas. As they collide with the walls of their container, they produce a force that causes **gas pressure**.

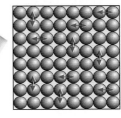

solid

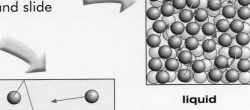

liquid

gas

- **Diffusion** is when substances mix without us stirring them up. This happens automatically in liquids and gases because their particles are free to move around.

7H Solutions

- When solids dissolve in a liquid their particles become intermingled. The solid is called the **solute**, the liquid is the **solvent** and the resulting mixture is a **solution**.
- We can collect the solvent (liquid) from the solution by **distillation**.

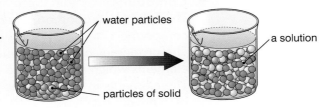

water particles

a solution

particles of solid

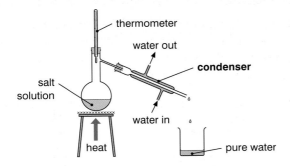

thermometer

water out

condenser

salt solution

water in

heat

pure water

- If a solvent contains two or more solutes, we can separate the solutes by **chromatography**.
- A solution that will not dissolve any more solid is called a **saturated** solution.
  The **solubility** of a substance varies with temperature.

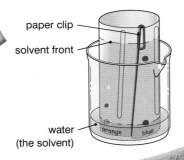

paper clip

solvent front

water (the solvent)

orange   blue

Key words

chromatography
distillation
neutralise
particles
product
reactant
solubility

hydrogen

oxygen

sulphur

These are all molecules of elements

● 8E Elements and atoms

- **Elements** are substances that cannot be broken down into any simpler substances. The smallest part of an element, that we can still recognise as the element, is an **atom**. Elements are made up of only one type of atom.
- When atoms bond together they form **molecules**.
- If the atoms in a molecule are not all the same type, then we have a **compound**.

These are all molecules of compounds

- Each chemical element has a **symbol** (for example, hydrogen's is H, helium's is He).
- We can show the number and type of each atom in a molecule by its chemical **formula** (for example, carbon dioxide is CO_2).
- The elements have been sorted out into a useful arrangement called the **Periodic Table**. This shows us patterns in the properties of elements.

● 8F Compounds and mixtures

- **Compounds** contain more than one type of atom bonded together. The ratio (or proportion) of each element is fixed for any particular compound.
- The properties of a compound are nothing like those of the elements which make up the compound.
- The elements in a compound can only be separated by some kind of chemical reaction.
- The amount of each substance in a mixture can vary.
- Because no new substances have been formed, it is usually possible to separate out the different substances in a mixture. (Methods such as filtration, evaporation, distillation and chromatography can be used.)

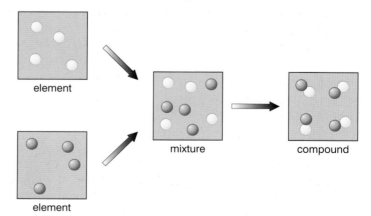

element

element

mixture

compound

- We can use melting points and boiling points to identify pure substances from values given in data books or databases. However, the melting point and boiling point of a mixture will vary depending on its composition.

● 8G Rocks and weathering

- Rocks are broken down by **weathering**.
- **Chemical weathering** happens when the rock is attacked by weakly acidic rain water (or by oxygen).
- Rocks are also broken down by **physical weathering**.

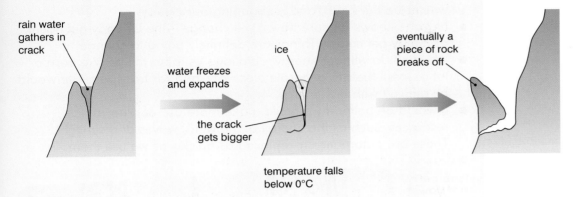

rain water gathers in crack

water freezes and expands

ice

the crack gets bigger

temperature falls below 0°C

eventually a piece of rock breaks off

- Changes in temperature also put rocks under great stress. The minerals in the mixture that make up the rock will each expand and contract at different rates. Again this cracks the rock and breaks bits off.
- The weathered rock is then **transported** to another place, mainly by moving water. On its journey the rock fragment will get smaller, smoother and rounder the further it is carried along. It will also wear away rock that it passes over. This is called **erosion**.
- Eventually, the rock fragment is **deposited** as a **sediment** (sedimentation).
  These sediments build up in layers. The sediments can be made from the remains of animals and plants as well as bits of rock. Other layers are formed when dissolved compounds come out of solution as solids as the water evaporates. These are called **evaporites**.

● 8H The rock cycle

- **Sedimentary rocks** are formed when layers of sediment are buried by more recent deposits. Under the pressure (compaction) and with the help of mineral 'cements' (left behind when water evaporates from between the grains of sediment), rocks are formed.
- **Metamorphic rocks** are formed when existing rock is put under increased pressure and/or temperature (without melting). The existing rock has its structure (and possibly its minerals) changed. Bands of minerals are visible if the metamorphic rock is formed under pressure.
- **Igneous rocks** are formed when molten rock solidifies. Slow cooling, inside the Earth's crust, produces rock with large crystals, such as granite. Faster cooling, at or near the Earth's surface, produces rock with small crystals, such as basalt.
- The processes of rock formation happen in a natural cycle that we can summarise in the **rock cycle** (see Book 8, page 135).

Key words

atom
compound
element
igneous
metamorphic
molecule
sedimentary

7I Energy

- Without knowing it, people have been damaging the environment by using energy resources at a great rate. When we burn fossil fuels (coal, oil and gas), they release their stores of energy. But at the same time, carbon dioxide is released into the atmosphere. That warms up the Earth, and is changing our climate.
- No-one knows for sure how it will change – the UK may get hotter, or it may get colder. Things are definitely going to change.
- We can't do without energy – it allows us to do things. We burn a lot of fossil fuels to generate electricity, and for transport. Life would be difficult with less energy.
- It would be better if we could make more use of renewable resources, such as the energy of the wind, waves and sunlight. These are automatically replaced as quickly as we use them.

These pylons carry electricity from a power station. Why would it be better if we made more use of the energy that comes to us from the Sun?

7J Electrical circuits

- It's electric current that flows around a circuit, not 'electricity'. You need a complete circuit of metal from the positive (+) end of the battery all the way round to the negative (−) end.
- We use ammeters to measure current (in amps, A).
- In a series circuit, the components are all connected end-to-end, and the current flows through them one after another. The components have resistance, which makes it difficult for the current to flow.
- If two components are connected in parallel (side-by-side), the current has to divide up, so that some flows through one and the rest through the other.
- A cell or battery provides the voltage (or 'push') needed to make the current flow. You can use a voltmeter to measure the voltage (in volts, V).

How must the current change to make this bulb brighter? What could you change in the circuit to do this?

7K Forces and their effects

- We can measure forces using a newtonmeter (in newtons, N).
- Weight is caused by the Earth's gravity, pulling us towards the centre of the Earth.
- If there wasn't another force to balance our weight, we'd fall through the floor or sink in the sea. The upward push of the floor, and the upthrust of the water, help to keep us in place.
- When things move, the force of friction tries to slow them down. If there were no friction to slow it down, a moving object would go on moving for ever. A streamlined shape can help to reduce friction.
- Your mass (in kg) tells you how much matter you are made of. The greater your mass, the greater your weight, because gravity pulls on your mass. But if you go somewhere where gravity is weaker, such as the Moon, your weight will be less, even though your mass stays the same.

Four forces are acting on this boat: one pulling down, one pushing up, one making it go faster and one slowing it down. Can you name them?

7L The solar system – and beyond

- The Sun is a luminous object – it is a source of light. The Earth and the other planets are non-luminous, but we can see them because they reflect sunlight.
- The planets travel in orbits around the Sun. These orbits are almost perfect circles.
- The Moon orbits the Earth – it's the Earth's satellite.
- If the Moon's orbit takes it in front of the Sun, the Sun's light is blocked off and we see an eclipse of the Sun (a solar eclipse). We are in the Moon's shadow.
- A lunar eclipse happens when the Moon's orbit takes it into the Earth's shadow.

There are nine planets in the Solar System – can you name them in order, starting with Mercury?

Key words

eclipse
energy
gravity
luminous
parallel
series

REVISION

8I Heating, cooling

- We use thermometers to measure temperatures (in °C) – that tells us how hot something is.
- Heat energy is energy moving from hotter places to colder places. There are three ways it can travel: conduction, convection and radiation. Because we know how heat travels, we can insulate houses to reduce the waste of energy.
- We can use the particle model of matter to explain how this works. In conduction, the vibrating particles of a solid pass energy along as they bump into each other. In convection, liquids and gases expand as they get hotter. This makes them less dense, so they float upwards.

- Radiation is different. It is energy travelling in the form of waves, which can pass through any transparent material and even through empty space.
- Materials usually expand as they get hotter. Their particles move apart. When a solid melts, it's because its particles have broken apart and are more free to move about. If a liquid is heated, its particles break free completely and escape to become a gas.

Balloonists can float upwards. What type of current is carrying them up?

8J Magnets and electromagnets

- Some metals and some other materials are magnetic. That means they are attracted by magnets, and can be made into permanent magnets.
- A magnet is strongest at its poles, which are usually near its ends. A north pole will attract a south pole, and two poles that are the same will repel each other.
- There is a magnetic field around a magnet – that's the space where it attracts magnetic materials. The Earth is like a giant magnet, with a field like the field of a bar magnet.
- Electromagnets are useful, because you can switch the electric current to make the magnet go on and off. An electromagnet is a coil of wire; the more turns of wire and the bigger the current, the stronger it is. Adding a soft iron core makes it much stronger.

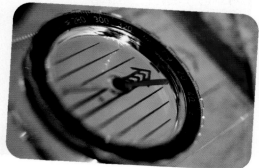

A compass needle points north – can you explain why?

8K Light

- Light travels in straight lines at a very high speed.
- To show how light travels, we draw rays. Rays of light are reflected by shiny surfaces, such as mirrors.
- When light travels into a transparent material such as glass, it bends. We say that it is refracted. Entering glass, it bends towards the normal. Leaving, it bends away from the normal.
- White light is a mixture of all the colours of the rainbow. When it is refracted, it is split into a spectrum.
- If an object looks red, it is because it is reflecting red light back to you. If you shine green light on a red object, it will look black, because there is no red light for it to reflect.

Binoculars use several lenses to bend light. Can you draw a diagram to show how light bends when it enters glass?

8L Sound and hearing

- Sounds are made by objects which are vibrating. We can use an oscilloscope to show up these vibrations. The bigger the vibrations, the louder the sound.
- The pitch of a sound depends on the frequency (in hertz, Hz) of the vibrations. More vibrations per second means a higher frequency, which means a higher pitch sound.
- Noise is unwanted sound, and it can be harmful to our hearing. When sound waves enter our ears, they make the eardrum vibrate. The three small bones in the ear pass on these vibrations to the cochlea. Loud noises can damage these fragile parts of the ear.
- Sound needs a material (solid, liquid or gas) to travel through – there must be something to vibrate!
- By understanding how sound travels and how it can be absorbed, we can try to reduce noise.

These miners are working with noisy equipment. How should they protect their hearing?

Key words

conduction
convection
frequency
magnetic field
reflection
refraction
temperature

Revision tips and exam technique

understand what you have written – and why you have written it. Make sure you have caught up on anything you missed. You will need it, to make sense of later work.

Every activity *you* do helps *your* memory.

Do you know the difference between **learning** and **revision**? Revision reminds you of things you already know – it *isn't* learning things for the first time. Before you can revise, you must learn, and there aren't any short cuts.

Learning

In fact you are learning all the time. You learn:
- when you do activities,
- when you answer questions,
- when you discuss work or argue with your partner about it,
- when you do homework.

Scientists have discovered that the more *you* have to think about things, and *do* things, the more likely you are to remember them. That explains why you remember practical work and projects where you had to find out things the best. Do some **active work** on everything you are trying to remember.

Learning takes time. Don't leave it until just before a test. Set aside a short time regularly to review the last three or four lessons. Check that you

Getting started on revision

Now make a revision timetable. Break down each main topic into smaller sections to work on. When you have covered a section, you can cross it off your list – a great feeling!

Where

Find somewhere at home where you won't be interrupted. People learn most effectively in quiet, cool places. If your family or neighbourhood is noisy, some gentle boring music playing in the background will smooth out lots of interruptions.

Make use of before- and after-school study clubs. Homework clubs at your local library have someone to help you find information.

How

Do regular small amounts of work in between your normal homework in the weeks before the exams.

Work in 30-minute blocks of time. It is hard to concentrate for longer. Give yourself a short break between sessions and change the topic you are working on.

> **Organising a revision block**
>
> Revise for 20 minutes using your favourite revision technique.
>
> Test your knowledge for 5 minutes.
>
> *Make sure your books are closed. You'll be amazed at what you can read through the corner of your eye!*
>
> Make a note of weak spots to be tackled in another session.
>
> *Pat yourself on the back for all that you remembered*
>
> Spend 5 minutes having a break – have a drink, play with the dog.

Schedule breaks carefully. If you've done lots of work you can reward yourself when your favourite programme is on.

Revision techniques

There are lots of different ways to revise. Try several until you find one that suits you best.

Spider diagrams suit me. I learn best from pictures.

Can you write definitions of key words?

I make lists, diagrams and charts.

I make crib notes on scrap paper... it's the writing that counts not the notes I make.

The animations on the CD make it really clear.

Working with a friend is a good idea. Talking about a topic helps you organise your thoughts. You can make up quiz questions and answers, then test each other. You could make up rhymes about pairs of words, or make up a song about a topic to sing to the tune of a chart hit.

Don't forget to have a go at practice questions. Use study support clubs to straighten out difficulties. Use books and CD ROMs to learn from, especially if there are gaps in your work.

> **It's never too late to do some revision.**

Writing the answers

You have to write using scientific words accurately to capture a mark. Use the glossary to learn what words mean. People miss out on marks because their answers are too general, vague or miss out a crucial scientific word. Sometimes the problem comes from everyday speech when we use words that have a precise scientific meaning wrongly. Try to practise using these words and ideas correctly.

...and the baby grows in the mother's tummy...

What? She's eaten it?

Shut the door. You'll let the cold in.

No, it's the heat that's transferred.

Draw label lines carefully so they end on the target. If there is a list of labels to choose from don't pick something else. Draw graph lines very carefully with a sharp pencil, it should not have the 'wobbles.'

Key words

active work
concentration
glossary
practice
schedule
techniques
timetable

GLOSSARY

accelerating speeding up. **p. 166**

acid rain rain with a pH value of 5.5 or below. **pp. 104–105**

addiction a state when the body has a physical craving for a substance. **pp. 28, 30**

air resistance the force caused by the air, which tends to slow things down. **p. 168**

alcohol a substance made in anaerobic respiration; it affects the nervous system and liver. **p. 31**

allele a version of a gene. **p. 6**

anabolic steroid a hormone that affects how we use energy to build tissues. **p. 32**

anaemia a medical condition due to having too few red blood cells. **p. 24**

antagonistic pair describes two muscles which work in opposite directions to each other. **pp. 22, 185**

artificial insemination a process in which a sample of sperm is introduced into the female reproductive system for fertilisation. **p. 9**

atmosphere the layer of gas surrounding a planet. **p. 148**

atmospheric pressure the pressure caused by molecules of gas in the air colliding with things. **p. 183**

average speed calculated by average speed = distance travelled/time taken. **p. 162**

balanced diet eating food that contains all the nutrients in the correct proportions. **p. 24**

balanced equation represents a chemical reaction by showing the formulae of reactants and products, so that the number of each type of atom is the same on either side of the equation: e.g. $2 \, Mg + O_2 \rightarrow 2 \, MgO$ **p. 74**

balanced forces when two or more forces cancel out, they are balanced. **p. 149**

biased describes data that is presented in such a way as to favour one side of an argument. **p. 111**

bioaccumulation a process in which substances, such as metals or pesticides in food, build up in the body. They pass to the next animal in a food chain when something is eaten and add to their stores. **p. 61**

biodiversity the range of different species within a habitat. **p. 48**

biomass the total dry mass of an organism or a population of organisms. **p. 42**

caffeine a stimulant substance found in tea, coffee, cola, etc. **p. 30**

cartilage a flexible slippery substance covering the end of a bone. **p. 21**

catalytic converter a honeycomb of precious metals fitted in a car exhaust system to reduce the pollutants given out. p. 105

chemical energy the energy stored in a chemical substance. p. 132

chlorophyll the green pigment in chloroplasts that harvests light energy. p. 40

chromosome structures found in a cell's nucleus. They are made of DNA and consist of a string of genes. p. 6

ciliated cells cells with small hair-like structures that move liquids along the tube. p. 28

cloche a small covering used by gardeners to protect plants in cold weather. p. 62

cloning involves taking small samples of tissue from an individual and using them to create new identical individuals. p. 11

compete two organisms compete when they both try to use the same resources. p. 58

component any device which is connected into an electric circuit. p. 138

compressing squashing or squeezing something, to reduce its volume. pp. 130, 182

conservation of mass the mass of reactants before a reaction equals the mass of products formed after the reaction. p. 121

constant speed when an object covers equal distances in equal times, its speed is constant (unchanging). p. 166

continuous variation a feature, such as height or weight, where individuals may be any size within a range. p. 4

contract get shorter or smaller. Muscle fibres shorten when they contract, and pull on bones. pp. 22, 185

copper nitrate the salt formed in the reaction between copper oxide and dilute nitric acid. Its formula is $Cu(NO_3)_2$. p. 93

copper sulphate the salt formed in the reaction between copper oxide and dilute sulphuric acid. Its formula is $CuSO_4$. p. 93

crop plants grown for harvesting. p. 54

deficiency disease occurs when the body does not get enough of a particular nutrient in food. p. 24

deforestation cutting down and clearing areas of forest. p. 48

discontinuous variation a feature, such as gender, in which individuals fall into groups, e.g. boys or girls. p. 4

Key words

on key people
Charles Darwin
inheritance
Sir Richard Doll
smoking
Theodor Boveri
chromosomes

GLOSSARY

displacement reaction
a reaction in which a more reactive metal takes the place of a less reactive metal in its compound. **pp. 93, 118**

distance
how far something has moved. **p. 162**

drag
the force caused by air, water, etc., which tends to slow things down. **p. 169**

drug
a substance that affects how the nervous system works; a medicinal drug is given by a doctor to help an illness. **p. 30**

dynamo
a machine which is turned to generate electricity. **p. 134**

eating disorder
a condition in which people do not eat a balanced diet. **p. 25**

economically important
has a large monetary value, e.g. a crop such as wheat or cocoa beans. **p. 54**

ecosystem
a collection of living organisms living within a particular type of environment. **p. 46**

effort
the force you apply to a lever to move the load. **p. 186**

electrical energy
energy carried by electricity. **p. 131**

endangered species
a species with a small population that is in danger of dying out. **p. 14**

endothermic reaction
a chemical reaction which takes in energy from its surroundings, making the temperature decrease. **p. 119**

epidermis
the outer layer of a leaf; also refers to the outer layer of skin. **p. 39**

eutrophication
pollution of rivers and lakes by fertilisers (or sewage and detergents). **p. 107**

exothermic reaction
a chemical reaction which gives out energy to its surroundings, making the temperature increase. **pp. 116, 118**

factor
something that might have an influence on what happens in an investigation. **p. 171**

fertiliser
a substance applied to soil to boost the mineral content. **p. 56**

fibre
a substance found in food that is not digested but is necesary for food to pass along the intestine. **p. 24**

fibrous root
a small thin root, often close to the surface. **p. 44**

flex
to bend a joint. **p. 22**

force
a push or a pull. **pp. 147, 166**

fossil fuel
a substance that stores the energy of living things which lived and died millions of years ago. **pp. 104, 135**

gamete
a sex cell, e.g. sperm or ovum. **p. 6**

gene — a section of DNA that carries the instructions for a feature. pp. 4, 6

general equation — a word equation that summarises a group of similar reactions, e.g. acid + alkali → a salt + water. pp. 72, 76, 81, 220

generator — a device which is turned to produce electricity. p. 134

genetic counselling — advice on the likelihood of inheriting a gene. p. 13

genetic diversity — the range of gene variations within a population. p. 14

genetic modification — involves transferring genes from one organism to another. p. 11

geocentric model — the idea that the Earth is at the centre of the universe, with the Sun, planets and stars moving around it. p. 151

glasshouse — a very large greenhouse used to grow commercial crops. p. 62

global warming — the increasing average temperatures around the world. p. 109

glucose — the sugar made in photosynthesis and used in respiration. p. 40

gravitational pull — the attractive force of gravity. p. 146

guard cells — cells around the pores (stomata) in a leaf. They can open or close the pore. p. 39

heliocentric model — the idea that the Sun is at the centre of the Solar System, with the Earth and other planets orbiting around it. p. 150

herbicide — a chemical that kills plants. p. 58

hydraulic — describes a system which works by applying pressure to a liquid (water, oil). p. 182

hydrocarbon — a compound containing hydrogen and carbon only. p. 116

hydroponics — a system of growing plants in a solution of minerals. p. 64

inbreeding — where close relatives mate together. p. 14

incomplete combustion — a reaction in which a substance burns in a limited supply of oxygen. p. 117

joint — a place where bones meet. p. 21

kinetic energy — the energy of a moving object. p. 154

lever — you press at one point on a lever to exert a force on an object at another point on the lever. p. 184

light gate — a device used to measure times automatically. p. 165

load — the force which a lever or other machine has to push on. p. 186

Key words
on key people
Carl Wilhelm Scheele
discovering elements
Richard S. Lindzen
global warming
Leo Baekeland
plastics

GLOSSARY

logging — cutting down trees. **p. 48**

mass — the amount of matter from which something is made (measured in kilograms). **p. 147**

minerals — compounds containing elements that animals and plants need to grow. **pp. 44, 48, 64**

model — a 'picture' constructed by scientists to help explain something. **pp. 76, 139**

moment — tells you about how effective a force is in turning about a pivot; calculated by:
moment = force × distance from pivot **p. 188**

muscle — tissue which contracts to exert a pulling force on a bone. **pp. 22, 185**

neutralisation — a chemical reaction in which an acid reacts with a base to form a salt and water. **pp. 76, 78**

nicotine — an addictive substance found in cigarette smoke. **p. 28**

nitrate — a mineral that plants use to make protein. **pp. 56, 73**

nuclear fuel — a substance, such as uranium, which is used in nuclear power stations. **p. 135**

orbit — the path of a planet around the Sun. **p. 152**

palisade layer — the layer of cells just under the surface of a leaf where most photosynthesis takes place. **pp. 39, 40**

pascal (Pa) — the unit of pressure, $1 \, Pa = 1 \, N/m^2$ **p. 183**

performance enhancers — drugs and other substances that enable an athlete to perform better. **p. 32**

pesticide — a chemical which kills animals that are a pest. **p. 61**

phlogiston — the substance once believed to be contained within a material that allowed it to burn. **p. 123**

phosphate — a mineral that plants need to grow; a major component of bone. **p. 56**

photosynthesis — the process in which plants use light energy to make glucose from carbon dioxide and water. **pp. 40, 46**

pivot — the fixed point about which a lever turns. **p. 184**

plant breeding — the process of breeding plants to obtain offspring with better features. **p. 55**

pneumatic — describes a system which works by applying pressure to air. **p. 183**

pollination — transfer of pollen from one flower to another. **p. 10**

polymer — a long chain molecule made up of many repeating units. **p. 124**

population boom this happens when an animal or plant reproduces very successfully and the numbers increase dramatically. **p. 60**

potassium a mineral that plants need to grow. **p. 56**

potassium nitrate the salt formed in the reaction between dilute potassium hydroxide and dilute nitric acid. Its formula is KNO_3. **p. 73**

potential difference another name for the voltage across a component in a circuit. **p. 138**

potential energy energy of something raised up, or stretched or squashed. **pp. 130, 154**

power supply a device used to provide a voltage in a circuit, to push a current around. **p. 155**

precipitation a chemical reaction in which an insoluble solid is formed when two solutions are mixed. **p. 120**

precision a more precise measurement has more figures: e.g. 27.54 s is more precise than 28 s. **pp. 163, 172**

pressure calculated by pressure = force/area. **p. 178**

principle of moments the rule for working out if a lever is balanced. **p. 189**

productivity the amount of saleable product from an animal or plant for the cost of raising it. **p. 8**

protein a nutrient needed for growth and repair. **p. 42**

qualitative data information gathered by observations from experiments. **p. 91**

quantitative data information gathered by making measurements during experiments. **p. 91**

Reactivity Series a list of the metals in order of their reactivity. **p. 91**

recessive describes a gene that is masked by a dominant version. **pp. 7, 13**

relax when a muscle stops contracting. **pp. 22, 185**

reliable describes data that we can expect to be reproduced if collected under the same conditions again. **pp. 197, 198, 199, 205**

respiration the process of releasing energy from glucose. **pp. 42, 46**

revolve when something turns around its own axis. **p. 152**

root hairs cells that are specialised for absorbing water and minerals from the soil. **p. 44**

salt a salt is usually a metal compound formed during a reaction involving an acid. **p. 72**

satellite an object which is in orbit around another. **p. 153**

Key words on key people **Michael Faraday** electricity **Isaac Newton** gravity **Albert Einstein** relativity

GLOSSARY

selective breeding choosing individuals with desirable features to be the parents of the next generation. p. 8

sickle-cell anaemia a medical condition resulting from having only sickle haemoglobin in red blood cells. p. 12

sickle-cell trait carrying one gene for sickle haemoglobin. p. 12

sodium hydroxide the most common alkali found in school laboratories. Its formula is NaOH. p. 78

sodium oxide the white solid formed when sodium metal reacts with oxygen. Its formula is Na_2O. p. 78

spin when something turns around its own axis. p. 152

starch a storage product made by plants from glucose. pp. 42, 54

stomata (plural) small pores in the surface of a cell. p. 39

streamlining giving something a shape which reduces drag. p. 168

stretching pulling on something to increase its length. p. 222

symbol equation a chemical equation in which the reactants and products are represented by their formulae. pp. 73, 120

systematic a logical, step-by-step approach; not random. p. 189

tap root a long tough root extending deep into the ground. p. 44

tar a component of cigarette smoke which can cause cancer. p. 28

tarnish a metal's reaction in air that forms a coating on the metal's surface. p. 86

tendon links a muscle to a bone. p. 22

thermal pollution hot water released into rivers (usually from power stations) that upsets the natural balance in the habitat. p. 107

thermit reaction the vigorous displacement reaction between iron(III) oxide and aluminium (used to weld lengths of railway track to each other). p. 93

timber wood from trees. p. 55

time the number of seconds which have passed between two events. p. 162

toxic poisonous. p. 61

transferring when energy passes from one place to another, or from one object to another. p. 130

transforming when energy changes from one form to another. p. 130

turbine a 'windmill' which is turned, to make a generator turn. p. 135

turning effect   tells you about how effective a force is in turning about a pivot; another name for moment. p. 187

unbalanced forces   when a single force acts, or when two or more forces act but do not cancel each other out, they are unbalanced. pp. 149, 167

upthrust   the upwards push of water (or air) which tends to make things float. p. 170

variety   a type of plant or animal that is different from others of the same species. p. 10

vein   blood vessel that conveys blood towards the heart. p. 39

voltage   a measure of the push of a cell or battery. p. 133

voltmeter   a meter used to measure voltages. p. 133

water culture solution   a solution of mineral salts in the correct proportions for plants. p. 64

weed   a plant growing among crop plants that competes with them. p. 58

weed killer   a substance that kills weeds. p. 58

weight   the force of gravity on an object (measured in newtons). pp. 146, 170

xylem   a kind of cell that conveys water through plants. p. 45

yield   the amount of product, for example, the milk produced by a cow each day. p. 58

Key words

on key people
Robert Boyle
gases
Georg von Békésy
the inner ear

ACKNOWLEDGEMENTS

AA Photolibrary: 98; **Action Plus:** Tony Henshaw 32r, Neil Tingle 124b, Glynn Kirk 172t, bl; **Alamy:** 107t, Holt Studios International 62, Joe Sohm 64, Profimedia.CZ s.r.o 201; **ASNNC:** 186; **Corbis:** 87tr, 103br, Robert Garvey 190tl; **Corel (NT):** 8m, 10t, b, 14, 23t, 32l, 36, 43, 52, 54b, 59t, 61, 102, 103tr, bl, 158, 162, 167b, 169b, 175, 182, 190br, 196bl, 197t, b, 212b, 215, 226t, 227t; **Digital Vision (NT):** 48r, 146, 147, 148, 154t, b, 155t, b, 159, 166t, m, 167t, 168, 169t, 170, 178, 179b, 190tr, 203t, b, 204t, b, 206m, b, 224t, 225t, b, 227b, 213bl, br; **Geoscience Features Picture Library:** 86br, bl; **Grabber:** 119; **Hulton Getty:** 106; **Ian Miles:** 163l, r; **Lawrie Ryan:** 90; **Marine Nationale:** 200l; **Mary Evans Picture Library:** 140r; **Martyn Chillmaid:** 58, 60, 86tr, tl, 87tl, 132t, 133, 134t, 135t, b, 136, 165; **M G Duff Marine:** 199; **NASA:** 150, 195t, 212t; **New Media:** 89; **Nordic Track:** 210; **Photodisc (NT):** 23b, 48l, 54a, d, 80tr, 166b, 179t, 184, 196br, 205, 206t, 224b, 226b; **Rail Images:** 93r; **Science Photolibrary:** 96t, 123, 156, 190bl, 211, Renee Lynn 8t, Genpharm International/Peter Arnold Inc. 9, Sinclair Stammers 11t, Bill Barksdale/Agstock 11b, Jackie Lewin/Royal Free Hospital 12, Steve Gschmeissner 26, Bob Gibbons 38, Eye of Science 39, 45, 196t, Pascal Goetgheluck 46, 80b, 95t, b, Chris Knapton 57r, Robert Brook 57l, 117, Peter Menzel 59b, Mark de Fraeye 70, Andrew McClenaghan 71, Dr P Marazzi 78, Jeremy Walker 80tl, Andrew Lambert Photography 91, 198b, Charles D Winters 93l, Jean-Loup Charnet 96b, Andy Harmer 104, Astrid & Hanns-Frieder Michler 107m, Colin Cuthbert 107b, British Antarctic Survey, Martin Bond 110, Jim Varney 124m, US Department of Energy 134b, David Parker 138, Dr Jeremy Burgess 140l, Sheila Terry 151, Royal Greenwich Observatory 172br, Tom McHugh 194l, National Library of Medicine 194r, James King-Holmes 195b, Steve Allen 198t, Simon Fraser 200r, Adam Hart-Davis 213t, Michael Donne 208, CMEABG-LYON-1/ISM 217; **Thorpe Park:** 202; **Topham Picturepoint:** 116.

Picture research by johnbailey@ntlworld.com and Stuart Sweatmore.

Every effort has been made to trace all the copyright holders, but if any have been overlooked the publisher will be pleased to make the necessary arrangements at the first opportunity.